Ha-Mashiach:

The Messiah of the Hebrew Scriptures

Other Books by Dr. Arnold G. Fruchtenbaum

A Passover Haggadah for Jewish Believers

An Historical and Geographical Study Guide of Israel: With a Supplement on Jordan

Ariel's Harmony of the Gospels

Faith Alone: The Condition of Our Salvation (An Exposition of the Book of Galatians and Other Relevant Topics)

God's Will & Man's Will: Predestination, Election, and Free Will

Ha-Mashiach: The Messiah of the Hebrew Scriptures

Israelology: The Missing Link in Systematic Theology

Jesus Was a Jew

The Feasts and Fasts of Israel: Their Historic and Prophetic Significance

The Historical and Geographical Maps of Israel and Surrounding Territories

The Remnant of Israel: The History, Theology, and Philosophy of the Messianic Jewish Community

The Sabbath

Yeshua: The Life of Messiah from a Messianic Jewish Perspective (published by Ariel Ministries in a multi-volume set and an abridged version)

Ariel's Bible Commentary Series:

The Messianic Jewish Epistles (Hebrews, James, I & II Peter, Jude)

Judges and Ruth

The Book of Genesis

Biblical Lovemaking: A Study of the Song of Solomon

Ariel's Come and See Series:

The Word of God: Its Nature and Content

What We Know About God: Theology Proper

Messiah Yeshua, Divine Redeemer: Christology from a Messianic Jewish Perspective

Ha-Mashiach:

The Messiah of the Hebrew Scriptures

A Study of Old Testament Prophecy
Concerning the First Coming of the Messiah

By Arnold G. Fruchtenbaum, Th.M., Ph.D.

Ha-Mashiach: The Messiah of the Hebrew Scriptures
(Author: Arnold G. Fruchtenbaum, Th.M., Ph.D.)
Copyright © 1998 by Ariel Ministries
5th Edition © 2019 by Ariel Ministries

ISBN: 978-1-935174-33-2

Library of Congress Control Number: 2014942582

This book was completed with the use of Logos Bible Software to acquire the following Bible texts for word processing: *Biblia Hebraica Stuttgartensia: With Werkgroep Informatica, Vrije Universiteit Morphology.* Logos Bible Software, 2006, edited by Eep Talstra. Hebrew Text: Copyright © 1990 Deutsche Bibelgesellschaft Stuttgart. Morphology: Copyright © 2006 Werkgroep Informatica, Vrije Universiteit. All rights reserved.

The Holy Bible, American Standard Version (ASV) of 1901, similar to the English Revised Version of 1881-1885, both being based upon the Hebrew Masoretic text for the OT and upon the Westcott-Hort Greek text for the NT. The machine-readable database Copyright © 1988 by the Ellis Enterprises, Inc., which by permission derived, reformatted, and corrected the machine-readable version of the ASV from the CompuBible Concordance Study System by NASSCO, Inc. of Lubbock, TX. Used by permission. However, the archaic language has been changed with one exception: The archaic *ye* has been retained in order to distinguish the second person plural from the singular *you*. The words "Jesus" and "Christ" have been replaced with "Yeshua" and "Messiah."

The New American Standard Bible (NASB), copyright © 1960, 1962, 1963, 1968, 1971, 1972, 1973, 1975, 1977, 1988 and electronic version © 1987, 1988 by The Lockman Foundation. All rights reserved. An updated edition of the ASV, completed in 1971.

The text of the NIV was acquired for word processing using Verse Search for Windows, from Bible Research Systems. Bible Research Systems, 2013 Wells Branch Parkway, Suite 304, Austin, Texas 78728-6901, U.S.A., Phone (512) 251-7541, Fax (512)251-4401. *Holy Bible, New International Version* (NIV) ® Copyright © 1973, 1978, 1984 International Bible Society.

Edited by Christiane Jurik, M.A.
2014-adjustments to the original cover design by Jesse Gonzales
Graphs on pp. 8, 38, and 108 by Matthew Lipsey

Printed in the United States of America

Published by

P.O. Box 792507
San Antonio, TX 78279-2507
Phone (210)344-7707
Web: ariel.org

This volume is dedicated to the memory of

Dr. Daniel Fuchs

Longtime director of Chosen People Ministries (ABMJ),
A lover of Israel to whom the passages studied
In this work meant so much.

Table of Contents

Introductory Note 1

Chapter 1: The *Torah* 3

Genesis 3:15 —The Seed of the Woman 4
Genesis 22:18—The Seed of Abraham 9
Genesis 49:10—The Seed of Judah 11
Numbers 23 & 24—The Predictions of Balaam 14
Deuteronomy 18:15-19—A Prophet Like Moses 19
Summary of The Law 21

Chapter 2: The *Nevi'im* 23

Isaiah 7:1-17—Born of a Virgin 24
Isaiah 8:9-10—The Promise of Immanuel 32
Isaiah 9:6-7—Unto Us a Son Is Given 33
Isaiah 11:1-2—The Stump of Jesse 36
Isaiah 40:3-5—The Herald of the King 39
Isaiah 42:1-6—The Servant of Jehovah 40
Isaiah 49:1-13—The Discouragement of the Servant 43
Isaiah 50:4-9—The Training of the Servant 47
Isaiah 52:13-53:12—The Suffering of the Servant 50
Isaiah 61:1-3—The Mission of the Servant 58
Jeremiah 23:5-6—Messiah the King 60
Micah 5:2—Bethlehem Ephrathah 62
Zechariah 9:9-10—Riding on a Donkey 63
Zechariah 11:1-17—The Two Shepherds 66
Zechariah 12:10—The Final Recognition of Messiah 73
Zechariah 13:7—The Good Shepherd 75
Malachi 3:1—The Messenger of the King 76

Chapter 3: The *K'tuvim* 79

1 Chronicles 17:10b-14—The Davidic Covenant 80
Psalm 2:7-12—The Son of God 83
Psalm 16:1-11—The Death of Messiah 85
Psalm 22:1-31—The Suffering & Exaltation of Messiah ... 87
Psalm 80:17—The Man of Your Right Hand 92
Psalm 110:1-7—A Priest After the Order of Melchizedek . 93
Proverbs 30:4—The Name of God's Son 96
Daniel 9:1-27—The Messianic Timetable 97

Chapter 4: Other Lines of Evidence   109

Introduction   110
The Plurality of the Godhead   111
The Unity of the Godhead   118
The Triunity of the Godhead   119
Conclusions   128

Chapter 5: Appendices   129

1   How the *Brit Chadasha* Quotes the *Tanach*   130
2   The Sons of God   139
3   Why Did Messiah Have to Die?   145
4   The Starting Point of the Seventy Sevens   152
5   How Did the Wise Men Know?   155
6   Messiah's Right to David's Throne   160
7   The Death of Judas Iscariot   166
8   Rabbinic Views of Messiah and Isaiah 53   171
9   *Brit Chadasha* Usage   180
10   Jewish Objections to Yeshua   185
11   Table of Messianic Prophecies   194

Introductory Note

This study is a survey of all the Messianic prophecies in the Hebrew Scriptures which were fulfilled at the first coming of Messiah. The Orthodox Jewish interpretation does not, of course, expect Messiah to come twice, but rather—as will be seen later—expects two Messiahs, each coming once. This study is presented from a Messianic Jewish perspective. The Scriptures we will analyze are the *Torah* (the Law), the *Nevi'im* (the Prophets), and the *K'tuvim* (the Writings).

Dr. Arnold G. Fruchtenbaum

CHAPTER 1:

THE TORAH

Genesis 3:15

The Seed of the Woman

[15] And I will put enmity between you and the woman, And between your seed and her seed; He shall bruise you on the head, And you shall bruise him on the heel. (NASB)

[15] וְאֵיבָה אָשִׁית בֵּינְךָ וּבֵין הָאִשָּׁה וּבֵין זַרְעֲךָ וּבֵין זַרְעָהּ הוּא יְשׁוּפְךָ רֹאשׁ וְאַתָּה תְּשׁוּפֶנּוּ עָקֵב: ס

Messianic prophecy begins as early as the third chapter of the book of Genesis. It is no surprise that the very first Messianic prophecy should occur within the context of the Fall. If sin had not entered the world, there would never have been a need for a redeeming Messiah. After the Fall, God curses the serpent who had caused the Fall, and declares enmity between the serpent and womanhood. This enmity is to extend to *her seed*, meaning the seed of the woman, and *your seed*, or the seed of the serpent. The seed of the woman refers to Christ, the Messiah, and the seed of the serpent will be the Antichrist.[1]

The Prophecy

This, the first Messianic prophecy, declares that the Messiah's descent will be reckoned after a woman, not a man. This is highly unusual. There are many genealogies in Scripture, beginning with the earliest in Genesis five and 10, through the first nine chapters of 1 Chronicles, to Matthew one and Luke three (among many others). Virtually all of these genealogies are lists of men's names. Legal descent, national and tribal identity, was always taken from the father, never from the mother (the sole exception to this is found in Ezra 2:61 and Nehemiah 7:63). It is very rare that a woman's name would be included at all unless she figured very prominently in Jewish history, and even then, she would warrant only a passing reference.

The fact that Moses traced this genealogy through the woman tells us that there will be something very different about the Messiah, something that necessitates tracing His ancestry through His mother, not His father. Moses gives no explanation here, and none will be given for several centuries until the time of the Prophet Isaiah—when he will prophesy (in chapter 7) that Messiah is to be born of a virgin and have no human father. The virgin birth hinted at in this verse also implies the humanity of the Messiah. The Redeemer will not be angelic nor simply divine, but

---

[1] A discussion of the Antichrist lies beyond the scope of this study, but see the author's book, *The Footsteps of the Messiah*, pages 135–146, for further details.

will be a man. Thus, Genesis 3:15 lays the groundwork for the Messiah to be the God-Man. These ideas are further developed in subsequent prophecies.

Finally, Genesis 3:15 states that Messiah the seed of the woman would *bruise your head*, meaning He would crush the head of the serpent—that is Satan (Rev. 12:9). In the process, Satan will manage to *bruise him on the heel* but will be unable to prevent his own destruction. The bruising of Messiah's heel took place at Yeshua's crucifixion—painful but, in the eternal sense, not fatal. The crushing of the serpent's head began with Yeshua's death and resurrection, a point made in Hebrews 2:14-18. Romans 16:20 sees the crushing of Satan's head as still future, and so, his final destruction will not come until he is thrown into the Lake of Fire, as described in Revelation 20:10.

Genesis Four, Five, and Six: Early Echoes of the Promise

These understandings about Genesis 3:15 come from our own historical perspective with the light of full revelation we have from the Scriptures; but how was this first Messianic promise understood by Adam and Eve? How was it understood by their progeny? We do have some early echoes of it in the book of Genesis. A study of the passages shows that the virgin birth would not be understood until Isaiah. However, the expectation of a God-Man Redeemer was understood.

Genesis 4:1

A literal translation of the Hebrew text for Genesis 4:1 would read:

And the man knew Eve his wife, she con-ceived and bare Cain and said "I have gotten a man: Jehovah."	וְהָאָדָם יָדַע אֶת־חַוָּה אִשְׁתּוֹ וַתַּהַר וַתֵּלֶד אֶת־קַיִן וַתֹּאמֶר קָנִיתִי אִישׁ אֶת־יְהוָה:

This is the same sentence construction as in the next verse:

Again she bare his brother: Abel.	וַתֹּסֶף לָלֶדֶת אֶת־אָחִיו אֶת־הָבֶל

Few Bible translators understand what Eve was saying here, which is why our English translations do not read as given above. Eve clearly understood from God's words in Genesis 3:15 that the serpent will be defeated by a God-Man. She obviously thought that Cain *is* Jehovah. Her basic theology was correct: Messiah would be both man and God. It is her application of the promise that was wrong. She assumed that Cain, her first child, was the promised God-Man. That she quickly realized her mistake is evident at the birth of Cain's brother whom she named Abel, meaning "vanity."

It is interesting to see how scholars have dealt with this verse at different times. Most English translations read, "I have gotten a man with *the help of* Jehovah." The words "with the help of" were added by the translators to avoid giving a reading which was unacceptable to them. But the Hebrew literally reads, "I have gotten a man: Jehovah." This is the same construction as the Hebrew for the immediately preceding words, "and she bare: Cain." The common English translation is not based on the Hebrew text but on the Greek *Septuagint* which reads "through God." This was followed by the Latin Vulgate which also reads "through God."

The *Jerusalem Targum*, an Aramaic translation, reads, "I have gotten a man: the angel of Jehovah." The rabbis gave a reading here which is much closer to the original Hebrew text. The *Targum Pseudo-Jonathan* reads, "I have gotten for a man the angel of the Lord." Another Aramaic translation is the *Targum Onqelos* which says, "from before the Lord." These Aramaic translations and paraphrases are seeing what the Hebrew is saying and the supernatural implications of it. In Christian theology, the Angel of Jehovah is seen as the second person of the triune God (something which is discussed later under "Other Lines of Evidence") but, of course, that was not the view of the Jewish translators of the *Targumim*.

The *Midrash Rabbah* on Genesis, 22:2, says of Genesis 4:1 "with the help of the Lord:"

> Rabbi Ishmael asked Rabbi Akiba, "Since you have served Nahum of Gimzo for 22 years and he taught that every *ach* and *rach* is a limitation but every *et* and *gam* is an extension, tell me what is the purpose of the *et* here." He replied, "if it is said 'I have gotten a man: the Lord' it would have been difficult to interpret, hence *et* 'with the help of the Lord' is required."

The footnote on page 181 of this *Midrash* says, "it might imply that she had begotten the Lord." The rabbis clearly understood the implications of the construction and so had to make the necessary adjustments in their translation.

The *Peshitta* says, "I have gotten a man to the Lord." A leading rabbi known as Saadia Gaon reads it "from with the Lord." Rashi translates it as "with the Lord," and Nachmanides translates it as "unto the Lord for the service of the Lord." Here again attempts are made to get around the obvious.

Genesis 5:21-29

[21] And Enoch lived sixty-five years, and became the father of Methuselah. [22] Then Enoch walked with God three hundred years after he became the father of Methuselah, and he had *other* sons and daughters. [23] So all the days of Enoch were three hundred and sixty-five years. [24] And Enoch walked with God; and he was not, for God took him. [25] And Methuselah lived one hundred and eighty—seven years, and became the father of Lamech. [26] Then Methuselah lived seven hundred and eighty-two years after he became the father of Lamech, and he had *other* sons and daughters. [27] So all the days of Methuselah were nine hundred and sixty-nine years,

and he died. [28] And Lamech lived one hundred and eighty-two years, and became the father of a son. [29] Now he called his name Noah, saying, "This one shall give us rest from our work and from the toil of our hands arising from the ground which the LORD cursed." (NASB)

In verse 24, we read of righteous Enoch who *was not, for God took him*. The New Testament tells us in Jude 14-15 that Enoch was a preacher of righteousness and a prophet. The name he gave to his son was indeed rich with prophetic significance. In Hebrew, *Methuselah* means "When he dies, it will come." Since there is no neuter in Hebrew, it actually reads "When he dies, he will come." This prophecy refers to the coming of the Flood. Simple arithmetic with the years given in Genesis shows that the Flood came in the year 1656 A.H.—the same year that Methuselah died (see chart on next page). Lamech understood the name of his father to be prophetic, but mistook it as referring to the birth of his son Noah. Noah will indeed be a man of tremendous significance in human history, but not in the way that Lamech thought.

Lamech clearly hoped that Noah, meaning "rest," will be the longed-for Messiah. It is clear from the ages and years given in Genesis 5 that Lamech was 56 years old when Adam died. Lamech would therefore have been given a clear firsthand account of all that happened in the Garden of Eden and all the words that God had spoken. It is very interesting, therefore, to see in Genesis 5:29 how Lamech expressed his own Messianic hope: He saw Messiah as a redeemer who will remove the curse of Adam's fall and all of its results. As with Eve, his basic theology was correct, but he misapplied it. Such a man would one day come, in fulfillment of the promise of Genesis 3:15—but Noah was not to be that man.

Genesis 6:1-4

Human creatures were not the only ones to understand the meaning and significance of God's words in Genesis 3:15. Satan, to whom those words were addressed, also understood them. In Genesis 6:1-4, we see Satan's first attempt to thwart God's Messianic program. Since Messiah is to be the seed of the woman, Satan's objective must be to corrupt this line of descent.

> [1] Now it came about, when men began to multiply on the face of the land, and daughters were born to them, [2] that the sons of God saw that the daughters of men were beautiful; and they took wives for themselves, whomever they chose. [3] Then the LORD said, "My Spirit shall not strive with man forever, because he also is flesh; nevertheless his days shall be one hundred and twenty years." [4] The Nephilim were on the earth in those days, and also afterward, when the sons of God came in to the daughters of men, and they bore *children* to them. Those were the mighty men who *were* of old, men of renown. (NASB)

At Satan's command, fallen evil angels, *the sons of God*, intermarried with human women, foreshadowing the supernatural conception of the Antichrist also hinted at in Genesis 3:15. The results of these marriages were grotesque creatures—the *Nephilim*. It was the appearance of these diabolic creatures which brought the judgment of the Flood upon the earth. By means of this judgment, God destroyed all the Nephilim and preserved a line through which Messiah would be born. Since this interpretation of the passage is disputed by some, a full explanation of it is given in Appendix 2.

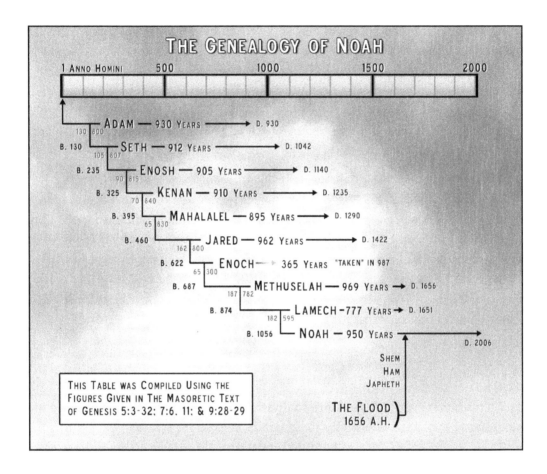

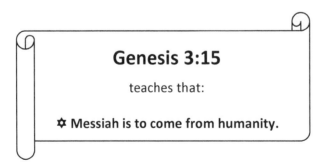

Genesis 22:18

The Seed of Abraham

¹⁸ "And in your seed all the nations of the earth shall be blessed, because you have obeyed My voice." (NASB)

¹⁸ וְהִתְבָּרֲכוּ בְזַרְעֲךָ כֹּל גּוֹיֵי הָאָרֶץ עֵקֶב אֲשֶׁר שָׁמַעְתָּ בְּקֹלִי:

Genesis 22, along with many other passages, deals with the Abrahamic Covenant, which is one of the eight covenants in Scripture. The term "seed" in the Hebrew text is always used in the singular, but in two different ways. It can be used as an absolute singular, referring to one individual person, or as a collective singular, referring to a group. Within the context of the Abrahamic Covenant, when "seed" is used in its collective sense, it always refers to the nation of Israel. An example of this is Genesis 22:17, which says, "your seed shall be as the stars and the sand." When used as an absolute singular, it refers to one specific individual—Messiah. This is highlighted in the New Testament by the Apostle Paul:

> Now the promises were spoken to Abraham and to his seed. He does not say, "And to seeds," as *referring* to many, but *rather* to one, "And to your seed," that is, Messiah.
>
> Galatians 3:16 (NASB)

Here Paul quotes Genesis 22:18, highlighting the absolute singular nature of "seed" and applying it to the Messiah. In Genesis 3:15, we learned that Messiah would be "the seed of the woman"; Messiah would be human. Within the Abrahamic Covenant, this is narrowed to Messiah being a descendant of one particular branch of humanity, a descendant of Abraham.

A second point made in this prophecy is that Gentiles—the nations—will be blessed through the seed of Abraham. This is not explained here but is developed in later prophecies (Isaiah 42:1-6 and 49:5-6).

Altogether, there are six different passages of Scripture that pertain to the Abrahamic Covenant: Genesis 12:1-3, 7; 13:14-17; 15:1-21; 17:1-21; and 22:15-18. A study of these passages shows that there is a total of fourteen specific provisions within this covenant. These cannot be discussed here, but if the covenant is reduced to its very basics, then it can be said to contain three main aspects: the land, the seed, and the blessing. The land aspect is developed further in Scripture by the Palestinian Covenant. The seed aspect is developed further by the Davidic Covenant, and since the seed is of importance in our present study, the Davidic Covenant will be discussed later under 1 Chronicles 17:10b-14 on page 80. The blessing aspect is further developed by the New Covenant.[2]

Genesis 22:18

teaches that:

✡ **The seed of the woman is limited to being a descendant of Abraham; Messiah is to be a Jew.**

---

[2] An in-depth study of these covenants goes beyond the purpose of this book. It is detailed in the author's other work, *Israelology: The Missing Link in Systematic Theology*, pages 570–587, 628–639, 791–805.

Genesis 49:10

The Seed of Judah

¹⁰ The scepter will not depart from Judah, nor the ruler's staff from between his feet, until he comes to whom it belongs and the obedience of the nations is his. (NIV)

10 לֹא־יָסוּר שֵׁבֶט מִיהוּדָה וּמְחֹקֵק מִבֵּין רַגְלָיו עַד כִּי־יָבֹא (שִׁילֹה) [שִׁילוֹ] וְלוֹ יִקְּהַת עַמִּים:

Genesis chapter 49 describes the prophecies proclaimed by Jacob concerning his sons. In verse 10, he makes a prophetic statement concerning Judah. The basic meaning of this statement is that Judah will not lose its tribal identity or its right to rule over the other tribes until someone comes. The exact wording of the statement varies between translations. Most versions obscure the real meaning by using the word "Shiloh," as if it were a proper name for Messiah. This word should, in fact, be taken as a possessive pronoun. The best translation is probably the NIV given above: "until he comes to whom it belongs." A more literal translation of the verse would read:

> The scepter will not depart from Judah, nor the ruler's staff from between his feet, until he comes whose right it is, and unto him shall the obedience of the peoples be.

Judah's identity and right to rule cannot be lost until one comes who has full rights to the scepter, full rights to rule. This is how the *Septuagint* translates the verse, as does the Syriac. This reading of the verse is further supported by comparison with a passage in Ezekiel 21:25-27:

> ²⁵ 'And you, O slain, wicked one, the prince of Israel, whose day has come, in the time of the punishment of the end,' ²⁶ thus says the Lord GOD, 'Remove the turban, and take off the crown; this will be no more the same. Exalt that which is low, and abase that which is high. ²⁷ 'A ruin, a ruin, a ruin, I shall make it. This also will be no more, until He comes whose right it is; and I shall give it to Him.' (NASB)

Ezekiel 21:25-27 is primarily concerned with the second coming of Messiah. Verse 25 refers to the Antichrist, the last Gentile to rule over Israel. In verse 26, the *turban* is the mitre of the priest (Exodus 28:4, 37, 39; 29:6; 39:28, 31; Leviticus 8:9, 16:4), and the *crown* is the royal crown. Just as Genesis 49:10 uses the royal scepter to represent the authority to rule, Ezekiel uses the royal crown to represent the same thing. Then the exact same phrase is used: "until he comes whose right it is." Both priesthood and kingship will be overthrown "until he comes whose right it is." It should be noted in passing that Ezekiel's reference to the priestly mitre indicates that Messiah will be a priest as well as a king—something that will be discussed further in Psalm 110. Both priesthood and kingship are to be removed from Israel until Messiah comes the second time, when both priesthood and kingship will be given to Him.

Returning to Genesis 49:10 and Messiah's first coming, we can see that this verse makes three points. Messiah has previously been declared to be a man, descended from Abraham. His descent is now limited to being a son of Judah. A second point is that Messiah is going to be a King. The scepter and the ruler's staff indicate royalty and authority. Third, it should be seen that Messiah must come before the tribe of Judah loses its identity. This establishes a clear time period for the prophecy. The records by which tribal identities were maintained were kept in the Jewish Temple. These records were lost with the destruction of the Temple in A.D. 70. Immediately after, the rabbis passed laws which would preserve the identity of the priestly tribe of Levi, but Jews from the other tribes lost their identity within a few generations. Since the tribe of Judah lost its pre-eminence and identity in A.D. 70, it can be clearly seen that Messiah must have come some time before that year. It is simply not possible for Messiah to come after A.D. 70.

This verse has been consistently regarded by the rabbis as being a Messianic verse. For example, the *Targum of Onqelos*, which is an Aramaic translation, translates it as, "the transmission of dominion shall not cease from the house of Judah nor the scribe from his children's children for ever until the Messiah comes to whom the kingdom belongs and whom nations shall obey." Onqelos clearly saw this verse as Messianic.

The rabbis have also interpreted this verse as being the source for one of the rabbinic names for Messiah: *Shiloh*. The amniotic sac in which a fetus is formed in the womb is called the *shilyah* in Hebrew. This is similar to *sheloh*, the Hebrew word for *Shiloh*. This is one of the rabbinic arguments against the divinity of Messiah. By calling him *Shiloh*, this was meant to be an indication that he was born from a *shilyah* and therefore, in their thinking, merely human. This is reflected in the following rabbinic statement: "The Messiah shall be called *Shiloh* to indicate that he was born of a woman and would therefore not be a divine being."

Rashi said, "until King Messiah will come, whose will be the kingdom, unto him [meaning the Messiah] shall the nations seek."

The *Midrash Rabbah* 97 on this passage reads as follows:

"Furthermore the royal Messiah will be descended from the tribe of Judah as it says [quoting Isaiah 11:10]. Thus from the tribe of Judah were descended Solomon who built the first Temple and Zerubbabel who built the second Temple and from him will be descended the royal Messiah who will rebuild the Temple. Now of the Messiah it is written [quoting Psalm 89:37]."

"Judah is a lion's whelp. Rabbi Hummah ben Rabbi Hannina said, 'This alludes to the Messiah the son of David who was descended from two tribes, his father from Judah and his mother from Dan, in connection with both of which "lion" is written [quoting Deuteronomy 33:22]'."

"The scepter alludes to the Messiah the son of David who will chastise the nations with a staff as it is written [quoting Psalm 2:9]."

"'until Shiloh comes' this indicates that all nations will bring a gift to Messiah the son of David as it says [quoting Isaiah 18:7]."

The *Midrash Rabbah* 98 says as follows:

"This alludes to the royal Messiah. 'Obedience of the people,' the Messiah will come and set on edge the teeth of the nations of the world."

The *Midrash Rabbah* 99, on Genesis 49:10, says "to whom kingship belongs," again taking "Shiloh" to be a possessive pronoun.

It is therefore very clear that the consistent rabbinic view of Genesis 49:10 was that it related to the Messiah.

Genesis 49:10

teaches that:

✡ **The seed of the woman and the seed of Abraham is now limited to being of the specific tribe of Judah.**
✡ **Messiah will be a king.**
✡ **Messiah had to come before A.D. 70.**

Numbers 23 & 24

The Predictions of Balaam

23:7 And he took up his discourse and said, "From Aram Balak has brought me, Moab's king from the mountains of the East, 'Come curse Jacob for me, And come, denounce Israel!' 8 "How shall I curse, whom God has not cursed? And how can I denounce, whom the Lord has not denounced? 9 "As I see him from the top of the rocks, And I look at him from the hills; Behold, a people who dwells apart, And shall not be reckoned among the nations. 10 "Who can count the dust of Jacob, Or number the fourth part of Israel? Let me die the death of the upright, And let my end be like his!"

18 Then he took up his discourse and said, "Arise, O Balak, and hear; Give ear to me, O son of Zippor! 19 "God is not a man, that He should lie, Nor a son of man, that He should repent; Has He said, and will He not do it? Or has He spoken, and will He not make it good? 20 "Behold, I have received a command to bless; When He has blessed, then I cannot revoke it. 21 "He has not observed misfortune in Jacob; Nor has He seen trouble in Israel; The Lord his God is with him, And the shout of a king is among them. 22 "God brings them out of Egypt, He is for them like the horns of the wild ox. 23 "For there is no omen against Jacob, Nor is there any divination against Israel; At the proper time it shall be said to Jacob And to Israel, what God has done. 24 "Behold, a people rises like a lioness, And as a lion it lifts itself; It shall not lie down until it devours the prey, And drinks the blood of the slain."

23:7 וַיִּשָּׂא מְשָׁלוֹ וַיֹּאמַר מִן־אֲרָם יַנְחֵנִי בָלָק מֶלֶךְ־מוֹאָב מֵהַרְרֵי־קֶדֶם לְכָה אָרָה־לִּי יַעֲקֹב וּלְכָה זֹעֲמָה יִשְׂרָאֵל: 8 מָה אֶקֹּב לֹא קַבֹּה אֵל וּמָה אֶזְעֹם לֹא זָעַם יְהוָה: 9 כִּי־מֵרֹאשׁ צֻרִים אֶרְאֶנּוּ וּמִגְּבָעוֹת אֲשׁוּרֶנּוּ הֶן־עָם לְבָדָד יִשְׁכֹּן וּבַגּוֹיִם לֹא יִתְחַשָּׁב: 10 מִי מָנָה עֲפַר יַעֲקֹב וּמִסְפָּר אֶת־רֹבַע יִשְׂרָאֵל תָּמֹת נַפְשִׁי מוֹת יְשָׁרִים וּתְהִי אַחֲרִיתִי כָּמֹהוּ:

18 וַיִּשָּׂא מְשָׁלוֹ וַיֹּאמַר קוּם בָּלָק וּשֲׁמָע הַאֲזִינָה עָדַי בְּנוֹ צִפֹּר: 19 לֹא אִישׁ אֵל וִיכַזֵּב וּבֶן־אָדָם וְיִתְנֶחָם הַהוּא אָמַר וְלֹא יַעֲשֶׂה וְדִבֶּר וְלֹא יְקִימֶנָּה: 20 הִנֵּה בָרֵךְ לָקָחְתִּי וּבֵרֵךְ וְלֹא אֲשִׁיבֶנָּה: 21 לֹא־הִבִּיט אָוֶן בְּיַעֲקֹב וְלֹא־רָאָה עָמָל בְּיִשְׂרָאֵל יְהוָה אֱלֹהָיו עִמּוֹ וּתְרוּעַת מֶלֶךְ בּוֹ: 22 אֵל מוֹצִיאָם מִמִּצְרָיִם כְּתוֹעֲפֹת רְאֵם לוֹ: 23 כִּי לֹא־נַחַשׁ בְּיַעֲקֹב וְלֹא־קֶסֶם בְּיִשְׂרָאֵל כָּעֵת יֵאָמֵר לְיַעֲקֹב וּלְיִשְׂרָאֵל מַה־פָּעַל אֵל: 24 הֶן־עָם כְּלָבִיא יָקוּם וְכַאֲרִי יִתְנַשָּׂא לֹא יִשְׁכַּב עַד־יֹאכַל טֶרֶף וְדַם־חֲלָלִים יִשְׁתֶּה:

24:3 And he took up his discourse and said, "The oracle of Balaam the son of Beor, And the oracle of the man whose eye is opened; 4 The oracle of him who hears the words of God, Who sees the vision of the Almighty, Falling down, yet having his eyes uncovered, 5 How fair are your tents, O Jacob, Your dwellings, O Israel! 6 "Like valleys that stretch out, Like gardens beside the river, Like aloes planted by the Lord, Like cedars beside the waters. 7 "Water shall flow from his buckets, And his seed shall be by many waters, And his king shall be higher than Agag, And his kingdom shall be exalted. 8 "God brings him out of Egypt, He is for him like the horns of the wild ox. He shall devour the nations who are his adversaries, And shall crush their bones in pieces, And shatter them with his arrows. 9 "He couches, he lies down as a lion, And as a lion, who dares rouse him? Blessed is everyone who blesses you, And cursed is everyone who curses you."

24:15 And he took up his discourse and said, "The oracle of Balaam the son of Beor, And the oracle of the man whose eye is opened, 16 The oracle of him who hears the words of God, And knows the knowledge of the Most High, Who sees the vision of the Almighty, Falling down, yet having his eyes uncovered. 17 "I see him, but not now; I behold him, but not near; A star shall come forth from Jacob, And a scepter shall rise from Israel, And shall crush through the forehead of Moab, And tear down all the sons of Sheth. 18 "And Edom shall be a possession, Seir, its enemies, also shall be a possession, While Israel performs valiantly. 19 "One from Jacob shall have dominion, And shall destroy the remnant from the city."

24:3 וַיִּשָּׂא מְשָׁלוֹ וַיֹּאמַר נְאֻם בִּלְעָם בְּנוֹ בְעֹר וּנְאֻם הַגֶּבֶר שְׁתֻם הָעָיִן: 4 נְאֻם שֹׁמֵעַ אִמְרֵי־אֵל אֲשֶׁר מַחֲזֵה שַׁדַּי יֶחֱזֶה נֹפֵל וּגְלוּי עֵינָיִם: 5 מַה־טֹּבוּ אֹהָלֶיךָ יַעֲקֹב מִשְׁכְּנֹתֶיךָ יִשְׂרָאֵל: 6 כִּנְחָלִים נִטָּיוּ כְּגַנֹּת עֲלֵי נָהָר כַּאֲהָלִים נָטַע יְהוָה כַּאֲרָזִים עֲלֵי־מָיִם: 7 יִזַּל־מַיִם מִדָּלְיָו וְזַרְעוֹ בְּמַיִם רַבִּים וְיָרֹם מֵאֲגַג מַלְכּוֹ וְתִנַּשֵּׂא מַלְכֻתוֹ: 8 אֵל מוֹצִיאוֹ מִמִּצְרַיִם כְּתוֹעֲפֹת רְאֵם לוֹ יֹאכַל גּוֹיִם צָרָיו וְעַצְמֹתֵיהֶם יְגָרֵם וְחִצָּיו יִמְחָץ: 9 כָּרַע שָׁכַב כַּאֲרִי וּכְלָבִיא מִי יְקִימֶנּוּ מְבָרֲכֶיךָ בָרוּךְ וְאֹרְרֶיךָ אָרוּר:

24:15 וַיִּשָּׂא מְשָׁלוֹ וַיֹּאמַר נְאֻם בִּלְעָם בְּנוֹ בְעֹר וּנְאֻם הַגֶּבֶר שְׁתֻם הָעָיִן: 16 נְאֻם שֹׁמֵעַ אִמְרֵי־אֵל וְיֹדֵעַ דַּעַת עֶלְיוֹן מַחֲזֵה שַׁדַּי יֶחֱזֶה נֹפֵל וּגְלוּי עֵינָיִם: 17 אֶרְאֶנּוּ וְלֹא עַתָּה אֲשׁוּרֶנּוּ וְלֹא קָרוֹב דָּרַךְ כּוֹכָב מִיַּעֲקֹב וְקָם שֵׁבֶט מִיִּשְׂרָאֵל וּמָחַץ פַּאֲתֵי מוֹאָב וְקַרְקַר כָּל־בְּנֵי־שֵׁת: 18 וְהָיָה אֱדוֹם יְרֵשָׁה וְהָיָה יְרֵשָׁה שֵׂעִיר אֹיְבָיו וְיִשְׂרָאֵל עֹשֶׂה חָיִל: 19 וְיֵרְדְּ מִיַּעֲקֹב וְהֶאֱבִיד שָׂרִיד מֵעִיר:

²⁰ And he looked at Amalek and took up his discourse and said, " Amalek was the first of the nations, But his end shall be destruction." ²¹ And he looked at the Kenite, and took up his discourse and said, "Your dwelling place is enduring, And your nest is set in the cliff. ²² "Nevertheless Kain shall be consumed; How long shall Asshur keep you captive?" ²³ And he took up his discourse and said, "Alas, who can live except God has ordained it? ²⁴ "But ships shall come from the coast of Kittim, And they shall afflict Asshur and shall afflict Eber; So they also shall come to destruction." ²⁵ Then Balaam arose and departed and returned to his place, and Balak also went his way. (NASB)

²⁰ וַיַּרְא אֶת־עֲמָלֵק וַיִּשָּׂא מְשָׁלוֹ וַיֹּאמַר רֵאשִׁית גּוֹיִם עֲמָלֵק וְאַחֲרִיתוֹ עֲדֵי אֹבֵד: ²¹ וַיַּרְא אֶת־הַקֵּינִי וַיִּשָּׂא מְשָׁלוֹ וַיֹּאמַר אֵיתָן מוֹשָׁבֶךָ וְשִׂים בַּסֶּלַע קִנֶּךָ: ²² כִּי אִם־יִהְיֶה לְבָעֵר קָיִן עַד־מָה אַשּׁוּר תִּשְׁבֶּךָּ: ²³ וַיִּשָּׂא מְשָׁלוֹ וַיֹּאמַר אוֹי מִי יִחְיֶה מִשֻּׂמוֹ אֵל: ²⁴ וְצִים מִיַּד כִּתִּים וְעִנּוּ אַשּׁוּר וְעִנּוּ־עֵבֶר וְגַם־הוּא עֲדֵי אֹבֵד: ²⁵ וַיָּקָם בִּלְעָם וַיֵּלֶךְ וַיָּשָׁב לִמְקֹמוֹ וְגַם־בָּלָק הָלַךְ לְדַרְכּוֹ: פ

Numbers, chapters 22-24, present us with the story of Balaam. Balaam was a Gentile astrologer, a seer, who came from the region of Babylonia. He established a considerable reputation for himself throughout the ancient world. It was widely regarded that "he whom Balaam cursed was cursed, and he whom Balaam blessed was blessed" (Num. 22:6).

At this point in the exodus from Egypt, the Israelites have arrived on the border of Moab and are about to enter the promised land. The king of Moab, one of the early anti-Semites of history, took objection to the prospect of new neighbors and decided to take action. He called for Balaam and commissioned him for a considerable amount of money to come and curse the Jews. Balaam tries very hard to fulfill his commission, but every time he opens his mouth to pronounce curses, God takes control of his tongue, and he finds himself blessing the Jews instead. The four oracles which he utters, put in his mouth by God, deal for the most part with the second coming of Messiah and His kingdom. There are, however, several statements which are of interest in our present study.

The First Oracle—Numbers 23:7-10

There are a few points worth noting in this first oracle. Balaam points out in verse 8 that he is unable to curse those whom God has not cursed. It is sometimes said that Israel's enjoyment of divine blessing is dependent on her obedience. At this point in her history, Israel is in disobedience, yet despite that, God is still watching over her. Regardless of her obedience or disobedience, Israel will always be God's chosen and covenant people. God will never permit Gentiles to put curses on Israel such that they would be of eternal effect, which Balaam's would have been. God therefore intervenes in this situation and overrules the intentions of men.

A second point to note is in verse 9. Israel will not be considered a nation. Throughout much of their history, the Jewish people have been unable to live in a land of their own. While the land of Canaan, or Palestine, or better still, the land of Israel, belongs to the Jews by divine right, their ability to occupy the land has been largely dependent on their obedience to God. To man, a people without a land cannot be a nation, which is why in verse 9 "they dwell alone . . . not reckoned among the nations." From the divine viewpoint, however, the people of Israel will always be a distinct nation. It makes no difference whether Israel is in the land or scattered abroad; God sees Israel not as the people of a particular place, but as the nation which is descended from Abraham, Isaac, and Jacob. This is why Jewish identity is determined by descent. Jewishness is not determined by place of birth or by religious beliefs, but purely by ancestry. It is irrelevant what an individual Jew may believe or disbelieve; his Jewish identity is determined by his descent. Judaism as a religion is, of course, determined by belief, but atheists and agnostics will still call themselves Jews on the basis of their lineage.

In the dispersion, the Jews have for centuries been "not reckoned among the nations"; that is, not given a separate national status. They have been called American Jews, Polish Jews, Russian Jews, and so on, which is not entirely wrong—an American Jew is a Jew who lives in America. But biblically speaking this cannot be correct. A Jew can never be American, Polish, or Russian—a Jew can only ever be a Jew with a quite distinct national identity. Even after four centuries, the Jews in Egypt were not called "Egyptians" but "Israel." As the Passover *Haggadah* states:

> "And there became a nation." By which we are informed that the Children of Israel were distinct, even in Egypt, as a peculiar nation.

This may not be recognized by Gentiles, but in God's eyes, Israel will always be separate, distinct, and unique among the nations of the world.

As Balaam prophetically looks forward to the future of this nation, he sees that God's final destiny for them is one of supreme blessing, and in verse 10b, he expresses his desire to share in that blessing.

The Second Oracle—Numbers 23:18-24

There are two key points made in this passage, found mainly in verse 21. First, Balaam sees a time in the future when Israel as a nation will be seen as sinless. Second, Balaam says that during this time of sinlessness, God Himself will be present as King. These prophecies relate to the second coming of Messiah, but it should still be noted that God will be present and rule in the midst of His people one day.

The Third Oracle—Numbers 24:3-9

Again, two points are emphasized. The first is a description of the future condition of Israel as one of supreme blessing. The second highlights the future condition of Israel's King (Num. 24:7b).

Having introduced the uniqueness of the nation of Israel in the first oracle, the second and third oracles go on to emphasize the uniqueness of the King who will one day rule over this nation.

The Fourth Oracle—Numbers 24:15-24

It is the fourth of the oracles which is of greatest interest in our study of first coming prophecies. The key prophecy is given in verse 17a, and it builds on the prophecy already given in Genesis 49:10.

A star shall come forth from Jacob, that is, Israel; coupled with this star is a scepter which, as in Genesis 49:10, represents kingship, since he who has the scepter has the right to rule. Therefore, the message is that Messiah will be a king. As we shall see, Messiah has three offices, one of which is king.

Balaam began his oracles by emphasizing the unique nature of the nation of Israel. He then went on to say that this nation, though scattered at first, would have a unique King to rule over it. He finishes here by declaring the awesome power of this King and noting, in verse 17a, that His coming would be heralded by the appearance of a star.

The significance of the closing words of chapter 24 should not be missed. Having completed his work, Balaam the Babylonian astrologer returns to "my people" (verse 14) and to "his place" (verse 25). With him, he takes the prophecy of a star announcing the birth of a unique and powerful King who will rule over Israel. As we shall see in Appendix 5 of our study, later generations of Babylonian astrologers recorded these words and kept watch for this star. At its appearing, they went and found the new-born King and worshipped Him.

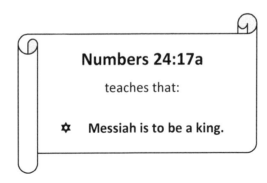

Numbers 24:17a

teaches that:

✡ **Messiah is to be a king.**

Deuteronomy 18:15-19

A Prophet Like Moses

¹⁵ "The LORD your God will raise up for you a prophet like me from among you, from your countrymen, you shall listen to him. ¹⁶ "This is according to all that you asked of the LORD your God in Horeb on the day of the assembly, saying, 'Let me not hear again the voice of the LORD My God, let me not see this great fire anymore, lest I die.' ¹⁷ "And the LORD said to me, 'They have spoken well. ¹⁸ 'I will raise up a prophet from among their countrymen like you, and I will put My words in his mouth, and he shall speak to them all that I command him. ¹⁹ 'And it shall come about that whoever will not listen to My words which he shall speak in My name, I Myself will require *it* of him. (NASB)

¹⁵ נָבִיא מִקִּרְבְּךָ מֵאַחֶיךָ כָּמֹנִי יָקִים לְךָ יְהוָה אֱלֹהֶיךָ אֵלָיו תִּשְׁמָעוּן: ¹⁶ כְּכֹל אֲשֶׁר־שָׁאַלְתָּ מֵעִם יְהוָה אֱלֹהֶיךָ בְּחֹרֵב בְּיוֹם הַקָּהָל לֵאמֹר לֹא אֹסֵף לִשְׁמֹעַ אֶת־קוֹל יְהוָה אֱלֹהָי וְאֶת־הָאֵשׁ הַגְּדֹלָה הַזֹּאת לֹא־אֶרְאֶה עוֹד וְלֹא אָמוּת: ¹⁷ וַיֹּאמֶר יְהוָה אֵלָי הֵיטִיבוּ אֲשֶׁר דִּבֵּרוּ: ¹⁸ נָבִיא אָקִים לָהֶם מִקֶּרֶב אֲחֵיהֶם כָּמוֹךָ וְנָתַתִּי דְבָרַי בְּפִיו וְדִבֶּר אֲלֵיהֶם אֵת כָּל־אֲשֶׁר אֲצַוֶּנּוּ: ¹⁹ וְהָיָה הָאִישׁ אֲשֶׁר לֹא־יִשְׁמַע אֶל־דְּבָרַי אֲשֶׁר יְדַבֵּר בִּשְׁמִי אָנֹכִי אֶדְרֹשׁ מֵעִמּוֹ:

Deuteronomy 18:18 contains a promise given by God to Moses. God promises Moses that He will raise up a prophet "like you." Why does God specify a prophet like Moses? What was different about Moses compared with other men called by God to be prophets? The unique status of Moses among the other prophets is explained in Numbers 12:5-8:

> ⁵ Then the LORD came down in a pillar of cloud and stood at the doorway of the tent, and He called Aaron and Miriam. When they had both come forward, ⁶ He said, "Hear now My words: If there is a prophet among you, I, the LORD, shall make Myself known to him in a vision. I shall speak with him in a dream. ⁷ "Not so, with My servant Moses, He is faithful in all My household; ⁸ With him I speak mouth to mouth, Even openly, and not in dark sayings, And he beholds the form of the LORD. Why then were you not afraid To speak against My servant, against Moses?" (NASB)

In this passage, Aaron and Miriam are railing against their brother Moses because they do not approve of the woman he has married. God Himself intervenes on Moses' behalf, declaring Moses' unique standing before Him. Even with great men like Elijah and Isaiah, God did not reveal

Himself directly but used dreams, visions, and other methods. Moses is the only man who received direct revelation from God. It is on this basis that Judaism developed its three-tier view of Scriptural inspiration.

Previously, we were told that Messiah would be a king. Now we are told that He will be a prophet too, and not an ordinary prophet, but One who will speak "mouth to mouth" with God and Who will see the very form of Jehovah.

Many writers have sought to draw up lists of similarities between Moses and Yeshua, the "prophet like unto Moses." Many of these parallels are rather contrived and somewhat fanciful. We can, however, point out four clear similarities between the ministries of Moses and Messiah:

1. **A Prophet** (Numbers 12:6-8)
    As explained above.

2. **A Redeemer** (Exodus 3:10)
    In Exodus 3:1-10, God sees the suffering of the people of Israel and declares His intention to redeem them out of the land of Egypt. Moses is the man chosen by God to lead the people out of their captivity. (Note that the Angel of Jehovah mentioned in verse 2 is further discussed in the part of this study called "Other Lines of Evidence.") As has already been seen, Messiah too will be a redeemer.

3. **A Mediator** (Exodus 20:18-21)
    To begin with, God spoke directly to the people of Israel (Exodus 19:16-25). The sound of God's voice was so overwhelming that the people asked Moses to mediate for them so that they would not hear God's voice, but only God's words repeated to them by Moses.

4. **An Intercessor** (Exodus 32:7-35)
    Often, during their long exodus from Egypt, it was only because of Moses' intercession on their behalf that Israel escaped the judgment of God and survived. This is particularly clear in Exodus 32:30-32.

Messiah will fit the Mosaic mold in each of these four areas: He will be a prophet, a redeemer, a mediator, and an intercessor.

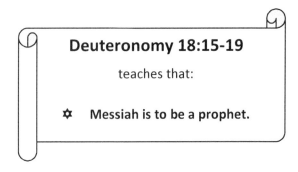

Deuteronomy 18:15-19

teaches that:

✿ **Messiah is to be a prophet.**

Summary of the Law

The Messianic prophecies in the Law which relate to the first coming of Messiah can be summarized in six key points. These relate either to His Person or His work or both.

The Seed

The subject of the seed was encountered three times:

1. *The Seed of the Woman*
   Messiah would be human, not an angel, nor purely God as God.

2. *The Seed of Abraham*
   Messiah would come from one specific part of humanity; He would be a Jew, not a Gentile.

3. *The Seed of Judah*
   Although there were twelve Jewish tribes, Messiah would come from one specific tribe, the tribe of Judah. This requires that Messiah come prior to the destruction of Jewish genealogical records in A.D. 70.

Both God and Man

Although Eve wrongly identified Cain as Messiah, she clearly understood that Messiah was to be a God-Man.

A King

More than once the symbol of the scepter was used to indicate that Messiah would be a king.

A Prophet Like Moses

Messiah would be a prophet, and specifically, He would be a prophet like Moses.

Removal of the Curse

Although Lamech wrongly identified his son Noah as Messiah, he clearly understood that Messiah, when He came, would remove the curse brought upon the earth by Adam's sin.

A Hint of the Virgin Birth

Although not as clearly stated as the five points above, there is a hint in Genesis 3:15 that Messiah would be born of a virgin. He would be reckoned as the seed of the woman and not of a man.

CHAPTER 2:

THE NEVI'IM

Isaiah 7:1-17

Born of a Virgin

1 When Ahaz son of Jotham, the son of Uzziah, was king of Judah, King Rezin of Aram and Pekah son of Remaliah king of Israel marched up to fight against Jerusalem, but they could not overpower it. 2 Now the house of David was told, "Aram has allied itself with Ephraim"; so the hearts of Ahaz and his people were shaken, as the trees of the forest are shaken by the wind. 3 Then the LORD said to Isaiah, "Go out, you and your son Shear-Jashub, to meet Ahaz at the end of the aqueduct of the Upper Pool, on the road to the Washerman's Field. 4 Say to him, 'Be careful, keep calm and don't be afraid. Do not lose heart because of these two smoldering stubs of firewood—because of the fierce anger of Rezin and Aram and of the son of Remaliah. 5 Aram, Ephraim and Remaliah's son have plotted your ruin, saying, 6 "Let us invade Judah; let us tear it apart and divide it among ourselves, and make the son of Tabeel king over it." 7 Yet this is what the Sovereign LORD says: " 'It will not take place, it will not happen, 8 for the head of Aram is Damascus, and the head of Damascus is only Rezin. Within sixty-five years Ephraim will be too shattered to be a people. 9 The head of Ephraim is Samaria, and the head of Samaria is only Remaliah's son. If you do not stand firm in your faith, you will not stand at all.' "

1 וַיְהִ֡י בִּימֵ֣י אָ֠חָז בֶּן־יוֹתָ֨ם בֶּן־עֻזִיָּ֜הוּ מֶ֣לֶךְ יְהוּדָ֗ה עָלָ֣ה רְצִ֣ין מֶֽלֶךְ־אֲ֠רָם וּפֶ֨קַח בֶּן־רְמַלְיָ֤הוּ מֶֽלֶךְ־יִשְׂרָאֵל֙ יְר֣וּשָׁלִַ֔ם לַמִּלְחָמָ֖ה עָלֶ֑יהָ וְלֹ֥א יָכֹ֖ל לְהִלָּחֵ֥ם עָלֶֽיהָ: 2 וַיֻּגַּ֣ד לְבֵ֣ית דָּוִ֗ד לֵאמֹר֙ נָ֣חָֽה אֲרָ֖ם עַל־אֶפְרָ֑יִם וַיָּ֤נַע לְבָבוֹ֙ וּלְבַ֣ב עַמּ֔וֹ כְּנ֥וֹעַ עֲצֵי־יַ֖עַר מִפְּנֵי־רֽוּחַ: 3 וַיֹּ֣אמֶר יְהוָה֮ אֶֽל־יְשַֽׁעְיָהוּ֒ צֵא־נָא֙ לִקְרַ֣את אָחָ֔ז אַתָּ֕ה וּשְׁאָ֖ר יָשׁ֣וּב בְּנֶ֑ךָ אֶל־קְצֵ֗ה תְּעָלַת֙ הַבְּרֵכָ֣ה הָעֶלְיוֹנָ֔ה אֶל־מְסִלַּ֖ת שְׂדֵ֥ה כוֹבֵֽס: 4 וְאָמַרְתָּ֣ אֵ֠לָיו הִשָּׁמֵ֨ר וְהַשְׁקֵ֜ט אַל־תִּירָ֗א וּלְבָבְךָ֙ אַל־יֵרַ֔ךְ מִשְּׁנֵ֨י זַנְב֧וֹת הָאוּדִ֛ים הָעֲשֵׁנִ֖ים הָאֵ֑לֶּה בָּחֳרִי־אַ֛ף רְצִ֥ין וַאֲרָ֖ם וּבֶן־רְמַלְיָֽהוּ: 5 יַ֗עַן כִּֽי־יָעַ֥ץ עָלֶ֛יךָ אֲרָ֖ם רָעָ֑ה אֶפְרַ֥יִם וּבֶן־רְמַלְיָ֖הוּ לֵאמֹֽר: 6 נַעֲלֶ֤ה בִֽיהוּדָה֙ וּנְקִיצֶ֔נָּה וְנַבְקִעֶ֖נָּה אֵלֵ֑ינוּ וְנַמְלִ֥יךְ מֶ֙לֶךְ֙ בְּתוֹכָ֔הּ אֵ֖ת בֶּן־טָֽבְאַֽל: ס 7 כֹּ֥ה אָמַ֖ר אֲדֹנָ֣י יְהוִ֑ה לֹ֥א תָק֖וּם וְלֹ֥א תִֽהְיֶֽה: 8 כִּ֣י רֹ֤אשׁ אֲרָם֙ דַּמֶּ֔שֶׂק וְרֹ֥אשׁ דַּמֶּ֖שֶׂק רְצִ֑ין וּבְע֗וֹד שִׁשִּׁ֤ים וְחָמֵשׁ֙ שָׁנָ֔ה יֵחַ֥ת אֶפְרַ֖יִם מֵעָֽם: 9 וְרֹ֤אשׁ אֶפְרַ֙יִם֙ שֹׁמְר֔וֹן וְרֹ֥אשׁ שֹׁמְר֖וֹן בֶּן־רְמַלְיָ֑הוּ אִ֚ם לֹ֣א תַאֲמִ֔ינוּ כִּ֖י לֹ֥א תֵאָמֵֽנוּ: ס

¹⁰ Again the LORD spoke to Ahaz, ¹¹ "Ask the LORD your God for a sign, whether in the deepest depths or in the highest heights." ¹² But Ahaz said, "I will not ask; I will not put the LORD to the test." ¹³ Then Isaiah said, "Hear now, you house of David! Is it not enough to try the patience of men? Will you try the patience of my God also? ¹⁴ Therefore the Lord himself will give you a sign: The virgin will be with child and will give birth to a son, and will call him Immanuel. ¹⁵ He will eat curds and honey when he knows enough to reject the wrong and choose the right. ¹⁶ But before the boy knows enough to reject the wrong and choose the right, the land of the two kings you dread will be laid waste. ¹⁷ The LORD will bring on you and on your people and on the house of your father a time unlike any since Ephraim broke away from Judah—he will bring the king of Assyria." (NIV)

10 וַיּוֹסֶף יְהוָה דַּבֵּר אֶל־אָחָז לֵאמֹר: 11 שְׁאַל־לְךָ אוֹת מֵעִם יְהוָה אֱלֹהֶיךָ הַעְמֵק שְׁאָלָה אוֹ הַגְבֵּהַּ לְמָעְלָה: 12 וַיֹּאמֶר אָחָז לֹא־אֶשְׁאַל וְלֹא־אֲנַסֶּה אֶת־יְהוָה: 13 וַיֹּאמֶר שִׁמְעוּ־נָא בֵּית דָּוִד הַמְעַט מִכֶּם הַלְאוֹת אֲנָשִׁים כִּי תַלְאוּ גַּם אֶת־אֱלֹהָי: 14 לָכֵן יִתֵּן אֲדֹנָי הוּא לָכֶם אוֹת הִנֵּה הָעַלְמָה הָרָה וְיֹלֶדֶת בֵּן וְקָרָאת שְׁמוֹ עִמָּנוּ אֵל: 15 חֶמְאָה וּדְבַשׁ יֹאכֵל לְדַעְתּוֹ מָאוֹס בָּרָע וּבָחוֹר בַּטּוֹב: 16 כִּי בְּטֶרֶם יֵדַע הַנַּעַר מָאֹס בָּרָע וּבָחֹר בַּטּוֹב תֵּעָזֵב הָאֲדָמָה אֲשֶׁר אַתָּה קָץ מִפְּנֵי שְׁנֵי מְלָכֶיהָ: 17 יָבִיא יְהוָה עָלֶיךָ וְעַל־עַמְּךָ וְעַל־בֵּית אָבִיךָ יָמִים אֲשֶׁר לֹא־בָאוּ לְמִיּוֹם סוּר־אֶפְרַיִם מֵעַל יְהוּדָה אֵת מֶלֶךְ אַשּׁוּר: פ

Chapters 7-12 of Isaiah constitute a single unit, sometimes referred to as "The Book of Immanuel" because the name "Immanuel" appears three times in the Hebrew text (7:14; 8:8, 10). The first prophecy which we will look at within this section of Scripture deals with the birth of Immanuel. In the Bible, when parents name a child, the meaning of the name shows the thinking of the parents. When God names the child, as here, the name shows the very nature of the child. Immanuel means "with us, God." The character of the child will be "God among us."

The Controversy

As mentioned in our discussion of Genesis 3:15, Isaiah 7:13-14 is a prophecy concerning the virgin conception and birth of the Messiah. This is perhaps the most controversial of the Messianic prophecies and therefore requires a closer textual analysis than others. The exact meaning of this passage is disputed by rabbis, liberal theologians, and even by some evangelical theologians.

The passage talks of a sign: "The virgin will be with child." There are two areas of controversy here:

1. **The Sign**

   Since the context of the chapter requires a short-range prophecy—giving a sign to King Ahaz—how can this be applied to the birth of a child some 700 years later, as claimed in Matthew 1:22-23?

2. **The Hebrew Word "***Almah***"**

   Does *almah* really mean virgin or simply young unmarried woman?

We will deal with both of these contentious issues before proceeding to discuss the passage itself.

Hermeneutics

Since Isaiah 7:13-14 requires an immediate sign to King Ahaz, many Evangelicals have taken this verse to be an example of "double fulfillment." This principle states that a prophecy may have more than one fulfillment. This verse may, accordingly, be both a sign for King Ahaz and the sign in Matthew 1:22-23 for the birth of Yeshua.

This author does not accept the principle of double fulfillment either here or in any other place in the Bible. If this principle were true, there would be no real need for the virgin birth at all. There is another, better principle of biblical interpretation which is "double reference." This principle states that one block of Scripture dealing with one person, one event, one time may be followed by another block of Scripture dealing with a different person, place, and time, without making any clear distinction between the two blocks or indicating that there is a gap of time between the two blocks. The fact of a gap of time is known only from other Scriptures. There are, therefore, two separate prophecies side-by-side each having their own fulfillment, but with only one fulfillment per prophecy. "Double Fulfillment" states that one prophecy can have two fulfillments. "Double Reference" states that the one piece of Scripture actually contains two prophecies, each having its own fulfillment.

As will be explained later, Isaiah 7:13-17 contains two quite separate prophecies with different purposes and having different fulfillments at different times.

The Hebrew Word *Almah*

The major debate, of course, is over the exact meaning of the Hebrew word *almah*, translated here as *virgin*. In describing a young woman, there are three Hebrew words which Isaiah could have used:

1. *Na'a'rah*

   Na'a'rah means "damsel" and can refer to either a virgin (as in 1 Kings 1:2) or a non-virgin (as in Ruth 2:6).

2. **Betulah**

   This is commonly considered to mean "a virgin," exclusively. It is argued that if Isaiah had really meant to say *a virgin*, then he would have used this word. It is true that this word is often used to mean *virgin*, but not always. For example:

   i. In Joel 1:8, it is used in reference to a widow.

   ii. In Genesis 24:16, because the word does not exclusively mean "virgin," the writer adds the phrase "had never known a man" in order to clarify what he means.

   iii. Again, in Judges 21:12, the phrase "had not known a man" has to be added to give the precise meaning.

3. **Almah**

   Almah means "a virgin," "a young virgin," "a virgin of marriageable age." This word is used seven times in the Hebrew Scriptures, and not once is it used to describe a married woman; this point is not debated.

   i. **Genesis 24:43.** In contrast to Genesis 24:16, verse 43 requires no additional qualifying remarks since the one word alone is sufficient to mean "virgin." Furthermore, it is used of Rebekah who was obviously a virgin at the time of her marriage to Isaac.

   ii. **Exodus 2:8.** Used in reference to Moses' sister Miriam, who was a virgin.

   iii. **Psalm 68:25.** Used in reference to the royal procession of virgins. Since the King in this context is God Himself, absolute virginity is required; it is unthinkable that God would allow unchaste, unmarried women in His procession.

   iv. **Song of Songs 1:3.** The context here is purity in marriage.

   v. **Song of Songs 6:8.** The word is used here in contrast to wives and concubines who would obviously be non-virgins.

   vi. **Proverbs 30:18-19.** The word is used in verse 19 in contrast to an adulteress in verse 20.

   vii. **Isaiah 7:14.** Since all of the above six verses mean "a virgin," what reason is there for making Isaiah 7:14 the only exception?

Since everyone agrees that *almah* means an unmarried woman, if the woman in Isaiah 7:14 were a non-virgin, then God would be promising a sign involving fornication and illegitimacy. It is unthinkable that God would sanction sin, and in any case, what would be so unusual about an illegitimate baby that could possibly constitute a sign?

As far as ancient Jewish writers were concerned, there was no argument about Isaiah 7:14 predicting a virgin birth. The *Septuagint* is a Greek translation of the Hebrew Scriptures made about 200 B.C., 200 years before the issue of Yeshua's Messiahship ever arose. The Jews, who made this translation, living much closer to the times of Isaiah than we do today, translated Isaiah 7:14 using the Greek word *parthenos* which very clearly and exclusively means "a virgin."

Therefore, there can be no doubt that the unique event, which God is promising as a sign, is the miraculous conception of a son by a girl who is still a virgin.

The Threat to the House of David—Isaiah 7:1-2

At this point in history, there was an empire arising which was threatening the smaller kingdoms of the Middle East—the Assyrian Empire.

Among these smaller kingdoms was Syria (or Aram), the northern kingdom of Israel (or Ephraim), and the southern kingdom of Judah. The kings of Israel and Syria joined forces against their common enemy (verses 1-2), but still did not have enough military might to withstand an Assyrian attack. They invited Judah to join forces with them, but Ahaz, king of Judah, refused. Israel and Syria then conspired, not only to dethrone Ahaz, when they might have succeeded, but to depose the entire House of David. This is the emphasis in verse 2. They would then establish a new dynasty in Judah more favorable to an alliance against Assyria. This is a direct attack upon God's eternal covenant with David. It is therefore doomed to failure.[3]

The Message to Ahaz—Isaiah 7:3-9

Ahaz is not a worshipper of the one true God, but has fallen into idolatry and is very much afraid of the approaching attack (verse 2). In verses 3-9, God gives a message to Ahaz. In verse 3, Isaiah is commissioned to meet with Ahaz, who is inspecting water supplies in preparation for a siege. Isaiah is also to take his son with him. His son is called Shear-Jashub, meaning "a remnant will return." The reason for taking his son is not explained until verses 15-16.

In verses 4-6, the message is given, describing the plot and telling Ahaz not to be afraid. The plot consists of overthrowing Ahaz and replacing him with the son of Tabeel. Isaiah was a master of the Hebrew language and loved playing word games. He does so here in verse 6. "Tabeel" means "God is good." By altering the vowel pattern very slightly, Isaiah changes this to mean "good for nothing." The one that means "God is good" will prove to be "good for nothing." Because of the Davidic Covenant, no conspiracy against the House of David can ever succeed. God clearly states this in verse 7, and, in verses 8-9, God will judge the two kings involved in the conspiracy.

---

[3] The Davidic Covenant is discussed under 1 Chronicles 17:10b–14 in the section on the Writings, page 80.

The Signs of Deliverance—Isaiah 7:10-17

The Offer of a Sign—Isaiah 7:10-11

Ahaz, however, is an idolater who does not trust in God and has made his own arrangements. He has sent letters and gifts to the Assyrian emperor, asking for assistance in his defense against these two kings. He has greater faith in the Assyrian Empire than in the God of Israel. So, in verse 10, God speaks a second time. He offers Ahaz a sign—whatever it takes to convince Ahaz not to fear, not to trust the Assyrians, but to trust in God. Whatever it takes, let him ask for it, and God will do it for him. The word for "sign" does not of itself mean a miracle; it could be a miraculous or a natural sign. Within this context, however, it is clear that it will take a miracle to convince Ahaz. God offers him a sign anywhere he wants—in heaven, on earth, under the earth—whatever it takes to convince him.

The Rejection of the Offer—Isaiah 7:12

In response, the idolatrous Ahaz suddenly becomes very spiritual. In verse 12, he refuses to "test" God or "tempt" Him. This is a reference to Deuteronomy 6:16, but he misapplies it. Nevertheless, it is evident that, even in idolatry, Ahaz was not ignorant of the true God! Deuteronomy 6:16 warns against *asking* for a sign, but here God is *offering* a sign and Ahaz is invited to respond. Ahaz does not want a sign, lest it come to pass and he be forced to abandon his alliance with Assyria.

Then come the crucial verses, 13 and 14.

The Sign to the House of David—Isaiah 7:13-14

In verse 13, Isaiah turns from addressing Ahaz as an individual to addressing the entire House of David. The English language does not distinguish between "you" referring to one person and "you" addressed to many people. In Hebrew, there *is* a difference, and there is a clear change between the singular "you" of verses 9, 11, 16, 17 and the plural "you" of verses 13-14. The sign therefore is not just for Ahaz, but for the whole House of David. This becomes clearer if we state the passage again with the singular [s] and plural [pl] words indicated:

> [10] Then the Lord spoke again to Ahaz, saying, [11] "Ask a sign for yourself [s] from the Lord your God; make it deep as Sheol or high as heaven." [12] But Ahaz said, "I will not ask, nor will I test the Lord!" [13] Then he said, "Listen now, O house of David! Is it too slight a thing for you [pl] to try the patience of men, that you [pl] will try the patience of my God as well? [14] "Therefore the Lord Himself will give you [pl] a sign: Behold, a virgin will be with child and bear a son, and she will call His name Immanuel. [15] "He will eat curds and honey at the time He knows enough to refuse evil and choose good. [16] "For before the boy will know enough to refuse evil and choose good, the land whose two kings you [s] dread will be forsaken. [17] "The Lord will bring on you

[s], on your people, and on your father's house such days as have never come since the day that Ephraim separated from Judah, the king of Assyria." (NASB, with comments added)

In verse 14, the Hebrew word for "behold" is a word that draws attention to an event which could be past, present, or future. However, grammatically, whenever "behold" is used with the Hebrew present participle, it always refers to a future event. That is the case here. Not only is the birth future, but the very conception is future. This is not referring to a pregnant woman about to give birth.

The text specifically says *"the* virgin" (the NIV and NKJV are correct at this point; the NASB like most translations says *"a* virgin," which is quite wrong). According to the rules of Hebrew grammar, when finding the use of a definite article (*the*), the reader should look for a reference in the immediate previous context. Having followed the passage from chapter 7:1, there has been no mention of any woman. Having failed with the immediate context, the second rule is the "principle of previous reference," something which has been dealt with much earlier and is common knowledge among the people. Where in Jewish Scripture or tradition is there any concept of "the virgin giving birth to a son"? The only possible reference is to Genesis 3:15. Contrary to the biblical norm, the Messiah would be reckoned after the seed of the woman. Why? Because He would have no human father; His would be a virgin conception and birth.

The key point of this should not be missed. God is promising that the House of David cannot be deposed or lose its identity until the birth of a virgin-born son. Again, this requires that Messiah be born prior to the destruction of the Temple and its genealogical records in A.D. 70.

The Sign to Ahaz—Isaiah 7:15-17

Having concluded that Isaiah 7:12-14 is a long-range prophecy concerning the birth of Messiah, that still leaves a problem. What about Ahaz? An event 700 years in the future is of little significance to him. There is however a second sign in verses 15-17, and this time it is specifically for Ahaz. The "you" in verse 16 is again singular, meaning Ahaz. Before Isaiah's son is old enough to make moral distinctions between right and wrong, the kings of Israel and Syria will be deposed and their threat removed. This was fulfilled within three years. Isaiah again uses the definite article before the term "boy." This time, there is another boy mentioned in the context: Isaiah's son. The boy of verse 16 cannot be the son of verse 14 but refers back to Isaiah's son in verse 3. Why else was Isaiah commanded to take him?

Summary of Isaiah 7:1-17

In Isaiah chapter 7, Ahaz, the king of Judah, is under threat of attack. This threat is not only to him personally but to the whole House of David. Through the Prophet Isaiah, God tells King Ahaz to be at peace and to be unafraid. Two reasons are given, two signs which guarantee God's promise of security. The first sign, in verses 13 and 14, is that no attempt to destroy the House of David will succeed until the birth of a virgin-born son. The term "virgin" is required both by the Hebrew vocabulary and the context. The second sign, in verses 15 and 16, is given to Ahaz personally. God promises that the attack upon him by Israel and Syria will not succeed, and before Isaiah's son, Shear-Jashub, reaches an age of moral maturity, the two enemy kings will cease to exist.

Isaiah 7:14

teaches that:

✿ Messiah would be born of a girl who is still a virgin; the explanation of Genesis 3:15.

✿ Messiah will be the God-Man.

✿ Messiah will be a king.

✿ Messiah must be born prior to the destruction of the Temple in A.D. 70.

Isaiah 8:9-10

The Promise of Immanuel

⁹ "Be broken, O peoples, and be shattered; And give ear, all remote places of the earth. Gird yourselves, yet be shattered; Gird yourselves, yet be shattered. ¹⁰ "Devise a plan but it will be thwarted; State a proposal, but it will not stand, For God is with us." (NASB)

רֹעוּ עַמִּים וָחֹתּוּ וְהַאֲזִינוּ כֹּל מֶרְחַקֵּי־אָרֶץ הִתְאַזְּרוּ ⁹
וָחֹתּוּ הִתְאַזְּרוּ וָחֹתּוּ: ¹⁰ עֻצוּ עֵצָה וְתֻפָר דַּבְּרוּ דָבָר וְלֹא
יָקוּם כִּי עִמָּנוּ אֵל: ס

saiah 7 describes how King Ahaz was under threat of attack. This threat was primarily directed against him, but also against the House of King David. When God made His covenant with David, He promised him an eternal dynasty.[4] This covenant assured the House of David of God's protection. God's response in Isaiah 7 was to offer a sign to King Ahaz assuring him of his security and to offer another sign which assured the preservation of the House of David. This meant that God was committed to preserving the line of David until "the virgin shall conceive and bear a son and call his name Immanuel." Clearly therefore, until this birth takes place, all conspiracies and uprisings against the House of David are doomed to failure.

It is this point which is reaffirmed in Isaiah 8:9-10. The real impact of these two verses is lost in English translations because of the failure to use the proper name *Immanuel*. Immanuel means "God with us," but it is quite wrong to translate it as such in verse 10. It is the same word as in 7:14 and 8:8 and should be translated the same way here: Immanuel. What is being said here is "attack if you want, but you will be defeated because of Immanuel." Until the virgin birth of Immanuel, the Messiah, God promises to preserve the security and identity of the House of David.

In A.D. 70, the Temple in Jerusalem was destroyed and along with it were lost all of the genealogical records of Israel. Since then, it has not been possible to identify the descendants of David. If the promise given in Isaiah 8:10 is true, it follows that Messiah must have been born before A.D. 70.

Isaiah 8:10

teaches that:

✡ **Messiah must be born prior to the destruction of the Temple in A.D. 70.**

---

[4] See discussion of 1 Chronicles 17:10b–14 on page 80.

Isaiah 9:6-7

Unto Us a Son Is Given

⁶ For a child will be born to us, a son will be given to us; And the government will rest on His shoulders; And His name will be called Wonderful Counselor, Mighty God, Eternal Father, Prince of Peace. ⁷ There will be no end to the increase of His government or of peace, On the throne of David and over his kingdom, To establish it and to uphold it with justice and righteousness From then on and forevermore. The zeal of the LORD of hosts will accomplish this. (NASB)

⁵ כִּי־יֶלֶד יֻלַּד־לָנוּ בֵּן נִתַּן־לָנוּ וַתְּהִי הַמִּשְׂרָה עַל־שִׁכְמוֹ וַיִּקְרָא שְׁמוֹ פֶּלֶא יוֹעֵץ אֵל גִּבּוֹר אֲבִיעַד שַׂר־שָׁלוֹם: ⁶ לְמַרְבֵּה הַמִּשְׂרָה וּלְשָׁלוֹם אֵין־קֵץ עַל־כִּסֵּא דָוִד וְעַל־מַמְלַכְתּוֹ לְהָכִין אֹתָהּ וּלְסַעֲדָהּ בְּמִשְׁפָּט וּבִצְדָקָה מֵעַתָּה וְעַד־עוֹלָם קִנְאַת יְהוָה צְבָאוֹת תַּעֲשֶׂה־זֹּאת: ס

Note that the Hebrew verse numbering differs from the English numbering for this passage.

Chapters 7-12 of Isaiah comprise the fifth major section of the book and constitute a single unit sometimes referred to as "The Book of Immanuel." The name Immanuel appears three times in this section, in verses 7:14, 8:8, and 8:10, but the unit as a whole deals with various facets of the Messiah. The two verses discussed here deal specifically with Messiah's origin, both human and divine.

Human Origin—Isaiah 9:6a

Isaiah 9:6a emphasizes the humanity of Messiah (His Messiahship is shown in verse 7). Isaiah sees a Son, given by God and being born into the human world, specifically, the Jewish world. The phrase "unto us a son is given" emphasizes the uniqueness of this gift of God. This is the same Son as in Psalm 2, which will be dealt with later.

Divine Origin—Isaiah 9:6b

In 9:6b, this son is given four names, each one having two parts. Each of these names is applicable to God; three of them exclusively so.

33

1.   **Wonderful Counselor** *(Pele-Yoeitz)*

     In some translations a comma is placed between these two words making them two separate names. The word "wonderful" is in the construct state and should be taken together with "counselor." There are some words in Hebrew which are used only of God and never of men. One example is *barah*, meaning "to create." This is used only of God and what God does. Another example is the word *"pele,"* rendered here in English as "wonderful." In English, "wonderful" may be freely used of many things, but in Hebrew it is reserved exclusively for that which is divine.

2.   **Mighty God** *(El-Gibbor)*

     Obviously never used of a mere man.

3.   **Eternal Father** *(Avi-Ad)*

     Literally: Father of Eternity. The Son who is to be born will be the Father of Eternity, meaning that He is the source of eternal life. Clearly this is to be no mere man.

4.   **Prince of Peace** *(Sar-Shalom)*

     This is the only one of the four names which can be used of man and God.

Furthermore, these four names are all used elsewhere in the book of Isaiah. In each case, they are used of God, never of man.

1.   **Wonderful Counselor**

     This can be found in Isaiah 25:1, "I will praise your name; for you have done wonderful things, even counsels of old." In Isaiah 28:29, it says, "This also comes forth from Jehovah of hosts, who is wonderful in counsel" (ASV). In both cases, the word "wonderful" clearly refers to God.

2.   **Mighty God**

     This is found in the very next chapter in Isaiah 10:21, which says, "to the mighty God." There are many liberal theologians who object to the concept of Messiah as a God-Man. When they translate verses such as Isaiah 9:6, they are forced to interfere with the text in order to justify their own presuppositions. In the New English Bible, for example, an entire phrase—completely absent in the Hebrew text—is inserted to make Isaiah 9:6 read, "in battle he will be Godlike." This is an impossible translation. In the Hebrew, there are only two words, *El Gibbor*, which mean "God Almighty." Furthermore, when the same words appear in Isaiah 10:21, the NEB then translates them correctly as "the mighty God." Clearly there is no integrity in such inconsistent translation.

3.   **Eternal Father**

     This can be compared with Isaiah 63:16b, which says, "you, O Jehovah, are our Father; our Redeemer from everlasting is your name" (ASV). The same words used in Isaiah 9:6 as a proper name are seen within this sentence. Here, they are clearly used of God.

4. **Prince of Peace**

Isaiah 26:3 says, "You will keep him in perfect peace, whose mind is stayed on you." The object and subject of the sentence is God Himself. In Isaiah 26:12, the work of peace is also attributed to God: "Lord, you will ordain peace for us." As stated above, "Prince of Peace" is sometimes used of men in the Hebrew text. If we limit our attention to the book of Isaiah, however, then the work of peace is the work of God only.

The Rule of the King—Isaiah 9:7

Isaiah 9:6 presents us with a being who is both God and man. Isaiah 9:7 shows us that this person is the Messiah of Israel: He is to sit upon the throne of David. Verse 7 is a reaffirmation of the Davidic Covenant.[5] In the Davidic Covenant, God promised David four things:

1. An eternal house or dynasty

2. An eternal kingdom

3. An eternal throne

4. An eternal son

Isaiah 9:7 further confirms that David's house, kingdom, and throne will be maintained eternally by the everlasting Son.

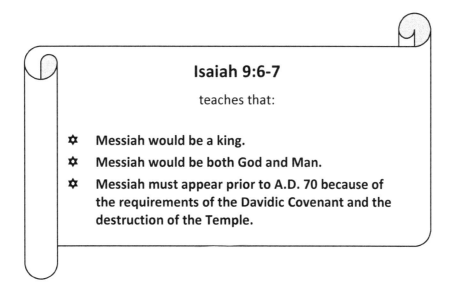

Isaiah 9:6-7

teaches that:

✡ **Messiah would be a king.**
✡ **Messiah would be both God and Man.**
✡ **Messiah must appear prior to A.D. 70 because of the requirements of the Davidic Covenant and the destruction of the Temple.**

---

[5] The Davidic Covenant is studied under 1 Chronicles 17:10b–14 on page 80.

Isaiah 11:1-2

The Stump of Jesse

[1] A shoot will come up from the stump of Jesse; from his roots a Branch will bear fruit. [2] The Spirit of the LORD will rest on him—the Spirit of wisdom and of understanding, the Spirit of counsel and of power, the Spirit of knowledge and of the fear of the LORD—[3] and he will delight in the fear of the LORD. (NIV)

וְיָצָא חֹטֶר מִגֵּזַע יִשָׁי וְנֵצֶר מִשָׁרָשָׁיו יִפְרֶה: [2] וְנָחָה עָלָיו רוּחַ יְהוָה רוּחַ חָכְמָה וּבִינָה רוּחַ עֵצָה וּגְבוּרָה רוּחַ דַּעַת וְיִרְאַת יְהוָה:

The emphasis in verse 1 is on Messiah's lowly origin. The picture given is of a tree which has been cut down, leaving only a dead stump. A single shoot remains growing low, near to the ground, eventually bearing fruit. It is interesting that this particular prophecy does not use the name of David, but uses the name of David's father, Jesse. David is normally associated with kingship, royalty, and wealth. It should not be forgotten, however, that in his youth, living in the house of Jesse, David was a poor shepherd boy. During the lifetime of David, the house of Jesse was raised from poverty in Bethlehem to honor and majesty in Jerusalem. The emphasis of verse 1 is that although Messiah will be a descendant of David, He will not appear until the House of David has been once again reduced to what it was in the days of Jesse. This verse concentrates on the lowly origin of Messiah at the time of His birth, rather than the majesty of His kingdom which will be seen at His second coming. From the stump of Jesse, however, grows a shoot, low to the ground, but not without fruit. Eventually this shoot will become a tree in its own right.

In verse 2, we are told that this One will have the sevenfold fullness of the Holy Spirit. The description used here is representative of the Jewish *Menorah* or seven-branched lampstand. The "Spirit of the Lord" is mentioned once, followed by three more references to "the Spirit of," each one followed by two attributes (see chart on page 38). When looking for the fulfillment of this prophecy in the life of Yeshua, we find that:

1. **Yeshua was born into the House of David.**

2. **He was born in Bethlehem, the home of Jesse.**

3. He was born in great poverty.

This is seen at the time of Mary's (*Miriam* in Hebrew) purification. It was required by the law, in Leviticus 12:1-8, that after the birth of a baby, the mother should go to the Temple and make a sacrifice for her cleansing. This had to be a blood sacrifice, and two offerings were acceptable. Normally, the sacrifice would consist of a lamb and a pigeon or dove, but provision was made for exceptionally poor families, from whom two pigeons or doves were acceptable. We are told in Luke's Gospel that Yeshua's mother could only afford two birds. Both Mary and Joseph were descendants of David, and so the abject poverty of the House of David is made clear.

4. In John 3:34, John the Baptist describes Yeshua as having the fullness of the Spirit.

"For He whom God has sent speaks the words of God; for He gives the Spirit without measure." The New Testament teaches that all who believe in Yeshua as Messiah are given a measure of the Holy Spirit. Because each believer only has a measure of the Spirit, each one has different gifts and ministries (1 Corinthians 12:13-14). No one ever has all of the gifts because God has ordained that the members of the Church be mutually dependent. Yeshua, however, was given the Spirit "without measure." In Scripture, the number seven signifies perfection, completeness, or fullness. The sevenfold nature of the Spirit in Isaiah 11:2 is therefore synonymous with the measureless fullness in John 3:34. It also corresponds to the "seven spirits" of Revelation 1:4, 3:1, 4:5, and 5:6.

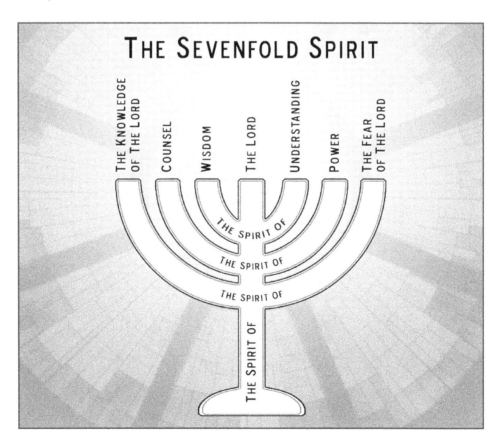

Isaiah 11:1-2

teaches that:

- ✡ Messiah would be born into the House of David.
- ✡ Messiah would not be born until the House of David had once again returned to the state of poverty which it was in during the days of David's father, Jesse. Messiah will be born into a house of lowliness.
- ✡ Messiah would have the sevenfold fullness of the Holy Spirit and act accordingly.

Isaiah 40:3-5

The Herald of the King

³ A voice is calling, "Clear the way for the LORD in the wilderness; Make smooth in the desert a highway for our God. ⁴ "Let every valley be lifted up, And every mountain and hill be made low; And let the rough ground become a plain, And the rugged terrain a broad valley; ⁵ Then the glory of the LORD will be revealed, And all flesh will see it together; For the mouth of the LORD has spoken." (NASB)

³ קוֹל קוֹרֵא בַּמִּדְבָּר פַּנּוּ דֶּרֶךְ יְהֹוָה יַשְּׁרוּ בָּעֲרָבָה מְסִלָּה לֵאלֹהֵינוּ: ⁴ כָּל־גֶּיא יִנָּשֵׂא וְכָל־הַר וְגִבְעָה יִשְׁפָּלוּ וְהָיָה הֶעָקֹב לְמִישׁוֹר וְהָרְכָסִים לְבִקְעָה: ⁵ וְנִגְלָה כְּבוֹד יְהֹוָה וְרָאוּ כָל־בָּשָׂר יַחְדָּו כִּי פִּי יְהֹוָה דִּבֵּר: ס

These verses do not deal with Messiah personally, but with His forerunner. In ancient times, a herald would be sent out to clear the road of obstacles or repair any pot-holes prior to a journey by the king. This passage states that such a forerunner will precede the arrival of the Messianic Kings. In the New Testament, the words are specifically applied to John the Baptist:

¹ Now in those days John the Baptist came, preaching in the wilderness of Judea, saying, ² "Repent, for the kingdom of heaven is at hand." ³ For this is the one referred to by Isaiah the prophet, saying, "The voice of one crying in the wilderness, 'Make ready the way of the Lord, make His paths straight!' " . . . ⁵ Then Jerusalem was going out to him, and all Judea, and all the district around the Jordan; ⁶ and they were being baptized by him in the Jordan River, as they confessed their sins.

Matthew 3:1-6 (NASB)

See also Mark 1:2-8; Luke 1:5-80 (especially verse 76); Luke 3:1-20 (especially verses 4-6); and John 1:6-8, 15-36 (especially verse 23).

Isaiah 40:3-5

teaches that:

✡ **Messiah would have a forerunner to prepare for His arrival.**

Isaiah 42:1-6

The Servant of Jehovah

¹ "Behold, My Servant, whom I uphold; My chosen one *in whom* My soul delights. I have put My Spirit upon Him; He will bring forth justice to the nations. ² "He will not cry out or raise His voice, Nor make His voice heard in the street. ³ "A bruised reed He will not break, And a dimly burning wick He will not extinguish; He will faithfully bring forth justice. ⁴ "He will not be disheartened or crushed, Until He has established justice in the earth; And the coastlands will wait expectantly for His law." ⁵ Thus says God the LORD, Who created the heavens and stretched them out, Who spread out the earth and its offspring, Who gives breath to the people on it, And spirit to those who walk in it, ⁶ "I am the LORD, I have called you in righteousness, I will also hold you by the hand and watch over you, And I will appoint you as a covenant to the people, As a light to the nations, (NASB)

הֵן עַבְדִּי אֶתְמָךְ־בּוֹ בְּחִירִי רָצְתָה נַפְשִׁי נָתַתִּי רוּחִי ¹
עָלָיו מִשְׁפָּט לַגּוֹיִם יוֹצִיא: ² לֹא יִצְעַק וְלֹא יִשָּׂא וְלֹא־
יַשְׁמִיעַ בַּחוּץ קוֹלוֹ: ³ קָנֶה רָצוּץ לֹא יִשְׁבּוֹר וּפִשְׁתָּה
כֵהָה לֹא יְכַבֶּנָּה לֶאֱמֶת יוֹצִיא מִשְׁפָּט: ⁴ לֹא יִכְהֶה וְלֹא
יָרוּץ עַד־יָשִׂים בָּאָרֶץ מִשְׁפָּט וּלְתוֹרָתוֹ אִיִּים יְיַחֵלוּ: פ
⁵ כֹּה־אָמַר הָאֵל יְהוָה בּוֹרֵא הַשָּׁמַיִם וְנוֹטֵיהֶם רֹקַע
הָאָרֶץ וְצֶאֱצָאֶיהָ נֹתֵן נְשָׁמָה לָעָם עָלֶיהָ וְרוּחַ לַהֹלְכִים
בָּהּ: ⁶ אֲנִי יְהוָה קְרָאתִיךָ בְצֶדֶק וְאַחְזֵק בְּיָדֶךָ וְאֶצָּרְךָ
וְאֶתֶּנְךָ לִבְרִית עָם לְאוֹר גּוֹיִם:

One of Isaiah's favorite designations for the Messiah is the term "servant." This Messianic title is found throughout chapters 42 to 66 of Isaiah's book. This is the first of five "servant" passages which we will study. Isaiah 42:1-6 can be broken down into four sections, each of which emphasizes a different aspect of the Messianic Person. The various points made can be detailed as listed below.

His Status—Isaiah 42:1

Verse 1 makes four points.

1. **He is the Servant of Jehovah.**
   This is the theme of the Gospel of Mark. Each of the four Gospel writers wrote for a different audience and highlighted different aspects of the life of Yeshua. Matthew emphasizes Messiah's royalty—Yeshua, the King of the Jews. Luke, the doctor, deals with the humanity

of Yeshua—Yeshua, the Messiah, the Son of Man. John concentrates on the divinity of Messiah—Yeshua, the Son of God. Mark sees Messiah primarily as the Servant of Jehovah. He focuses on those aspects of Yeshua's life which best demonstrate the way in which Yeshua perfectly completed the assignments given to Him as described in the Prophets and particularly the servant-passages of Isaiah.

2. **He is Jehovah's Chosen One in whom Jehovah will greatly delight.**

3. **He is anointed with the Spirit.**
   This is a reaffirmation of Isaiah 11:2.

4. **He will benefit the Gentile nations.**
   Although Messiah will come primarily for the Jewish nation, there will be some way by which the Gentiles (the nations) will also benefit. This is not explained here but is developed further in Isaiah 49:6, our next passage.

Most rabbis, apart from Rashi, saw verse 1 as being Messianic.

1. *Targum Pseudo-Jonathan*
   "Behold My Servant, the Messiah, I will draw Him near, My Chosen One in whom My *Memra* is well pleased."

2. **Rabbi David Kimchi**
   "Behold My Servant . . . This is King Messiah."

His Manner—Isaiah 42:2

Verse 2 describes the manner in which He will conduct Himself. Messiah will not be a street preacher. The Gospels describe Yeshua as teaching primarily in the synagogues. He also taught large groups of people on the hillsides; but these were people who came to Him, who sought Him out. At no time did Yeshua deliberately seek attention on the streets of the cities, but rather His reputation went ahead of Him, and it was the crowds who went looking for Him. This is not to say that there is anything wrong with street preaching. On the contrary, the New Testament encourages it and describes the apostles as doing so; but that was not Messiah's mode of operation.

His Way—Isaiah 42:3

Verse 3 emphasizes His character traits. He will be characterized by mercy, truth, and justice. Those who come to Him for help will be accepted and treated with great tenderness.

His Success—Isaiah 42:4

Verse 4 teaches that, ultimately, Messiah will not fail nor be discouraged. There will be discouragements along the way, as will be seen in the next passage, but these will be temporary. All of the objectives laid down for His first coming will be accomplished.

His Mission—Isaiah 42:5-6

Verses 5-6 teach that the coming of the Messiah will benefit two groups of people. First, the Messiah will be "the Covenant of the People," meaning He will be the One to fulfill God's covenant-promises to Israel. Second, He will be "the Light to the nations," the One to bring salvation-light to the Gentiles.

Isaiah 42:1-6

teaches that:

✿ The Messiah would be anointed by the Holy Spirit.

✿ The Messiah would conduct Himself in meekness and gentleness.

✿ Although Messiah's mission would appear to end in failure, it would in fact be a complete success. The success of His mission required His death.

✿ Messiah's mission includes Gentile salvation.

Isaiah 49:1-13

The Discouragement of the Servant

[1] Listen to Me, O islands, And pay attention, you peoples from afar. The LORD called Me from the womb; From the body of My mother He named Me. [2] And He has made My mouth like a sharp sword; In the shadow of His hand He has concealed Me, And He has also made Me a select arrow; He has hidden Me in His quiver. [3] And He said to Me, "You are My Servant, Israel, In Whom I will show My glory." [4] But I said, "I have toiled in vain, I have spent My strength for nothing and vanity; Yet surely the justice *due* to Me is with the LORD, And My reward with My God." [5] And now says the LORD, who formed Me from the womb to be His Servant, To bring Jacob back to Him, in order that Israel might be gathered to Him (For I am honored in the sight of the LORD, And My God is My strength), [6] He says, "It is too small a thing that You should be My Servant To raise up the tribes of Jacob, and to restore the preserved ones of Israel; I will also make You a light of the nations So that My salvation may reach to the end of the earth." [7] Thus says the LORD, the Redeemer of Israel, *and* its Holy One, To the despised One, To the One abhorred by the nation, To the Servant of rulers, "Kings shall see and arise, Princes shall also bow down; Because of the LORD who is faithful, the Holy One of Israel who has chosen You." [8] Thus says the LORD, "In a favorable time I have answered You, And in a day of salvation I have helped You; And I will keep You and give You for a covenant of the people, To restore the land, to make *them* inherit the desolate heritages;

שִׁמְעוּ אִיִּים אֵלַי וְהַקְשִׁיבוּ לְאֻמִּים מֵרָחוֹק יְהוָה [1] מִבֶּטֶן קְרָאָנִי מִמְּעֵי אִמִּי הִזְכִּיר שְׁמִי: [2] וַיָּשֶׂם פִּי כְּחֶרֶב חַדָּה בְּצֵל יָדוֹ הֶחְבִּיאָנִי וַיְשִׂימֵנִי לְחֵץ בָּרוּר בְּאַשְׁפָּתוֹ הִסְתִּירָנִי: [3] וַיֹּאמֶר לִי עַבְדִּי־אָתָּה יִשְׂרָאֵל אֲשֶׁר־בְּךָ אֶתְפָּאָר: [4] וַאֲנִי אָמַרְתִּי לְרִיק יָגַעְתִּי לְתֹהוּ וְהֶבֶל כֹּחִי כִלֵּיתִי אָכֵן מִשְׁפָּטִי אֶת־יְהוָה וּפְעֻלָּתִי אֶת־אֱלֹהָי: [5] וְעַתָּה אָמַר יְהוָה יֹצְרִי מִבֶּטֶן לְעֶבֶד לוֹ לְשׁוֹבֵב יַעֲקֹב אֵלָיו וְיִשְׂרָאֵל לֹא יֵאָסֵף וְאֶכָּבֵד בְּעֵינֵי יְהוָה וֵאלֹהַי הָיָה עֻזִּי: [6] וַיֹּאמֶר נָקֵל מִהְיוֹתְךָ לִי עֶבֶד לְהָקִים אֶת־שִׁבְטֵי יַעֲקֹב וּנְצִירֵי יִשְׂרָאֵל לְהָשִׁיב וּנְתַתִּיךָ לְאוֹר גּוֹיִם לִהְיוֹת יְשׁוּעָתִי עַד־קְצֵה הָאָרֶץ: ס [7] כֹּה אָמַר־יְהוָה גֹּאֵל יִשְׂרָאֵל קְדוֹשׁוֹ לִבְזֹה־נֶפֶשׁ לִמְתָעֵב גּוֹי לְעֶבֶד מֹשְׁלִים מְלָכִים יִרְאוּ וָקָמוּ שָׂרִים וְיִשְׁתַּחֲווּ לְמַעַן יְהוָה אֲשֶׁר נֶאֱמָן קְדֹשׁ יִשְׂרָאֵל וַיִּבְחָרֶךָּ: [8] כֹּה אָמַר יְהוָה בְּעֵת רָצוֹן עֲנִיתִיךָ וּבְיוֹם יְשׁוּעָה עֲזַרְתִּיךָ וְאֶצָּרְךָ וְאֶתֶּנְךָ לִבְרִית עָם לְהָקִים אֶרֶץ לְהַנְחִיל נְחָלוֹת שֹׁמֵמוֹת:

9 Saying to those who are bound, 'Go forth,' To those who are in darkness, 'Show yourselves.' Along the roads they will feed, And their pasture will be on all bare heights. 10 "They will not hunger or thirst, Neither will the scorching heat or sun strike them down; For He who has compassion on them will lead them, And will guide them to springs of water. 11 "And I will make all My mountains a road, And My highways will be raised up. 12 "Behold, these shall come from afar; And lo, these *will come* from the north and from the west, And these from the land of Sinim." 13 Shout for joy, O heavens! And rejoice, O earth! Break forth into joyful shouting, O mountains! For the LORD has comforted His people, And will have compassion on His afflicted. (NASB)

לֵאמֹר לַאֲסוּרִים צֵאוּ לַאֲשֶׁר בַּחֹשֶׁךְ הִגָּלוּ עַל־ 9
דְּרָכִים יִרְעוּ וּבְכָל־שְׁפָיִים מַרְעִיתָם: 10 לֹא יִרְעָבוּ
וְלֹא יִצְמָאוּ וְלֹא־יַכֵּם שָׁרָב וָשָׁמֶשׁ כִּי־מְרַחֲמָם
יְנַהֲגֵם וְעַל־מַבּוּעֵי מַיִם יְנַהֲלֵם: 11 וְשַׂמְתִּי כָל־הָרַי
לַדָּרֶךְ וּמְסִלֹּתַי יְרֻמוּן: 12 הִנֵּה־אֵלֶּה מֵרָחוֹק יָבֹאוּ
וְהִנֵּה־אֵלֶּה מִצָּפוֹן וּמִיָּם וְאֵלֶּה מֵאֶרֶץ סִינִים: 13 רָנּוּ
שָׁמַיִם וְגִילִי אָרֶץ יִפְצְחוּ הָרִים רִנָּה כִּי־נִחַם יְהוָה
עַמּוֹ וַעֲנִיָּו יְרַחֵם: ס

This is the second of the five "servant" passages in Isaiah. The first passage, 42:1-6, introduced the Servant. This passage, 49:1-13, now tells us more about the mission of the Servant and develops the promise in Isaiah 42 that He would bring blessing to the Gentiles. This will result from His initial rejection by the nation of Israel, although assurance is given that He will, finally, be accepted by Israel.

The Servant's Discouragement—Isaiah 49:1-4

Verses 1-4 highlight a temporary discouragement in the life of Messiah. In verse 1, the words of Messiah Himself are being spoken prophetically by Isaiah. He says that from His very conception He has been given a specific mission by God. In Matthew 1:21, we are told that the angel said to Joseph at the time of Mary's conception, "you are to call Him Yeshua because He will save His people from their sins." Here again, we have a reference to a mother but not a father, which is consistent with the virgin birth prophesied in Isaiah 7:14.

In verse 2, Messiah has been specifically called and equipped for His task.

In verse 3, Messiah, the Servant of Jehovah, is called "Israel *par excellence*" because He will be the only Jew to completely and perfectly fulfill the Mosaic Law.

It is in verse 4 that the note of discouragement comes. As is seen elsewhere, the Servant, despite His perfection, will be rejected, and it is this which causes His sadness. Yet He still has hope: "my reward is with my God." From a New Testament point of view, the only place in the life of Yeshua where this can find fulfillment is in the Garden of Gethsemane. In the Gospels, one reason for His discouragement is His fear of experiencing spiritual death, and He prays that the cup of God's wrath might pass from Him (Matthew 26:38-39 and Mark 14:34-36). Isaiah 49 highlights a second reason for discouragement. He had ministered to the nation of Israel for three and a half years, and although He had come as their Messiah, the Jewish nation rejected Him.

God's Answer—Isaiah 49:5-6

The Lord replies with words of encouragement in verses 5-6. He begins in verse 5 by summarizing the Servant's original commission:

1. **To bring Israel to spiritual salvation**

2. **To gather the dispersed Israel to physical restoration**
    Given Israel's rejection of the Servant, how can these objectives now be accomplished? The Lord continues in verse 6 by giving the Servant a third objective:

3. **To be a light to, and bring salvation to, the Gentile nations**
    Israel's rejection of Messiah at His first coming is part of God's plan. It need not be a source of discouragement. It was always God's plan that, for a period of time, the first two objectives would be set aside in order that salvation may go out to the Gentiles. It was noted in Isaiah 42:1 that the Gentiles would somehow benefit from Messiah's coming; now we are told exactly how.

The Rejection and Exaltation of the Messiah—Isaiah 49:7

Verse 7a confirms that Israel will reject Messiah, but verse 7b goes on to say that the rejection will only be for a time and Messiah will one day be accepted.

The Restoration by the Messiah—Isaiah 49:8-13

In verse 8, when Messiah's mission to the Gentiles is complete, then will come the final restoration of Israel. The rest of the passage through to verse 13 elaborates on this final restoration. Messiah will become the covenant for the people (singular, meaning Israel), showing that the Jews have at last accepted Him. With Israel's acceptance of Messiah comes the in-gathering of the dispersed Jews; in verse 12, even from as far away as *the land of Sinim*. "Sinim" is the modern Hebrew word for "China," but it is uncertain if that was the meaning in the Old Testament. The word does certainly imply the Far East. If there are Jews in the Far East, they will be re-gathered. It is interesting to note that at the time Isaiah wrote this, the Jewish people were not yet dispersed from the land; China, or anywhere in the Far East, would have been the last place to have looked for a Jew.

Summary

At the present time, Yeshua is still being rejected as Messiah by Israel. It is often said that if Yeshua had really been the true Messiah, then He would have been welcomed by the Jewish leaders of His day. This passage makes it very clear, however, that that is the exact *opposite* of the truth. Every man who has been hailed as Messiah by Jewish leadership has proved to be a false Messiah. Isaiah says quite specifically that Messiah will initially be rejected. Rejection is stated as being one of the credentials of Messiahship. Israel's national rejection of Yeshua substantiates His claim to be Messiah.

The purpose of the rejection the salvation of the Gentiles. For a limited time, there will be more Gentile believers than Jewish believers. In Acts 15:14, God is said to be "taking from the Gentiles a people for Himself." In Romans 11:25-26, it says that this will continue "until the full number of the Gentiles has come in. And so, all Israel shall be saved." Note that these things were written by the Jewish leaders of the first Jewish Church in Jerusalem. The tendency that there are more Gentile than Jewish believers will continue until the Church is numerically complete, at which point the rapture will occur. God will then again deal with Israel, and as Paul says above, "all Israel will be saved." Paul is building on what is written in Isaiah 49:7: Messiah is to be despised and abhorred by Israel, but is later destined for glory and honor, to be worshipped by kings and princes worldwide.

Isaiah 49:1-3

teaches that:

✿   The Messiah's first coming would be rejected by Israel.

✿   For a time, the message of salvation through Messiah will go out to the Gentiles.

✿   Eventually, Israel will receive Messiah; He will become their New Covenant.

✿   Israel's acceptance of Messiah will herald the re-gathering of all Jews to the land of Israel.

Isaiah 50:4-9

The Training of the Servant

⁴ The Lord GOD has given Me the tongue of disciples, That I may know how to sustain the weary one with a word. He awakens Me morning by morning, He awakens My ear to listen as a disciple. ⁵ The Lord GOD has opened My ear; And I was not disobedient, Nor did I turn back. ⁶ I gave My back to those who strike Me, And My cheeks to those who pluck out the beard; I did not cover My face from humiliation and spitting. ⁷ For the Lord GOD helps Me, Therefore, I am not disgraced; Therefore, I have set My face like flint, And I know that I shall not be ashamed. ⁸ He who vindicates Me is near; Who will contend with Me? Let us stand up to each other; Who has a case against Me? Let him draw near to Me. ⁹ Behold, the Lord GOD helps Me; Who is he who condemns Me? Behold, they will all wear out like a garment; The moth will eat them. (NASB)

⁴ אֲדֹנָי יְהוִה נָתַן לִי לְשׁוֹן לִמּוּדִים לָדַעַת לָעוּת אֶת־יָעֵף דָּבָר יָעִיר בַּבֹּקֶר בַּבֹּקֶר יָעִיר לִי אֹזֶן לִשְׁמֹעַ כַּלִּמּוּדִים: ⁵ אֲדֹנָי יְהוִה פָּתַח־לִי אֹזֶן וְאָנֹכִי לֹא מָרִיתִי אָחוֹר לֹא נְסוּגֹתִי: ⁶ גֵּוִי נָתַתִּי לְמַכִּים וּלְחָיַי לְמֹרְטִים פָּנַי לֹא הִסְתַּרְתִּי מִכְּלִמּוֹת וָרֹק: ⁷ וַאדֹנָי יְהוִה יַעֲזָר־לִי עַל־כֵּן לֹא נִכְלָמְתִּי עַל־כֵּן שַׂמְתִּי פָנַי כַּחַלָּמִישׁ וָאֵדַע כִּי־לֹא אֵבוֹשׁ: ⁸ קָרוֹב מַצְדִּיקִי מִי־יָרִיב אִתִּי נַעַמְדָה יָּחַד מִי־בַעַל מִשְׁפָּטִי יִגַּשׁ אֵלָי: ⁹ הֵן אֲדֹנָי יְהוִה יַעֲזָר־לִי מִי־הוּא יַרְשִׁיעֵנִי הֵן כֻּלָּם כַּבֶּגֶד יִבְלוּ עָשׁ יֹאכְלֵם:

The New Testament gives us an account of a 12-year-old Yeshua visiting the Temple in Jerusalem for the first time (Luke 2:41-50). He was fully conversant with the Hebrew Scriptures and able to debate deep spiritual matters with the leading theologians of the day. Furthermore, when Yeshua is later rebuked by His mother for remaining in the Temple, He replies, "Did you not know I would be in My Father's house?" This one statement shows that, by the age of 12, Yeshua knew that Joseph was not His father, knew that God was His Father, and therefore understood that He was the Messiah of Israel. Since it is clear that in His humanity Yeshua was not omniscient, how did He acquire His knowledge and learning? The New Testament does not explain. There are several aspects of Yeshua's life which are revealed only in the Old Testament; this is one of them.

Isaiah 50:4-9 gives us a picture of the learning process which Yeshua went through.

The Messiah Taught—Isaiah 50:4

Verse 4 describes the learning or disciplining of the Servant. During His boyhood in Nazareth, every morning, Yeshua was awakened by His Father in the early hours of the morning to receive instruction. In this way, Yeshua learned who He was, what His mission was, and how to act and react accordingly.

The Messiah Despised—Isaiah 50:5-6

In verse 5, we are told that Yeshua learned all that was required of Him, that He must suffer and die. By the time Yeshua's ministry became public, He was not rebellious and did not draw back. When the time came (verse 6), He willingly submitted Himself to His tormentors. The abuses described here are all fully described in the Gospels during both His religious and civil trials.

> [22] When He had said this, one of the officers standing nearby struck Yeshua, saying, "Is that the way You answer the high priest?" [23] Yeshua answered him, "If I have spoken wrongly, bear witness of the wrong; but if rightly, why do you strike Me?"
>
> John 18:22-23[6]

> [63] Now the men who were holding Yeshua in custody were mocking Him, and beating Him, [64] and they blindfolded Him and were asking Him, saying, "Prophesy, who is the one who hit You?" [65] And they were saying many other things against Him, blaspheming.
>
> Luke 22:63-65

> [65] Some began to spit at Him, and to blindfold Him, and to beat Him with their fists, and to say to Him, "Prophesy!" And the officers received Him with slaps in the face.
>
> Mark 14:65

> [26] Then he released Barabbas for them; but after having Yeshua scourged, he delivered Him to be crucified. [27] Then the soldiers of the governor took Yeshua into the Praetorium and gathered the whole *Roman* cohort around Him. [28] They stripped Him, and put a scarlet robe on Him. [29] And after twisting together a crown of thorns, they put it on His head, and a reed in His right hand; and they kneeled down before Him and mocked Him, saying, "Hail, King of the Jews!" [30] They spat on Him, and took the reed and began to beat Him on the head. [31] After they had mocked Him, they took His robe off and put His garments on Him, and led Him away to crucify *Him*.
>
> Matthew 27:26-31

---

[6] All verses in this chapter are from the NASB.

¹⁶ The soldiers took Him away into the palace (that is, the Praetorium), and they called together the whole *Roman* cohort. ¹⁷ They dressed Him up in purple, and after twisting a crown of thorns, they put it on Him; ¹⁸ and they began to acclaim Him, "Hail, King of the Jews!" ¹⁹ They kept beating His head with a reed, and spitting on Him, and kneeling and bowing before Him. ²⁰ After they had mocked Him, they took the purple off Him, and put His *own* garments on Him. And they led Him out to crucify Him.

Mark 15:16-20

The Messiah Aided by Jehovah—Isaiah 50:7-9

In verses 7-9, Yeshua is able to endure the sufferings which led to His death (although His death is not actually mentioned here) because He knows that God is with Him throughout.

Isaiah 50:4-9

teaches that:

✿ Messiah would receive special training from God the Father.

✿ Messiah's first coming would be characterized by suffering.

✿ Messiah would be obedient in submitting Himself to physical abuse.

Isaiah 52:13-53:12

The Suffering of the Servant

¹³ Behold, my servant shall deal wisely, he shall be exalted and lifted up, and shall be very high. ¹⁴ Like as many were astonished at you (his visage was so marred more than any man, and his form more than the sons of men), ¹⁵ so shall he sprinkle many nations; kings shall shut their mouths at him: for that which had not been told them shall they see; and that which they had not heard shall they understand.

⁵³:¹ Who has believed our message? and to whom has the arm of Jehovah been revealed? ² For he grew up before him as a tender plant, and as a root out of a dry ground: he has no form nor comeliness; and when we see him, there is no beauty that we should desire him. ³ He was despised, and rejected of men; a man of sorrows, and acquainted with grief: and as one from whom men hide their face he was despised; and we esteemed him not. ⁴ Surely he has borne our griefs, and carried our sorrows; yet we did esteem him stricken, smitten of God, and afflicted. ⁵ But he was wounded for our transgressions, he was bruised for our iniquities; the chastisement of our peace was upon him; and with his stripes we are healed. ⁶ All we like sheep have gone astray; we have turned every one to his own way; and Jehovah has laid on him the iniquity of us all.

¹³ הִנֵּה יַשְׂכִּיל עַבְדִּי יָרוּם וְנִשָּׂא וְגָבַהּ מְאֹד: ¹⁴ כַּאֲשֶׁר שָׁמְמוּ עָלֶיךָ רַבִּים כֵּן־מִשְׁחַת מֵאִישׁ מַרְאֵהוּ וְתֹאֲרוֹ מִבְּנֵי אָדָם: ¹⁵ כֵּן יַזֶּה גּוֹיִם רַבִּים עָלָיו יִקְפְּצוּ מְלָכִים פִּיהֶם כִּי אֲשֶׁר לֹא־סֻפַּר לָהֶם רָאוּ וַאֲשֶׁר לֹא־שָׁמְעוּ הִתְבּוֹנָנוּ:

⁵³:¹ מִי הֶאֱמִין לִשְׁמֻעָתֵנוּ וּזְרוֹעַ יְהוָה עַל־מִי נִגְלָתָה: ² וַיַּעַל כַּיּוֹנֵק לְפָנָיו וְכַשֹּׁרֶשׁ מֵאֶרֶץ צִיָּה לֹא־תֹאַר לוֹ וְלֹא הָדָר וְנִרְאֵהוּ וְלֹא־מַרְאֶה וְנֶחְמְדֵהוּ: ³ נִבְזֶה וַחֲדַל אִישִׁים אִישׁ מַכְאֹבוֹת וִידוּעַ חֹלִי וּכְמַסְתֵּר פָּנִים מִמֶּנּוּ נִבְזֶה וְלֹא חֲשַׁבְנֻהוּ: ⁴ אָכֵן חֳלָיֵנוּ הוּא נָשָׂא וּמַכְאֹבֵינוּ סְבָלָם וַאֲנַחְנוּ חֲשַׁבְנֻהוּ נָגוּעַ מֻכֵּה אֱלֹהִים וּמְעֻנֶּה: ⁵ וְהוּא מְחֹלָל מִפְּשָׁעֵנוּ מְדֻכָּא מֵעֲוֹנֹתֵינוּ מוּסַר שְׁלוֹמֵנוּ עָלָיו וּבַחֲבֻרָתוֹ נִרְפָּא־לָנוּ: ⁶ כֻּלָּנוּ כַּצֹּאן תָּעִינוּ אִישׁ לְדַרְכּוֹ פָּנִינוּ וַיהוָה הִפְגִּיעַ בּוֹ אֵת עֲוֹן כֻּלָּנוּ:

⁷ He was oppressed, yet when he was afflicted he opened not his mouth; as a lamb that is led to the slaughter, and as a sheep that before its shearers is dumb, so he opened not his mouth. ⁸ By oppression and judgment he was taken away; and as for his generation, who (among them) considered that he was cut off out of the land of the living for the transgression of my people to whom the stroke (was due)? ⁹ And they made his grave with the wicked, and with a rich man in his death; although he had done no violence, neither was any deceit in his mouth. ¹⁰ Yet it pleased Jehovah to bruise him; he has put him to grief: when you shall make his soul an offering for sin, he shall see (his) seed, he shall prolong his days, and the pleasure of Jehovah shall prosper in his hand. ¹¹ He shall see of the travail of his soul, (and) shall be satisfied: by the knowledge of himself shall my righteous servant justify many; and he shall bear their iniquities. ¹² Therefore will I divide him a portion with the great, and he shall divide the spoil with the strong; because he poured out his soul unto death, and was numbered with the transgressors: yet he bare the sin of many, and made intercession for the transgressors. (ASV)

⁷ נִגַּשׂ וְהוּא נַעֲנֶה וְלֹא יִפְתַּח־פִּיו כַּשֶּׂה לַטֶּבַח יוּבָל וּכְרָחֵל לִפְנֵי גֹזְזֶיהָ נֶאֱלָמָה וְלֹא יִפְתַּח פִּיו: ⁸ מֵעֹצֶר וּמִמִּשְׁפָּט לֻקָּח וְאֶת־דּוֹרוֹ מִי יְשׂוֹחֵחַ כִּי נִגְזַר מֵאֶרֶץ חַיִּים מִפֶּשַׁע עַמִּי נֶגַע לָמוֹ: ⁹ וַיִּתֵּן אֶת־רְשָׁעִים קִבְרוֹ וְאֶת־עָשִׁיר בְּמֹתָיו עַל לֹא־חָמָס עָשָׂה וְלֹא מִרְמָה בְּפִיו: ¹⁰ וַיהוָה חָפֵץ דַּכְּאוֹ הֶחֱלִי אִם־תָּשִׂים אָשָׁם נַפְשׁוֹ יִרְאֶה זֶרַע יַאֲרִיךְ יָמִים וְחֵפֶץ יְהוָה בְּיָדוֹ יִצְלָח: ¹¹ מֵעֲמַל נַפְשׁוֹ יִרְאֶה יִשְׂבָּע בְּדַעְתּוֹ יַצְדִּיק צַדִּיק עַבְדִּי לָרַבִּים וַעֲוֺנֹתָם הוּא יִסְבֹּל: ¹² לָכֵן אֲחַלֶּק־לוֹ בָרַבִּים וְאֶת־עֲצוּמִים יְחַלֵּק שָׁלָל תַּחַת אֲשֶׁר הֶעֱרָה לַמָּוֶת נַפְשׁוֹ וְאֶת־פֹּשְׁעִים נִמְנָה וְהוּא חֵטְא־רַבִּים נָשָׂא וְלַפֹּשְׁעִים יַפְגִּיעַ: ס

The most crucial passage in the whole book of Isaiah is 52:13-53:12. This long section of Isaiah is so clear in its description of the suffering Messiah that it has caused enormous problems for teachers of Judaism. It is quite common today to hear rabbis say that this passage speaks not of Messiah, but of Israel suffering in a Gentile world. They may even go as far as to say that this has always been the traditional view of Judaism. At that point, they are entirely dependent on the ignorance of their listeners. All of the ancient Jewish writings—the Mishnah, the Gemara, (the Talmud), the Midrashim, and many others—all regard this portion of Scripture as relating to the Messianic Person. The first rabbi to suggest otherwise was Rashi, around A.D. 1050. Every rabbi prior to Rashi, without exception, viewed this passage as describing Messiah. When Rashi first proposed that this passage spoke of the nation of Israel, he sparked a fierce debate with his contemporaries. The most famous of these was Rambam, perhaps better known as Maimonides. Rambam stated very clearly that Rashi was completely wrong in going contrary to the traditional Jewish viewpoint.[7] As evangelists, particularly from the early 1800s onward, began to make greater use of this passage in their work among the Jewish people, an increasing number of rabbis found Rashi's view an attractive way of countering Christian teaching. Reading through the passage will show that there are several statements which could not possibly be applied to the nation of Israel. This passage is not read in synagogues; public readings of Isaiah will jump from Isaiah 52 to Isaiah 54.

Previously, in Isaiah 49, it was said that Messiah would at first be rejected by Israel, but would eventually be accepted at some later stage. This passage of Isaiah is dealing with that final acceptance when the leaders of Israel will acknowledge their failure at Messiah's first coming and, using these very words in Isaiah, make their national confession. This description of Messiah, then, is not given as something still to happen, but from a point of time in the future, immediately prior to Messiah's second coming, looking back to His first coming.

After this introduction, we will now study the whole passage which divides easily into five sections, each having three verses. The first line of each section is the title of that section.

Behold My Servant Shall Deal Wisely — Isaiah 52:13-15

Isaiah 52:13-15 summarizes chapter 53 of Isaiah; verses 1-12 of chapter 53 elaborate on these three verses. By referring to the Messiah as the Servant, Isaiah connects Him with the previous Servant of Jehovah passages. In 42:1-6, Isaiah described the mission of the Servant; in 49:1-13, the mission of the Servant was accompanied by difficulties; in 50:4-9, the Servant was seen as suffering physically but short of death, and no reason was given for His sufferings. Now, in 52:13-53:12, it is revealed that His physical sufferings will lead to His death, and the reason for His suffering and death will be given.

Verse 13: The emphasis in this verse is the exaltation of Messiah, speaking of His ascension to heaven and sitting down at the right hand of God the Father. "Exaltation" speaks of Yeshua's resurrection, "lifted up" describes His ascension, and "very high" refers to His session at the right hand of God the Father. **Summary:** The Servant will act wisely, and His actions will gain Him a position of glory.

Verse 14: This verse explains that prior to His exaltation, Messiah is to suffer humiliation. His body was so badly disfigured that He no longer resembled a man. In the sufferings of Yeshua, this would have happened at His scourging. The 40 lashes were given with a multi-strand whip, each strand having a nail or a piece of glass attached to it. These literally lifted the flesh off bones, not only from the back but also by wrapping around to all parts of the body. There were many who were never crucified because they did

---

[7] See Appendix 8 for a discussion of these rabbinic sources.

not survive the initial scourging. By the end of His scourging, when Pilate said, "behold the man," Yeshua was so disfigured He was hardly recognizable as a man. **Summary:** The Servant will suffer and be terribly disfigured.

Verse 15: Despite the appalling suffering of verse 14, in verse 15, Messiah is destined for eventual success and victory. Those who once mocked Him will be silenced by Him. A day will come when their mouths will be closed in awe at Him. **Summary:** The Servant's suffering will eventually gain the silent attention of world rulers when they begin to understand the purpose of His sufferings.

With this overview, chapter 53 now elaborates on these points.

Who Has Believed Our Message? — Isaiah 53:1-3

Verse 1: The emphasis of verse 1 is on the unbelief of Israel. The Jewish people did not believe the message; the message that Yeshua is the Messiah. Isaiah, besides referring to Messiah as "the Servant of Jehovah," also refers to Him as "the Arm of Jehovah" as he does here. Earlier, in 40:10, Isaiah declared that the Arm will rule for God; in 51:5, the Gentiles will trust in the Arm; in 51:9, the Arm will redeem; in 52:10, the Arm will provide salvation. Now, in 53:1, Isaiah reveals the identity of the Arm to be the same as the Servant of Jehovah, the Messiah. **Summary:** Israel expresses surprise at what was just stated in 52:13-15.

Verse 2: Some of the reasons for this disbelief are given in verse 2. There was nothing about His first coming which seemed unusual. He was born in normal—indeed rather poor—circumstances. This is a reaffirmation of Isaiah 11:1. Furthermore, there was nothing in His outward appearance to draw men to Him. This militates against the portraits and portrayals of Yeshua so often seen. Yeshua was a Jewish man with a Jewish beard and dark eyes, and He was probably not very tall. According to this verse, He was not particularly good looking. **Summary:** Israel confesses that, when the Servant was with them, they did not notice anything special about His outward appearance that would have attracted them to Him; His childhood and growth were no different than those of others.

Verse 3: In this verse, we are told that His whole life was characterized by rejection and suffering. Men turned away from Him, and at no time was He accorded the respect due to royalty. **Summary:** The Messiah was despised and rejected, and people in general did their best to avoid Him.

Surely He Has Borne Our Griefs, and Carried Our Sorrows — Isaiah 53:4-6

Verse 4: The emphasis in verse 4 is on the substitutionary nature of Messiah's suffering. At the time (verse 4b), Israel did not understand this, but considered His sufferings to be a punishment from God. He was seen to be suffering for His own sins, not for the sins of others. **Summary:** The nation which formerly despised the Servant now recognizes that He suffered vicariously. They thought that He was suffering for His own sins, but now realize He was suffering for theirs.

Verse 5: They now recognize that "he was wounded for our transgressions, he was bruised for *our* iniquities," that His death was indeed substitutionary so that "with his stripes *we* are healed." **Summary:** The nation confesses that the substitutionary sufferings resulted in reconciliation and spiritual healing for He was the chastisement for their sins.

Verse 6: Messiah was not suffering for His own sins but, in verse 6, "Jehovah has laid on him the iniquity of us all." Messiah was suffering for the sins of Israel. **Summary:** Israel confesses that it was they who sinned and went astray, and God laid the iniquity of Israel upon the Servant, and therefore He suffered.

Note the personal pronouns throughout this passage: "we," "our," etc. Isaiah was not a Gentile but a Jew, talking to a Jewish nation. The pronouns mean that Isaiah and the Jews must be included; they cannot refer to Gentiles. Furthermore, none of the things happening to this individual could be said to apply to the nation of Israel. Isaiah is clearly talking of one person. The nation is only included in the pronouns.

He Was Oppressed; Yet When He Was Afflicted, He Opened Not His Mouth — Isaiah 53:7-9

Verse 7: According to this verse, in the course of His affliction, Messiah remains silent. This was true of Yeshua at both His Jewish and Roman trials (Matthew 26:63, 27:12-14; Luke 23:9). He uttered no words against the manifold accusations brought against Him. This is hardly true of Israel. One thing Israel has not been is silent in her sufferings; she has written many books describing her suffering and accusing those responsible. The modern state of Israel has not remained silent in the face of Arab attacks; she has bombed Iraqi nuclear installations and Palestinian military encampments. This verse about suffering in silence cannot possibly be applied to the nation of Israel past or present. But it does fit the Messianic Person. **Summary:** The Servant humbly subjected Himself to the suffering and unjust treatment saying nothing in His own defense or making any complaint.

Verse 8:   The Messiah undergoes a legal trial at which He is condemned to death. He is then "cut off"—legally executed. He suffered the penalty of the law for "the transgression of my people to whom the stroke was due." He was executed for the transgressions of the people. "Transgression" is a word for sin which emphasizes the breaking of a law. This One, who is Messiah, is quite distinct from "my people," who are Israel. Throughout both Old and New Testaments, "my people" is always a reference to Israel. Messiah will be killed because of the sins of Israel. Here, for the first time in Scripture, it clearly states that Messiah is to die. There have been many previous references to His suffering, but it was never suggested that He would die. It is important to remember that Messianic prophecy was a progressive revelation. **Summary:** After a judicial trial and judgment, the Servant was taken away for execution, and Israel did not realize that He died for the sins of the people.

Verse 9:   This verse talks about the burial of Messiah. Having been executed as a criminal, it would have been expected for Him to be given a criminal's grave. God intervenes, however, and, though treated with injustice and dishonor in execution, He is justly laid in a place of honor: in a rich man's tomb. Yeshua was indeed taken down from the cross and laid in the tomb of a rich man, Joseph of Arimathea (Matthew 27:57-60). God ordains this because "there was no deceit in his mouth"; His death was purely substitutionary. **Summary:** The Servant was assigned a criminal's grave, but, in divine justice, He was instead buried in a rich man's tomb.

Yet It Pleased Jehovah to Bruise Him — Isaiah 53:10-12

Verse 10:   Note who is ultimately responsible for Messiah's death. It is not the Jews, nor the Romans, but is Jehovah Himself. It was God's will to bruise Him and God Himself who made "his soul an offering for sin." The only one able and qualified to provide salvation to the world is God. Messiah's death was not accidental nor due to force of circumstance, but part of God's divine plan. It is a biblical principle that there is no remission of sin without the shedding of blood. As a temporary measure, a system of animal sacrifice was instituted, but these sacrifices only covered sin, they did not remove it. Even then, the covering only lasted for one year until the next *Yom Kippur*, the next Day of Atonement. But Messiah will be the final sacrifice for sin, the sacrifice which finally removes sin, and the One who will provide it will be God Himself. God is the One who is ultimately responsible for the death of Messiah.[8] And then comes a strange line: "He shall see his seed, he shall prolong his days." If He has been killed, how can He see His spiritual progeny? If He is dead, how can His days be prolonged? The only way that these things can happen is by means of the resurrection, which will be described later. Having been told for the first time that Messiah will die, we are

---

[8] See Appendix 3 for a more detailed discussion of this important doctrine.

immediately given clear indication that He will be raised from the dead. After resurrection, Messiah will see the success of His mission, and because of that, "the pleasure of the Lord shall prosper in His hand." **Summary:** God was pleased to allow the Servant to suffer and die because this was how He was going to make atonement for the people; though the Servant dies, He will see His posterity, and His days will be prolonged.

Verse 11: The Messiah who has died will be able to see the results of His sufferings. By His self-knowledge, as the Messiah who died for sin, He will be able to bring justification to many. While He died for all, His death is applied only to those who believe. For those who believe, "he shall bear their iniquities." **Summary:** God will be satisfied with the work of His Servant, for He dies a substitutionary death for His people and by His death justifies many, as He bears their iniquity.

Verse 12: He will finally come into His kingdom, "because he poured out his soul unto death." He was reckoned as a sinner although He was not, but rather He bore the sins of others and has, by His death and resurrection, made intercession for others' transgressions. **Summary:** The Servant will be greatly blessed in the end above all others because He died on behalf of others and thus bore their sin and now intercedes for them.

Summary of Isaiah 52-53

Having read through the passage, it should now be very clear that this prophecy cannot possibly be applied to the nation of Israel. Israel is not silent. Israel has never been legally tried and condemned; Israel as a nation has never died through legal execution. All of the ancient rabbis without exception held the view that this is a Messianic passage. There is of course an apparent conflict between passages such as this that describe Messiah as suffering and other passages which describe Messiah as conquering, ruling, and reigning in Jerusalem. To believers, this is easily understood as Messiah coming twice, once to suffer and a second time to establish His kingdom and to rule in peace in Jerusalem. The ancient rabbis resolved the problem in a different way: by inventing the concept of two Messiahs. They taught that the first Messiah, whom they called "Messiah son of Joseph," who suffered in Egypt, would come to suffer and die in fulfillment of the servant passages, one of which they listed as Isaiah 53. The second Messiah, "Messiah son of David," would then come and raise the first Messiah back to life. He would then establish His kingdom to rule and to reign. They clearly recognized the teaching of death and resurrection contained in the Messianic prophecies, but failed to correctly interpret that Messiah must first come to die for our sins and then come a second time to rule in Jerusalem.

To summarize why this passage must refer to Messiah and not Israel, the following ten points should be noted:

1. This was the view of all the ancient rabbis (see Appendix 8).

2. The distinctive pronouns *we*, *us*, and *our* must refer to Isaiah and his Jewish audience while the *he, him, his* refer to the Messiah.

3. Throughout the passage, the Servant is portrayed as a singular personality and not a nation; there is no allegory or personification of the Servant as Israel.

4. In verse 9, the Servant's suffering is voluntary, willing, and silent, which has never been true of Israel.

5. In verse 8, the Servant dies for "my people"; Isaiah's people were the Jews; the Servant and Israel are therefore clearly distinguished.

6. The Servant is an innocent sufferer (verses 4-6, 8-9), but Israel always suffers for its own sins as Isaiah himself stated in 1:4-8.

7. The Servant suffers a substitutionary death (verses 4-6, 8, 10, 12) while Israel does not suffer on behalf of the Gentiles, but because of the Gentiles.

8. The sufferings of the Servant bring justification and spiritual healing to those who accept it (verses 5b, 11b), but Israel has not done this for the Gentiles.

9. The Servant dies (verses 8, 12), but the people of Israel always survive.

10. The Servant is resurrected (verses 10-11), but since the people of Israel have never passed away, they have no need for a resurrection.

Isaiah 52:13-53:12 teaches that:

✿ **Messiah would be born in natural circumstances with no unusual characteristics.**

✿ **Messiah's first coming would be characterized by suffering.**

✿ **Messiah's first coming would be characterized by rejection.**

✿ **Messiah would undergo a legal trial and be condemned to death.**

✿ **Messiah would be executed.**

✿ **Messiah would be buried in a rich man's tomb.**

✿ **Messiah would be resurrected.**

✿ **The Messiah's sufferings and death were to be substitutionary. He died so that we, being freed from our sins, may enter a new relationship with God.**

✿ **Messiah would bring justification to all who believe in Him.**

Isaiah 61:1-3

The Mission of the Servant

¹ The Spirit of the Lord GOD is upon me, Because the LORD has anointed me To bring good news to the afflicted; He has sent me to bind up the brokenhearted. To proclaim liberty to captives, And freedom to prisoners; ² To proclaim the favorable year of the LORD, And the day of vengeance of our God; To comfort all who mourn, ³ To grant those who mourn in Zion, Giving them a garland instead of ashes, The oil of gladness instead of mourning, The mantle of praise instead of a spirit of fainting. So they will be called oaks of righteousness, The planting of the LORD, that He may be glorified. (NASB)

רוּחַ אֲדֹנָי יְהוִה עָלָי יַעַן מָשַׁח יְהוָה אֹתִי לְבַשֵּׂר ¹
עֲנָוִים שְׁלָחַנִי לַחֲבֹשׁ לְנִשְׁבְּרֵי־לֵב לִקְרֹא לִשְׁבוּיִם
דְּרוֹר וְלַאֲסוּרִים פְּקַח־קוֹחַ: ² לִקְרֹא שְׁנַת־רָצוֹן
לַיהוָה וְיוֹם נָקָם לֵאלֹהֵינוּ לְנַחֵם כָּל־אֲבֵלִים: ³ לָשׂוּם
לַאֲבֵלֵי צִיּוֹן לָתֵת לָהֶם פְּאֵר תַּחַת אֵפֶר שֶׁמֶן שָׂשׂוֹן
תַּחַת אֵבֶל מַעֲטֵה תְהִלָּה תַּחַת רוּחַ כֵּהָה וְקֹרָא
לָהֶם אֵילֵי הַצֶּדֶק מַטַּע יְהוָה לְהִתְפָּאֵר:

This prophecy falls into the third category of Messianic prophecies mentioned in Appendix 9—prophecies which combine references to the first and second comings with no clear indication of any gap of time in between. Verses 1 and 2a deal with the first coming; verses 2b and 3 deal with the second coming. This is very clear from Yeshua's reading of the passage, described in Luke 4:16-21:

> ¹⁶ And He came to Nazareth, where He had been brought up; and as was His custom, He entered the synagogue on the Sabbath, and stood up to read. ¹⁷ And the book of the prophet Isaiah was handed to Him. And He opened the book, and found the place where it was written, ¹⁸ "The Spirit of the Lord is upon me, because He anointed Me to preach the gospel to the poor. He has sent Me to proclaim release to the captives, and recovery of sight to the blind, to set free those who are downtrodden, ¹⁹ to proclaim the favorable year of the Lord." ²⁰ And He closed the book, and gave it back to the attendant, and sat down; and the eyes of all in the synagogue were fixed upon Him. ²¹ And He began to say to them, "Today this Scripture has been fulfilled in your hearing."

Yeshua read verses 1 and 2a and then stopped. These words were now fulfilled, but the fulfillment of the rest of the passage still awaits His return.

The First Coming—Isaiah 61:1-2a

Verse 1 reaffirms Isaiah 11:2 and 42:1. Messiah will be anointed with the Holy Spirit for His mission and His task. This anointing took place in the life of Yeshua at His baptism (Matthew 3:16). It was at this point that He began His public ministry and openly claimed to be Messiah. During His first coming, Messiah is prophesied to do four things:

1. **Preach good news (or the gospel) to men.**

2. **Proclaim liberty to the captives.**
    In the Jewish context, the nation of Israel was enslaved to the Mosaic Law because the people were unable to keep it. Anyone who commits sin becomes a slave to sin. Since no Jew was able to keep perfectly all 613 commandments, they were enslaved to the curse of the law. Yeshua came to preach deliverance from the law through faith in Him.

3. **To open the prison of them who are bound.**
    This is further explained in the New Testament in the letter to the Hebrews 2:14-16. Because of Israel's failures under the law, they were bound by a Satanic fear of death. Part of Yeshua's mission at His first coming was to remove the keys of death and Hades from Satan so that he who believes in Yeshua, Jew or Gentile, need have no more fear of death and need not be imprisoned by that fear.

4. **To proclaim the acceptable year of Jehovah's favor.**
    With the death of Messiah, the dispensation of law was ended, and the dispensation of grace began. Under the grace of God, our salvation comes purely from accepting that Messiah died and rose again on our behalf. This is a personal decision which must be made at some point in a person's life; no one can be born a Christian in the New Testament sense of the term.

The Second Coming—Isaiah 61:2b-3

This aspect of the passage lies outside the scope of this study. For further information on the second coming see the author's book, *The Footsteps of the Messiah*.

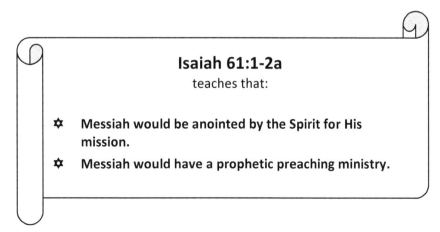

Isaiah 61:1-2a
teaches that:

✡   **Messiah would be anointed by the Spirit for His mission.**
✡   **Messiah would have a prophetic preaching ministry.**

Jeremiah 23:5-6

Messiah the King

⁵ "Behold, *the* days are coming," declares the LORD, "When I shall raise up for David a righteous Branch; And He will reign as king and act wisely And do justice and righteousness in the land. ⁶ "In His days Judah will be saved, And Israel will dwell securely; And this is His name by which He will be called, 'The LORD our righteousness.' (NASB)

⁵ הִנֵּה יָמִים בָּאִים נְאֻם־יְהוָה וַהֲקִמֹתִי לְדָוִד צֶמַח צַדִּיק וּמָלַךְ מֶלֶךְ וְהִשְׂכִּיל וְעָשָׂה מִשְׁפָּט וּצְדָקָה בָּאָרֶץ: ⁶ בְּיָמָיו תִּוָּשַׁע יְהוּדָה וְיִשְׂרָאֵל יִשְׁכֹּן לָבֶטַח וְזֶה־שְּׁמוֹ אֲשֶׁר־יִקְרְאוֹ יְהוָה צִדְקֵנוּ: ס

These verses deal primarily with the second coming of Messiah, but there is an aspect of them which relates to His first coming, too. Verse 5 tells of a man who will be a son of David, who will rule and reign as king. The kingship of Messiah is yet to come, but this verse clearly speaks of Messiah as a descendant of David and thus stresses His humanity. In verse 6, however, this man is given a name which is applicable to God alone: "Jehovah our righteousness." Modern translations generally render this as LORD. This is intended to convey the four letters YHVH which are read as Jehovah or Yahweh. (In Hebrew, יהוה. Reading from right to left these are the letters *yod heh vav heh.*) Throughout the Hebrew Scriptures, the name YHVH is given to God alone, yet here the man of verse 5 is clearly given the name of God in verse 6. This again presents us with the clear concept of Messiah as God-Man.

One of the arguments presented by Rabbinic Judaism to refute this teaching is to point out that throughout the Scriptures there are examples of names which contain the name of God. For example, the name Jeremiah means "Jehovah will establish" or "Jehovah will hurl." Or again, the name Isaiah means "Jehovah is salvation," and there are many other names which contain "Jehovah" in them. It needs to be realized, however, that in none of these cases are all four of the letters YHVH found. Usually only two letters are used, sometimes three, but nowhere are all four letters of the name of God ever used in relation to a human being. Despite this, Jeremiah 23:5 clearly speaks of a man—a human descendant of King David. In 23:6, he is given a name which is the name of God alone.

This is something which was not, in fact, disputed by the ancient rabbis, who always interpreted this as a Messianic passage. It is only relatively recently that rabbis have tried to argue otherwise. Four quotations from rabbinic writings can be given to show this.

In the *Midrash* on Proverbs 19:21 (c. A.D. 200-500), it says:

Rabbi Hunah said "Eight names are given to the Messiah which are: Yinnon, Shiloh, David, Menachem, Jehovah, Justi de Nostra, Tzemmach, Elias."

The fifth name listed is *Jehovah*, the name of God, and this is based on the words of Jeremiah 23:6. The seventh name is *Tzemmach*, or "Branch," and this is based on Jeremiah 23:5.

In the *Midrash* on Lamentations 1:16, it says:

What is the name of the Messiah? Rav Ava ben Kahanna said, "Jehovah is his name and this is proved by, 'this is his name . . . [quoting Jeremiah 23:6].' "

In the *Talmud* (*Babba Bathra* Tractate 75b), it says:

Shmuel ben Nachman said in the name of Rabbi Yohanan, "the following three will be named with the name of the Holy One blessed be he—the upright, as it is said, '. . . [quotes Isaiah 43:7]', the Messiah, as it is written 'and this is his name whereby he shall be called The Lord our righteousness [quoting Jeremiah 23:6]'. . ."

In the *Midrash* on Psalm 21:1, it says:

God calls King Messiah by his own name, but what is his name? The answer is 'Jehovah is a man of war' and concerning Messiah we read "Jehovah our righteousness this is his name."

And so, it can be seen that in ancient rabbinic writings, and even in the *Talmud* itself, Jeremiah 23:6 is applied to Messiah; Messiah is given the name of *Jehovah*.

Jeremiah 23:5-6
teaches that:

✡ The Messiah would be a God-Man.
✡ The Messiah would be Jehovah Himself; Jehovah would become a man.
✡ The Messiah would be a descendant of David and therefore a king. Jeremiah here reaffirms the Davidic Covenant.

Micah 5:2

Bethlehem Ephrathah

² "But as for you, Bethlehem Ephrathah, Too little to be among the clans of Judah, From you One will go forth for Me to be ruler in Israel. His goings forth are from long ago, From the days of eternity." (NASB)

¹ וְאַתָּה בֵּית־לֶחֶם אֶפְרָתָה צָעִיר לִהְיוֹת בְּאַלְפֵי יְהוּדָה מִמְּךָ לִי יֵצֵא לִהְיוֹת מוֹשֵׁל בְּיִשְׂרָאֵל וּמוֹצָאֹתָיו מִקֶּדֶם מִימֵי עוֹלָם:

Note that the Hebrew verse numbering differs from the English numbering in this passage.

This verse adds to Isaiah 7:14. It has already been shown that a great many Scriptures point to the divine as well as human nature of the Messiah. This has been clear from as early as Genesis chapters 3 and 4 and continues through to the prophecy of Micah. Micah was a contemporary of Isaiah, prophesying at the same time, but in a different part of Judea. In Isaiah 7:14, we read that Messiah was to be born of a virgin; here in Micah 5:2, we read where that birth is to take place. Messiah is to be born, not in Jerusalem as might have been expected, but in Bethlehem. This was perhaps hinted at in Isaiah 11:1, but is now stated clearly. This is Bethlehem Ephrathah, as distinguished from another Bethlehem in Galilee. Bethlehem Ephrathah is situated south of Jerusalem and is the birth place of David and of Judah. The One to be born is said to "go forth for Me"; He is being born in order to fulfill a particular mission, a specific purpose of God. About His human origin, He is to be born in Bethlehem; but regarding His divine origin, He is said to be "from long ago, from the days of eternity." The Hebrew words for "from long ago, from the days of eternity" are the strongest Hebrew expressions ever used for eternity past. They are used of God the Father in Psalm 90:2. What is true of God the Father is also said to be true of this One who is to be born in Bethlehem. These words are also used in Proverbs 8:22-23 (the voice of Wisdom speaking).

Again, we have a passage which shows that Messiah is to be human—being born at some specific point in time and at some specific place, yet having existed since all eternity past, and therefore being divine.

Micah 5:2
teaches that:

✡ Messiah would be born in Bethlehem, the city of David.
✡ He would be divine as well as human, having existed from eternity past.

Zechariah 9:9-10

Riding on a Donkey

⁹ Rejoice greatly, O daughter of Zion! Shout *in triumph*, O daughter of Jerusalem! Behold, your king is coming to you; He is just and endowed with salvation, Humble, and mounted on a donkey, Even on a colt, the foal of a donkey. ¹⁰ And I will cut off the chariot from Ephraim, And the horse from Jerusalem; And the bow of war will be cut off. And He will speak peace to the nations; And His dominion will be from sea to sea, And from the River to the ends of the earth. (NASB)

⁹ גִּילִי מְאֹד בַּת־צִיּוֹן הָרִיעִי בַּת יְרוּשָׁלַ͏ִם הִנֵּה מַלְכֵּךְ יָבוֹא לָךְ צַדִּיק וְנוֹשָׁע הוּא עָנִי וְרֹכֵב עַל־חֲמוֹר וְעַל־עַיִר בֶּן־אֲתֹנוֹת: ¹⁰ וְהִכְרַתִּי־רֶכֶב מֵאֶפְרַיִם וְסוּס מִירוּשָׁלַ͏ִם וְנִכְרְתָה קֶשֶׁת מִלְחָמָה וְדִבֶּר שָׁלוֹם לַגּוֹיִם וּמָשְׁלוֹ מִיָּם עַד־יָם וּמִנָּהָר עַד־אַפְסֵי־אָרֶץ:

The third category of Messianic prophecy mentioned in the first appendix is the kind where first and second coming prophecies are blended together without obvious distinction. Zechariah 9:9-10 is an example of this. Verse 9 relates to the first coming, while verse 10 relates to the second coming. This can be established from other passages of Scripture, but is not clear from the text itself.

The First Coming—Zechariah 9:9

The background to these verses is an invasion of Israel by a foreign king, prophesied in verses 1-8. These verses were fulfilled by Alexander the Great. In verse 9, in contrast to this invading Gentile king, we find reference to a future Jewish king. Israel is told to rejoice because "*your* king" (Israel's king) is coming (not "*against* you," but) "*to* you." Jerusalem is to rejoice because, unlike Alexander, this king will have the following character traits:

1. **Just**
   He is characterized by righteousness, a point also made by Jeremiah 23:5-6. In contrast, Alexander the Great died in a drunken stupor.

2. **Offering salvation**
   In contrast to Alexander who came with conquest, destruction, and death.

3. **Lowly and humble**

Lowly here has the sense of being brought low through oppression. Messiah was indeed oppressed. Alexander came with pomp and power. Furthermore, in contrast to the Greek conqueror on his white steed, this king is to come riding on a donkey. Specifically, He is to ride on the foal of a donkey—a creature not yet broken, one which has never been ridden before. The fulfillment of this prophecy is found in the Gospels of the New Testament in the triumphal entry of Yeshua into Jerusalem at the beginning of the last week of His life (Matthew 21:1-11). This marked His official presentation as the Messianic King. Yeshua instructs His disciples to go to Bethphage and find a colt which had never been ridden before. The miraculous aspect of this should not be missed. By nature, the animal should have bucked Yeshua off the moment He got on, but instead of throwing Him, it submitted to Him.

The Second Coming—Zechariah 9:10

Verse 10 deals with the events of the second coming, in which all weapons of war are to be removed from the land, but this lies outside the scope of this study.

The Rabbinic View

Here we see very clearly the two lines of Messianic prophecy side by side in the same passage. First, Messiah is described as being lowly and oppressed, but then, in the very next sentence, He is seen as a king whose dominion extends to the ends of the whole earth. When the ancient rabbis looked at these two contradictory prophecies, they reconciled them by saying that there would be two different Messiahs. First would come Messiah, whom they called the son of Joseph, to fulfill the suffering passages. He would then be followed by Messiah the son of David, the conquering Messiah.

That the rabbis took this passage as Messianic can be seen from the *Talmud* in *Sanhedrin* 98b-99a:

> Rabbi Hillel said: "Israel can expect no Messiah because they consumed him in the days of Hezekiah." The retort: "When did Hezekiah live? Was it not in the days of the First Temple? Yet Zechariah during the time of the second Temple prophesied and said . . . [quoting 9:9]."

Also, *Pesikta* (*Piska* 53) states:

> This refers to Messiah. He is called anee [lowly] because He was oppressed all these years in prison, and the sinners of Israel denied Him . . . For the merits of the Messiah, the Holy One, blessed be He, will protect and redeem you.

The Talmudic tractate *Sanhedrin* 98a makes a similar statement:

> Rabbi Joseph the son of Levi objects that it is written in one place "Behold one like the son of man comes with the clouds of heaven," but in another place it is written "lowly and riding upon an ass." The solution is, if they be righteous he shall come with the clouds of heaven, but if they not be righteous he shall come lowly riding upon an ass.

This is an alternative rabbinic interpretation to explain the two lines of Messianic prophecy. This says that either one line of prophecy or the other will be fulfilled, but not both. If Israel is righteous, Messiah will come riding on the clouds; but if she is sinful, then He will come riding on a donkey. The Scriptures, however, clearly require the fulfillment of both types of prophecy.

The New Testament view is much simpler than either of the rabbinic views given above. It teaches that there would be one Messiah, but He would come twice, first to die and then a second time to rule, thereby fulfilling all the prophetic statements concerning Him.

Zechariah 9:9-10
teaches that:

✡ **Messiah's first coming would be characterized by humility.**

✡ **Messiah's official presentation as the Messianic King would come when He rides into Jerusalem on the foal of a donkey.**

Zechariah 11:1-17

The Two Shepherds

¹ Open your doors, O Lebanon, That a fire may feed on your cedars. ² Wail, O cypress, for the cedar has fallen, Because the glorious *trees* have been destroyed; Wail, O oaks of Bashan, For the impenetrable forest has come down. ³ There is a sound of the shepherds' wail, For their glory is ruined; There is a sound of the young lions' roar, For the pride of the Jordan is ruined. ⁴ Thus says the LORD my God, "Pasture the flock *doomed* to slaughter. ⁵ "Those who buy them slay them and go unpunished, and *each of* those who sell them says, 'Blessed be the LORD, for I have become rich!' And their own shepherds have no pity on them. ⁶ "For I shall no longer have pity on the inhabitants of the land," declares the LORD; "but behold, I shall cause the men to fall, each into another's power and into the power of his king; and they will strike the land, and I shall not deliver them from their power." ⁷ So I pastured the flock doomed to slaughter, hence the afflicted of the flock. And I took for myself two staffs: the one I called Favor, and the other I called Union; so I pastured the flock. ⁸ Then I annihilated the three shepherds in one month, for my soul was impatient with them, and their soul also was weary of me. ⁹ Then I said, "I will not pasture you. What is to die, let it die, and what is to be annihilated, let it be annihilated; and let those who are left eat one another's flesh." ¹⁰ And I took my staff, Favor, and cut it in pieces, to break my covenant which I had made with all the peoples. ¹¹ So it was broken on that day,

¹ פְּתַח לְבָנוֹן דְּלָתֶיךָ וְתֹאכַל אֵשׁ בַּאֲרָזֶיךָ: ² הֵילֵל בְּרוֹשׁ כִּי־נָפַל אֶרֶז אֲשֶׁר אַדִּרִים שֻׁדָּדוּ הֵילִילוּ אַלּוֹנֵי בָשָׁן כִּי יָרַד יַעַר (הַבָּצוּר) [הַבָּצִיר] ³ קוֹל יִלְלַת הָרֹעִים כִּי שֻׁדְּדָה אַדַּרְתָּם קוֹל שַׁאֲגַת כְּפִירִים כִּי שֻׁדַּד גְּאוֹן הַיַּרְדֵּן: ⁴ כֹּה אָמַר יְהוָה אֱלֹהָי רְעֵה אֶת־צֹאן הַהֲרֵגָה: ⁵ אֲשֶׁר קֹנֵיהֶן יַהֲרֻגֵן וְלֹא יֶאְשָׁמוּ וּמֹכְרֵיהֶן יֹאמַר בָּרוּךְ יְהוָה וַאעְשִׁר וְרֹעֵיהֶם לֹא יַחְמוֹל עֲלֵיהֶן: ⁶ כִּי לֹא אֶחְמוֹל עוֹד עַל־יֹשְׁבֵי הָאָרֶץ נְאֻם־יְהוָה וְהִנֵּה אָנֹכִי מַמְצִיא אֶת־הָאָדָם אִישׁ בְּיַד־רֵעֵהוּ וּבְיַד מַלְכּוֹ וְכִתְּתוּ אֶת־הָאָרֶץ וְלֹא אַצִּיל מִיָּדָם: ⁷ וָאֶרְעֶה אֶת־צֹאן הַהֲרֵגָה לָכֵן עֲנִיֵּי הַצֹּאן וָאֶקַּח־לִי שְׁנֵי מַקְלוֹת לְאַחַד קָרָאתִי נֹעַם וּלְאַחַד קָרָאתִי חֹבְלִים וָאֶרְעֶה אֶת־הַצֹּאן: ⁸ וָאַכְחִד אֶת־שְׁלֹשֶׁת הָרֹעִים בְּיֶרַח אֶחָד וַתִּקְצַר נַפְשִׁי בָּהֶם וְגַם־נַפְשָׁם בָּחֲלָה בִי: ⁹ וָאֹמַר לֹא אֶרְעֶה אֶתְכֶם הַמֵּתָה תָמוּת וְהַנִּכְחֶדֶת תִּכָּחֵד וְהַנִּשְׁאָרוֹת תֹּאכַלְנָה אִשָּׁה אֶת־בְּשַׂר רְעוּתָהּ: ¹⁰ וָאֶקַּח אֶת־מַקְלִי אֶת־נֹעַם וָאֶגְדַּע אֹתוֹ לְהָפֵיר אֶת־בְּרִיתִי אֲשֶׁר כָּרַתִּי אֶת־כָּל־הָעַמִּים:

covenant which I had made with all the peoples. ¹¹ So it was broken on that day, and thus the afflicted of the flock who were watching me realized that it was the word of the LORD. ¹² And I said to them, "If it is good in your sight, give *me* my wages; but if not, never mind!" So they weighed out thirty *shekels* of silver as my wages. ¹³ Then the LORD said to me, "Throw it to the potter, *that* magnificent price at which I was valued by them." So I took the thirty shekels of silver and threw them to the potter in the house of the LORD. ¹⁴ Then I cut my second staff, Union, in pieces, to break the brotherhood between Judah and Israel. ¹⁵ And the LORD said to me, "Take again for yourself the equipment of a foolish shepherd. ¹⁶ "For behold, I am going to raise up a shepherd in the land who will not care for the perishing, seek the scattered, heal the broken, or sustain the one standing, but will devour the flesh of the fat *sheep* and tear off their hoofs. ¹⁷ "Woe to the worthless shepherd Who leaves the flock! A sword will be on his arm And on his right eye! His arm will be totally withered, And his right eye will be blind." (NASB)

וַתֻּפַר בַּיּוֹם הַהוּא וַיֵּדְעוּ כֵן עֲנִיֵּי הַצֹּאן הַשֹּׁמְרִים אֹתִי כִּי דְבַר־יְהוָה הוּא: ¹² וָאֹמַר אֲלֵיהֶם אִם־טוֹב בְּעֵינֵיכֶם הָבוּ שְׂכָרִי וְאִם־לֹא חֲדָלוּ וַיִּשְׁקְלוּ אֶת־שְׂכָרִי שְׁלֹשִׁים כָּסֶף: ¹³ וַיֹּאמֶר יְהוָה אֵלַי הַשְׁלִיכֵהוּ אֶל־הַיּוֹצֵר אֶדֶר הַיְקָר אֲשֶׁר יָקַרְתִּי מֵעֲלֵיהֶם וָאֶקְחָה שְׁלֹשִׁים הַכֶּסֶף וָאַשְׁלִיךְ אֹתוֹ בֵּית יְהוָה אֶל־הַיּוֹצֵר: ¹⁴ וָאֶגְדַּע אֶת־מַקְלִי הַשֵּׁנִי אֵת הַחֹבְלִים לְהָפֵר אֶת־הָאַחֲוָה בֵּין יְהוּדָה וּבֵין יִשְׂרָאֵל: ס ¹⁵ וַיֹּאמֶר יְהוָה אֵלָי עוֹד קַח־לְךָ כְּלִי רֹעֶה אֱוִלִי: ¹⁶ כִּי הִנֵּה־אָנֹכִי מֵקִים רֹעֶה בָּאָרֶץ הַנִּכְחָדוֹת לֹא־יִפְקֹד הַנַּעַר לֹא־יְבַקֵּשׁ וְהַנִּשְׁבֶּרֶת לֹא יְרַפֵּא הַנִּצָּבָה לֹא יְכַלְכֵּל וּבְשַׂר הַבְּרִיאָה יֹאכַל וּפַרְסֵיהֶן יְפָרֵק: ס ¹⁷ הוֹי רֹעִי הָאֱלִיל עֹזְבִי הַצֹּאן חֶרֶב עַל־זְרוֹעוֹ וְעַל־עֵין יְמִינוֹ זְרֹעוֹ יָבוֹשׁ תִּיבָשׁ וְעֵין יְמִינוֹ כָּהֹה תִכְהֶה: ס

The whole of chapter 11 deals with the first coming of the Messiah and the events surrounding it. The chapter divides into three sections. Verses 1-3 describe a great devastation upon the land of Israel from north to south. This was fulfilled by the first and second revolts against Rome in A.D. 70 and 135. Verses 4-14 describe the events of the first coming and the rejection of the true shepherd, Messiah, leading to the destruction of A.D. 70. Verses 15-17 describe the choosing of a false shepherd, leading to the destruction of A.D. 135.

The Devastation of the Land—Zechariah 11:1-3

The kind of devastation described in verses 1-3 only happened in A.D. 70 as a result of the first Jewish uprising against Rome. The prophecy of these first three verses could be said to be fully completed by the year A.D. 135 with the further destruction of the second uprising.

The Jewish Temple was often referred to as a place of cedar or as a house of cedar (1 Kings 5:5-6), so the destruction described in verses 1 and 2 is probably an allusion to the future destruction of the Temple, which was still being rebuilt at the time of Zechariah's prophecy. In verse 3a, the shepherds, that is the Jewish leaders, are to wail because of the ruin of their glory. When Jerusalem and the Temple were destroyed, their glory was indeed ruined. Finally, verse 3b concentrates on the ruination of the Jordan valley. This is also mentioned in Jeremiah 12:5, 49:19, and 50:44.

The rest of this chapter deals with the two causes of the destruction: the rejection of the true shepherd and the acceptance of the false shepherd.

The Rejection of the True Shepherd—Zechariah 11:4-14

The Commission to the Prophet—Zechariah 11:4-6

In verses 4-6, the prophet Zechariah is given a commission; he is given a role to act out as a message to the people. The part he is to play is that of Messiah at His first coming. Messiah is symbolized as the character of a shepherd, feeding a flock. The flock (verse 4) is symbolic of Israel. The sheep are being destroyed by their owners, symbolic of Rome, and even "their own shepherds," symbolic of the Jewish leaders, "have no pity on them." In verse 5, the flock has been abandoned by man; but further, in verse 6, it was also abandoned by God. God states that He will cause each and every man to fall "into the power of his king." At first this seems a little confusing since, at the time of the Roman occupation, Israel had no king. However, we read in the Gospels that when Yeshua, the True Shepherd, stood at His trial, Pontius Pilate declared to the people, "Here is your king." But the Pharisees rejected Yeshua and cried out, "We have no king but Caesar" (John 19:15). Since Messiah was rejected as king and only Caesar was recognized as king, it was to that king that God handed them over for judgment. In the war with the Romans in A.D. 70, 1,100,000 Jews were killed and 97,000 were taken into slavery.

The Carrying out of the Commission—Zechariah 11:7-11

In verses 7-11, Zechariah carries out his commission. In verse 7, he feeds the flock doomed to slaughter, but especially "the poor" of the flock or "the afflicted," according to some translations. "The poor and the needy" is a common phrase in the Prophets and is always a reference to the righteous remnant of Israel. While at many times in their history Israel as a whole is rebellious and unrighteous, there has always remained within Israel a small group of righteous, believing people, termed "the remnant of Israel."

While Messiah will come to minister to the whole of Israel, there will be a special emphasis in His ministry towards the believing remnant within Israel. The fulfillment of this is seen in Matthew 9:35-36. Zechariah employs two staffs in this work. One is given the name "Favor," and the other is given the name "Union." The staff called Favor was for the protection of the flock; the staff called Union was to keep the flock together and preserve its unity.

In verse 8, Zechariah faces the opposition of three other shepherds. In the context of the ministry of Yeshua, these three shepherds are symbolic of the Pharisees, the Sadducees, and the Scribes, the key sections of Jewish leadership during the period of the first coming. One of the results of Yeshua's ministry was the destruction of these three groups. The reason for their destruction is the mutual antagonism described in verse 8. The fulfillment of this is seen in Yeshua's denunciation of the religious leaders of Israel, described in Matthew 23:1-37. The hostility of the leaders toward Yeshua is also seen in their plotting His execution and bribing Judas Iscariot to betray Him.

Although verse 7 described the faithful shepherding of the flock, in verse 9 there is an abrupt cessation in the feeding of the flock. In the ministry of Yeshua, this part of the prophecy was fulfilled in the events of Matthew chapter 12:22-45. This chapter describes the crucial, pivotal point in Yeshua's ministry: the rejection of His Messiahship on the grounds of demon possession. Prior to His rejection, Yeshua openly declared His claim to be Messiah. After His rejection, Yeshua made no further claims and forbade anyone—His disciples and those individuals whom He healed—to disclose His Messiahship. Prior to His rejection, Yeshua openly performed many signs and miracles. After His rejection, He performed no signs—except the "sign of Jonah." Prior to the rejection, Yeshua healed all who came to Him, these healings being evidence of His claim to be Messiah. After the rejection, healing was refused if requested on the basis of His Messiahship and granted only in cases of personal need, on the basis of personal faith. Prior to the rejection, Yeshua taught the people—fed the flock—openly and clearly as in the Sermon on the Mount. After the rejection, Yeshua changed to the exclusive use of parables in order to hide the truth from the masses. The accusation of demon possession constituted the "unpardonable sin," and the moment the religious leaders committed this sin, pulling with them people of Israel, the judgment of A.D. 70 was inevitable. Note that the unpardonable sin and the judgment of it relate exclusively to "this generation"—the Jewish people of that time only (Matthew 12:39, 41, 42, 45; 23:36). With the committing of the unpardonable sin, Yeshua stops feeding the flock as a whole and deals only with individuals within the nation.

In verse 10, Zechariah takes the staff named Favor and breaks it. This symbolizes God's removal of Israel's protection and the inevitability of the A.D. 70 judgment; the fulfillment of this is seen in Luke 19:41-44 and 21:24. Note that "peoples" is in the plural, meaning "Gentile nations"; Israel is now vulnerable to Gentile attacks, and in A.D. 70, the attack of the Romans was to be devastating indeed.

In verse 11, the "afflicted of the flock"—that is the believing remnant—see the breaking of the staff Favor as the word of God and understand the significance of it. During the ministry of Yeshua, the Jewish believers did indeed understand that judgment was coming, that it was from the hand of the Lord, and that it was inevitable. In Luke 21:20-24, Yeshua had instructed them to flee from Jerusalem when the time of her destruction came:

[20] "But when you see Jerusalem surrounded by armies, then recognize that her desolation is at hand. [21] "Then let those who are in Judea flee to the mountains, and let those who are in the midst of the city depart, and let not those who are in the country enter the city; [22] because these are days of vengeance, in order that all things which are written may be fulfilled. [23] "Woe to those who are with child and to those who nurse babes in those days; for there will be great distress upon the land, and wrath to this people, [24] and they will fall by the edge of the sword, and will be led captive into all the nations; and Jerusalem will be trampled underfoot by the Gentiles until the times of the Gentiles be fulfilled. (NASB)

In A.D. 66, when the Romans besieged Jerusalem, the believers within the city realized that the time of judgment had arrived and that they were not to join the fight but should leave for the mountains. Later in that year, the siege was temporarily lifted, and the entire Jewish Christian community of Jerusalem and the whole land (some 100,000 people) left Israel and found refuge in Pella, east of the Jordan River. In A.D. 68, the siege was re-imposed, and in A.D. 70, the final destruction came. The main point here is that the "afflicted of the flock," the ones who had been given special emphasis in the ministry of Messiah, understood that God's protection had been lifted, that the nation was under judgment, and so they acted in accordance with Yeshua's words in Luke 21. Because of their faithful obedience to the words of their Messiah, not one Jewish believer lost his life; not one Jewish believer was taken into slavery.

The Price of the Good Shepherd—Zechariah 11:12-14

Verses 12-14 describe the value placed upon the work of the good shepherd. In verse 12, the good shepherd approaches the leadership of Israel and asks for his wages, to be paid according to what they think he is worth. He is paid thirty pieces of silver. While today that may sound like a reasonable amount, it was, in fact, a display of contempt. Under the Mosaic Law, thirty pieces of silver was the compensation value for a dead slave (Exodus 21:32). The work of the good shepherd is therefore judged to be equivalent to that of a dead slave. Being paid thirty pieces of silver was more insulting than being paid nothing at all.

The words of verse 13 are extremely important here. It is Zechariah who has been paid the thirty pieces of silver, but who is it that is really being insulted? "Then the Lord said to me, 'throw it to the potter, that magnificent price [sarcasm] at which I was valued by them.'" It is the Lord who is the Good Shepherd. It is the Lord whose work is so despised as to be valued at only the thirty pieces of silver. Thus, it becomes very clear that Zechariah is merely an actor playing out a prophetic role, a common means of giving prophecies in the Scriptures, and that this role is to be fulfilled by Jehovah Himself, when He becomes a man, as spelled out in previous prophecies.

Zechariah is then told to take the thirty pieces of silver and throw them away by throwing them into the potter's area of the Temple compound. These words found their fulfillment when Judas Iscariot was paid thirty pieces of silver by the Jewish leaders to betray Yeshua. Afterwards, Judas did what Zechariah did and threw the coins into the potter's section of the Temple compound. All of this is described in Matthew 26:14-16 and 27:3-10 (see Appendix 7). It should be noted that the thirty pieces of silver were paid to Judas by the chief priests, who would have taken the money from the Temple treasury. This money was intended for the specific purpose of purchasing sacrifices. Although they did not realize it, that is exactly what the priests did. They purchased a sacrifice; Yeshua was to be the final sacrifice for sin (see Appendix 3).

The response to the contempt of verse 13 is in verse 14. Zechariah takes the second staff, called "Union," and breaks it. This again is a prophetic act, this time signifying that the flock is to be scattered and the unity of Israel destroyed. During the war against the Romans from A.D. 66-70, various factions developed amongst the Zealots. They began fighting amongst themselves, destroying each other's food stocks and killing each other. Ultimately, it was the civil strife within Jerusalem which caused it to fall easily to Rome. The destruction of unity therefore led to the scattering of the flock; the great dispersion of Jewry, the Diaspora, did indeed begin in A.D. 70.

The Foolish Shepherd—Zechariah 11:15-17

While the leadership rejects the Good Shepherd of verses 4-14, they accept a foolish, or unrighteous, shepherd instead. In verse 15, Zechariah is told to play a second role, not of a good shepherd as before, but this time that of a foolish shepherd who will bring only harm to the flock.

In the year 132, Simon bar Cochba led the second Jewish revolt against Rome. He was supported in this by many of the rabbis, but most significantly, midway through the revolt, the chief rabbi, Rabbi Akiba, declared Bar Cochba to be the Messiah. At the start of the revolt, the Messianic Jews had taken up swords and joined in what was, initially, the defense of the land. With Rabbi Akiba's declaration, however, the revolt became a Messianic movement, and the believing Jews were forced to withdraw from the battle, unable to support Bar Cochba as Messiah. Thus, Rabbi Akiba together with the various Jewish councils passed a long list of laws prohibiting any kind of association with the Jewish believers in the land. Eventually, the Romans returned after their defeat by Bar Cochba and began a scorched earth policy. By the time Bar Cochba made his last stand in A.D. 135, virtually the entire land of Israel had been burned and the people were starving *en masse*. The destruction of Zechariah 11:1-3 was therefore fulfilled to a further degree than in the year A.D. 70.

Zechariah 11:1-17

teaches that:

✡ Messiah's first coming would be rejected, especially by the Jewish leaders.

✡ While the nation as a whole would reject Messiah, there would be a small remnant of believing people who would accept Him.

✡ The leadership of Israel would sell Him out for thirty pieces of silver.

✡ The results of this rejection were to be twofold. First, protection would be removed, leaving Israel vulnerable to Gentile attack. Second, unity would be removed, and Israel would be scattered.

✡ Because they turned away from the true Messiah, they would foolishly accept a false messiah. This led to the second devastation of the Land in A.D. 135.

✡ If the destruction described in Zechariah 11:1-3 was fulfilled in A.D. 70, then Messiah must have come before A.D. 70.

✡ Messiah is the Good Shepherd (John 10:11-18).

Zechariah 12:10

The Final Recognition of Messiah

[10] "And I will pour out on the house of David and on the inhabitants of Jerusalem, the Spirit of grace and of supplication, so that they will look on Me whom they have pierced; and they will mourn for Him, as one mourns for an only son, and they will weep bitterly over Him, like the bitter weeping over a first-born. (NASB)

[10] וְשָׁפַכְתִּי עַל־בֵּית דָּוִיד וְעַל יוֹשֵׁב יְרוּשָׁלַם רוּחַ חֵן וְתַחֲנוּנִים וְהִבִּיטוּ אֵלַי אֵת אֲשֶׁר־דָּקָרוּ וְסָפְדוּ עָלָיו כְּמִסְפֵּד עַל־הַיָּחִיד וְהָמֵר עָלָיו כְּהָמֵר עַל־הַבְּכוֹר:

The whole of Zechariah 12 deals with events surrounding the second coming of Messiah and specifically with the Campaign of Armageddon.[9] However, verse 10 is of relevance to our study of first coming prophecies. The Messiah was rejected by the Jewish leadership at His first coming, and it is an absolute prerequisite of His second coming that Jewish leaders should repent of their original rejection and ask God for His return. Zechariah 12:10 describes the grief which will one day be experienced by Jewish leaders over the death of Messiah. In the context of our present study, three points are made in this verse:

1. Zechariah confirms that Messiah will be rejected by the Jewish leaders.

2. We have already been told by Isaiah that Messiah will die, but now we are told that His will be a violent death: He will be pierced.

3. It is the Lord who is speaking, and He says that "they will look on *me* whom they have pierced." It is Jehovah who was pierced. Again we are told that Messiah will be God Himself. The word for "pierced" means "to thrust through." This was fulfilled during Yeshua's crucifixion when a Roman soldier thrust a spear into His side, as recorded in John 19:31-37.

That some rabbis took this passage as Messianic is clear from the *Talmud* in *Succah* 52a:

Why is this mourning in Messianic times? There is a difference in interpretation between Rabbi Dosa and the Rabanan [sages]. One opinion is that they mourn for Messiah Ben Joseph who is killed, and another explanation is that they mourn for the slaying of the evil inclination. It is well according to him who explains that the cause is the slaying of the Messiah since that well agrees with this verse. If it refers to the slaying of the evil

---

[9] This is obviously outside the scope of this study but is dealt with in the author's *The Footsteps of the Messiah*.

inclination, it must be asked, is this an occasion for mourning? Is it not rather an occasion for rejoicing? Why then should they weep?

Zechariah 12:10
teaches that:

✡ Messiah's first coming would be rejected by the leaders of Israel.
✡ Messiah would die a violent death by means of piercing.
✡ Messiah would be both God and Man.

Zechariah 13:7

The Good Shepherd

[7] "Awake, O sword, against My Shepherd, And against the man, My Associate," Declares the LORD of hosts. "Strike the Shepherd that the sheep may be scattered; And I will turn My hand against the little ones. (NASB)

חֶרֶב עוּרִי עַל־רֹעִי וְעַל־גֶּבֶר עֲמִיתִי נְאֻם יְהוָה [7]
צְבָאוֹת הַךְ אֶת־הָרֹעֶה וּתְפוּצֶיןָ הַצֹּאן וַהֲשִׁבֹתִי יָדִי
עַל־הַצֹּעֲרִים:

Zechariah 13:7 is a one verse summary of the whole of Zechariah chapter 11. The Shepherd of verse 13:7 is the Good Shepherd of 11:4-14. This verse again states that Messiah will be a God-Man. The humanity of Messiah is obvious: "and against the man." The words which follow are never adequately translated into English, and so the divinity of Messiah is not made obvious. What is translated as "my associate" is, in the Hebrew, "my equal." The verse should really read, "and against the man, my equal." Of course, in order to be equal with God, Messiah must actually be God. This may not be obvious in English translations, but is very clear in the original Hebrew.

The second part of this verse emphasizes the violent nature of Messiah's death and again states that His death will be the cause of the dispersion of Israel. The shepherd was struck in A.D. 30 when Yeshua was crucified, and the sheep were scattered in A.D. 70 when Israel was dispersed. These words are applied to Yeshua's disciples in Matthew 26:31-32, but the primary reference here is to the dispersion of A.D. 70. In verse 7b, even the little ones, the innocent common people, are to suffer because of the rejection of Messiah, the Good Shepherd, by the leaders of Israel.

Zechariah 13:7
teaches that:

✡ Messiah would be a God-Man.
✡ Messiah's death would be violent.
✡ Messiah's death would cause the dispersion of Israel.

Malachi 3:1

The Messenger of the King

[1] "Behold, I am going to send My messenger, and he will clear the way before Me. And the Lord, whom you seek, will suddenly come to His temple; and the messenger of the covenant, in whom you delight, behold, He is coming," says the LORD of hosts. (NASB)

[1] הִנְנִי שֹׁלֵחַ מַלְאָכִי וּפִנָּה־דֶרֶךְ לְפָנָי וּפִתְאֹם יָבוֹא אֶל־הֵיכָלוֹ הָאָדוֹן אֲשֶׁר־אַתֶּם מְבַקְשִׁים וּמַלְאַךְ הַבְּרִית אֲשֶׁר־אַתֶּם חֲפֵצִים הִנֵּה־בָא אָמַר יְהוָה צְבָאוֹת׃

Only two prophecies in the Hebrew Scriptures deal with the forerunner of the Messiah. The first is in Isaiah 40:3-5, and the second is here in Malachi 3:1. The forerunner of Messiah's second coming is clearly identified in Malachi 4:5-6 as the Prophet Elijah. The forerunner of Messiah's first coming, however, is never named, neither here nor in Isaiah. Only in the New Testament is he revealed as John the Baptist.

> [7] And as these were going *away*, Yeshua began to speak to the multitudes about John, . . . [10] "This is the one about whom it is written, 'Behold, I send My messenger before Your face, Who will prepare Your way before You.' [11] "Truly, I say to you, among those born of women there has not arisen *anyone* greater than John the Baptist; yet he who is least in the kingdom of heaven is greater than he.
>
> Matthew 11:7a, 10, 11 (NASB)

Malachi is the last of the Old Testament prophets. His name in Hebrew means "my messenger" or "my angel." The Hebrew word for "my messenger" in verse 3:1 is in fact *malachi* (מַלְאָכִי). The next prophetic voice to be heard in Israel, 400 years after Malachi, will be the voice of *malachi*, "My messenger"—John the Baptist.

The rest of verse 1 talks about the first coming of Messiah. It says that He will suddenly come to His Temple. This is the second Temple, rebuilt by Zerubbabel and remodeled by Herod the Great. It was to this Temple that Yeshua came, on two separate occasions, in order to cleanse it of money-changers (John 2:13-22; Matthew 21:12-13). The text specifically says *"his* temple." This Temple belongs to Messiah. He has full rights to the Temple and can do with it as He pleases. When Yeshua cleansed it, He was exercising His lordship, His authority, His ownership.

Verses 2-5 of this passage go on to talk about Messiah's cleansing of the people at His second coming.

Malachi 3:1

teaches that:

✡ **Messiah's first coming would be preceded by a herald.**

CHAPTER 3

The K'tuvim

1 Chronicles 17:10b-14

The Davidic Covenant

^{10b} Moreover, I tell you that the LORD will build a house for you. ¹¹ "And it shall come about when your days are fulfilled that you must go to be with your fathers, that I will set up one of your descendants after you, who shall be of your sons; and I will establish his kingdom. ¹² "He shall build for Me a house, and I will establish his throne forever. ¹³ "I will be his father, and he shall be My son; and I will not take My lovingkindness away from him, as I took it from him who was before you. ¹⁴ "But I will settle him in My house and in My kingdom forever, and his throne shall be established forever." (NASB)

וָאַגִּד לָךְ וּבַיִת יִבְנֶה־לְּךָ יְהוָה: ¹¹ וְהָיָה כִּי־מָלְאוּ יָמֶיךָ לָלֶכֶת עִם־אֲבֹתֶיךָ וַהֲקִימוֹתִי אֶת־זַרְעֲךָ אַחֲרֶיךָ אֲשֶׁר יִהְיֶה מִבָּנֶיךָ וַהֲכִינוֹתִי אֶת־מַלְכוּתוֹ: ¹² הוּא יִבְנֶה־לִּי בָיִת וְכֹנַנְתִּי אֶת־כִּסְאוֹ עַד־עוֹלָם: ¹³ אֲנִי אֶהְיֶה־לּוֹ לְאָב וְהוּא יִהְיֶה־לִּי לְבֵן וְחַסְדִּי לֹא־אָסִיר מֵעִמּוֹ כַּאֲשֶׁר הֲסִירוֹתִי מֵאֲשֶׁר הָיָה לְפָנֶיךָ: ¹⁴ וְהַעֲמַדְתִּיהוּ בְּבֵיתִי וּבְמַלְכוּתִי עַד־הָעוֹלָם וְכִסְאוֹ יִהְיֶה נָכוֹן עַד־עוֹלָם:

So far in our study, we have already encountered the Adamic Covenant, in Genesis 3:15, and the Abrahamic Covenant, in Genesis 22:18. Another of the eight covenants in Scripture which is crucial to a study of the Messianic Person is the Davidic Covenant. This is found in two segments of Scripture. The first concentrates on David's immediate son, Solomon, and the second deals with David's distant son, Messiah.

2 Samuel 7:11b-16

The first passage is in the scroll of the Prophets, in 2 Samuel 7:11b-16:

^{11b} The Lord also declares to you that the Lord will make a house for you. ¹² "When your days are complete and you lie down with your fathers, I will raise up your descendant after you, who will come forth from you, and I will establish his kingdom. ¹³ "He shall build a house for My name, and I will establish the throne of his kingdom forever. ¹⁴ "I will be a father to him and he will be a son to Me; when he commits iniquity, I will correct him with the rod of men and the strokes of the sons of men, ¹⁵ but My lovingkindness shall not depart from him, as I took it away from Saul, whom I removed from before you. ¹⁶ "And your house and your kingdom shall endure before Me forever; your throne shall be established forever." (NASB)

This passage deals with a son who will proceed from the loins of David himself, a son who will be David's immediate successor. In verse 16, God promises David three things as part of the covenant:

1. An eternal house or dynasty
2. An eternal kingdom
3. An eternal throne

As immediate proof of God's faithfulness to this covenant, David's line will be maintained by a son who will build the Temple which David was not permitted to build. This, of course, will be Solomon's temple. When this son sins, as Solomon indeed did by falling into idolatry, he will be disciplined, but God's covenant love will remain with him.

1 Chronicles 17:14

The parallel passage in 1 Chronicles 17: 14 is very similar, yet there are significant differences. In 2 Samuel, the son is immediate; in 1 Chronicles, he is distant. In 2 Samuel, the son is a sinner; in 1 Chronicles, there is no mention of sin. In 2 Samuel, the reference is to Solomon; in 1 Chronicles, the reference is to Messiah.

The three promises of 2 Samuel are repeated here, but a fourth is also added: an eternal son. "I will settle *him* in my house forever." David's line will eventually culminate in the birth of a person whose eternality will guarantee David's dynasty, kingdom, and throne forever.

Previously, "the seed" was to be born of a woman, Abraham, Jacob, and Judah. Now we are told which family within the tribe of Judah will bring forth this seed—the family of David. Messiah is to be a son of David. This automatically requires that Messiah come prior to A.D. 70 since all of Israel's genealogical records were destroyed in that year, along with the Temple which was destroyed by the Romans. Within a few decades of A.D. 70, it was impossible to prove who was a son of David and who was not.

There is one further limitation placed upon the descent of Messiah. We are told that He will come from one of David's sons, but in Jeremiah 22:24-30, we are told of one family, cursed by the prophet, which was excluded. This is the family of Coniah, also known as Jeconiah or Jehoiachin. Because of the kind of man that he was in the days of Jeremiah, God pronounced a curse on him. The curse, given in Jeremiah 22:30, is that no descendant of Jeconiah will ever have the right to sit on the throne of David. Messiah therefore had to be born a son of David but apart from Jeconiah.

We are told in Matthew's Gospel that Joseph, husband of Mary, the mother of Yeshua, was a son of David via Solomon and Jeconiah. He and his children were therefore under God's curse and would never fall heir to the throne of David. Luke's Gospel clearly gives Yeshua's lineage as being via Mary back to Nathan and David and, therefore, proves the legitimacy of Yeshua's claim to be Messiah.

1 Chronicles 17:10b-14

teaches that:

- ✡ Messiah would be a son of David, but descended through a line other than Jeconiah.
- ✡ Since all tribal and genealogical records were destroyed with the Temple in A.D. 70, Messiah must have come before that time.
- ✡ Messiah would live eternally.
- ✡ Messiah would be a king.

Psalm 2:7-12

The Son of God

⁷ "I will surely tell of the decree of the Lᴏʀᴅ: He said to Me, 'You are My Son, Today I have begotten You. ⁸ 'Ask of Me, and I will surely give the nations as Your inheritance, And the very ends of the earth as Your possession. ⁹ 'You shall break them with a rod of iron, You shall shatter them like earthenware.' " ¹⁰ Now therefore, O kings, show discernment; Take warning, O judges of the earth. ¹¹ Worship the Lᴏʀᴅ with reverence, And rejoice with trembling. ¹² Do homage to the Son, lest He become angry, and you perish in the way, For His wrath may soon be kindled. How blessed are all who take refuge in Him! (ɴᴀsʙ)

7 אֲסַפְּרָה אֶל חֹק יְהוָה אָמַר אֵלַי בְּנִי אַתָּה אֲנִי הַיּוֹם יְלִדְתִּיךָ: 8 שְׁאַל מִמֶּנִּי וְאֶתְּנָה גוֹיִם נַחֲלָתֶךָ וַאֲחֻזָּתְךָ אַפְסֵי־אָרֶץ: 9 תְּרֹעֵם בְּשֵׁבֶט בַּרְזֶל כִּכְלִי יוֹצֵר תְּנַפְּצֵם: 10 וְעַתָּה מְלָכִים הַשְׂכִּילוּ הִוָּסְרוּ שֹׁפְטֵי אָרֶץ: 11 עִבְדוּ אֶת־יְהוָה בְּיִרְאָה וְגִילוּ בִּרְעָדָה: 12 נַשְּׁקוּ־בַר פֶּן־יֶאֱנַף וְתֹאבְדוּ דֶרֶךְ כִּי־יִבְעַר כִּמְעַט אַפּוֹ אַשְׁרֵי כָּל־חוֹסֵי בוֹ:

The book of Psalms could be summarized in a single sentence: "The Psalms are the poetic versions of the messages of the law and the Prophets." The book is often regarded as purely devotional reading. While it is certainly very useful as such, it would be wrong to limit it to only that. The book is full of profound doctrine and deep spiritual truths couched in poetic terms.

The whole of Psalm 2 deals with the second coming of Messiah—the events before, during, and after it, and in particular the Campaign of Armageddon.[10] There are, however, some elements which are relevant to the first coming, particularly in verses 7-12. These verses cannot possibly be applied to David. While David was a great king, God never gave him authority over all the nations (verse 8), nor did he ever rule the uttermost ends of the earth. These verses speak of Messiah who, as the psalmist would have heard from the prophets, will rule over the entire world. Even Rashi admits, "Our rabbis expound it as relating to King Messiah."

Among the titles given to Messiah is the term "Son of God." This is applied to Messiah twice in Psalm 2, in verses 7 and 12. This Messiah, who is to be king in Jerusalem and over the whole world, is also uniquely the Son of God. In the Hebrew Scriptures, the phrase "sons of God" in the plural always applies to angels, either fallen or unfallen. The phrase "Son of God" in the singular is always and only applied to the Messiah.

---

[10] This is discussed in the author's book, *The Footsteps of the Messiah*.

Psalm 2:7-12

teaches that:

✡   Messiah would be the Son of God.

✡   Messiah will be a king in Jerusalem.

✡   Messiah will also rule over the Gentiles.

Psalm 16:1-11

The Death of Messiah

A Mikhtam of David.

¹ Preserve me, O God, for I take refuge in You. ² I said to the LORD, "You my Lord; I have no good besides You." ³ As for the saints who are in the earth, They are the majestic ones in whom is all my delight. ⁴ The sorrows of those who have bartered for another *god* will be multiplied; I shall not pour out their libations of blood, Nor shall I take their names upon my lips.

⁵ The LORD is the portion of my inheritance and my cup; You support my lot. ⁶ The lines have fallen to me in pleasant places; Indeed, my heritage is beautiful to me.

⁷ I will bless the LORD who has counseled me; Indeed, my mind instructs me in the night. ⁸ I have set the LORD continually before me; Because He is at my right hand, I will not be shaken. ⁹ Therefore my heart is glad and my glory rejoices; My flesh also will dwell securely. ¹⁰ For You will not abandon my soul to Sheol; Nor will You allow Your Holy One to undergo decay. ¹¹ You will make known to me the path of life; In Your presence is fullness of joy; In you right hand there are pleasures forever. (NASB)

מִכְתָּם לְדָוִד

¹ שָׁמְרֵנִי אֵל כִּי־חָסִיתִי בָךְ: ² אָמַרְתְּ לַיהוָה אֲדֹנָי אָתָּה טוֹבָתִי בַּל־עָלֶיךָ: ³ לִקְדוֹשִׁים אֲשֶׁר־בָּאָרֶץ הֵמָּה וְאַדִּירֵי כָּל־חֶפְצִי־בָם: ⁴ יִרְבּוּ עַצְּבוֹתָם אַחֵר מָהָרוּ בַּל־אַסִּיךְ נִסְכֵּיהֶם מִדָּם וּבַל־אֶשָּׂא אֶת־שְׁמוֹתָם עַל־שְׂפָתָי: ⁵ יְהוָה מְנָת־חֶלְקִי וְכוֹסִי אַתָּה תּוֹמִיךְ גּוֹרָלִי: ⁶ חֲבָלִים נָפְלוּ־לִי בַּנְּעִמִים אַף־נַחֲלָת שָׁפְרָה עָלָי: ⁷ אֲבָרֵךְ אֶת־יְהוָה אֲשֶׁר יְעָצָנִי אַף־לֵילוֹת יִסְּרוּנִי כִלְיוֹתָי: ⁸ שִׁוִּיתִי יְהוָה לְנֶגְדִּי תָמִיד כִּי מִימִינִי בַּל־אֶמּוֹט: ⁹ לָכֵן שָׂמַח לִבִּי וַיָּגֶל כְּבוֹדִי אַף־בְּשָׂרִי יִשְׁכֹּן לָבֶטַח: ¹⁰ כִּי לֹא־תַעֲזֹב נַפְשִׁי לִשְׁאוֹל לֹא־תִתֵּן חֲסִידְךָ לִרְאוֹת שָׁחַת: ¹¹ תּוֹדִיעֵנִי אֹרַח חַיִּים שֹׂבַע שְׂמָחוֹת אֶת־פָּנֶיךָ נְעִמוֹת בִּימִינְךָ נֶצַח:

The emphasis of Psalm 16:1-2 is that Messiah's refuge is in God and, in verse 3, that His delight is with the saints, the believing remnant, echoing the sentiments of Zechariah 11. In verses 4-9, the psalmist says that God the Father will be the Messiah's total trust in life, even to the point of death. Even in death, Messiah still trusts in God (verses 10-11).

The point of the song is that even though God allows Messiah to die, yet "You will not abandon my soul to Sheol; Nor will You allow Your Holy One to undergo decay." Messiah will be resurrected back to life.

Psalm 16:1-11

teaches that:

- ✡ Messiah would enjoy a unique relationship with God the Father. This aspect of His life is particularly emphasized in the Gospel of John.
- ✡ Messiah would die.
- ✡ Messiah would be raised back to life.

Psalm 22:1-31

The Suffering & Exaltation of Messiah

For the choir director; upon Aijeleth
Hashshahar. A Psalm of David.

¹ My God, my God, why have You forsaken
me? Far from my deliverance are the words of
my groaning. ² O my God, I cry by day, but You
do not answer; And by night, but I have no rest.
³ Yet You are holy, O You who are enthroned
upon the praises of Israel. ⁴ In You our fathers
trusted; They trusted, and You did deliver
them. ⁵ To You they cried out, and were
delivered; In You they trusted, and were not
disappointed. ⁶ But I am a worm, and not a
man, A reproach of men, and despised by the
people. ⁷ All who see me sneer at me; They
separate with the lip, they wag the head,
saying, ⁸ "Commit *yourself* to the LORD; let Him
deliver him; Let Him rescue him, because He
delights in him." ⁹ Yet You are He who does
bring me forth from the womb; You did make
me trust when upon my mother's breasts. ¹⁰
Upon You I was cast from birth; You have been
my God from my mother's womb. ¹¹ Be not far
from me, for trouble is near; For there is none
to help. ¹² Many bulls have surrounded me;
Strong *bulls* of Bashan have encircled me. ¹³
They open wide their mouth at me, As a
ravening and a roaring lion. ¹⁴ I am poured out
like water, And all my bones are out of joint;
My heart is like wax; It is melted within me. ¹⁵
My strength is dried up like a potsherd, And my
tongue cleaves to my jaws; And You do lay me
in the dust of death.

¹ לַמְנַצֵּחַ עַל־אַיֶּלֶת הַשַּׁחַר מִזְמוֹר לְדָוִד׃

² אֵלִי אֵלִי לָמָה עֲזַבְתָּנִי רָחוֹק מִישׁוּעָתִי דִּבְרֵי
שַׁאֲגָתִי׃ ³ אֱלֹהַי אֶקְרָא יוֹמָם וְלֹא תַעֲנֶה וְלַיְלָה וְלֹא־
דוּמִיָּה לִי׃ ⁴ וְאַתָּה קָדוֹשׁ יוֹשֵׁב תְּהִלּוֹת יִשְׂרָאֵל׃ ⁵ בְּךָ
בָּטְחוּ אֲבֹתֵינוּ בָּטְחוּ וַתְּפַלְּטֵמוֹ׃ ⁶ אֵלֶיךָ זָעֲקוּ
וְנִמְלָטוּ בְּךָ בָטְחוּ וְלֹא־בוֹשׁוּ׃ ⁷ וְאָנֹכִי תוֹלַעַת וְלֹא־
אִישׁ חֶרְפַּת אָדָם וּבְזוּי עָם׃ ⁸ כָּל־רֹאַי יַלְעִגוּ לִי
יַפְטִירוּ בְשָׂפָה יָנִיעוּ רֹאשׁ׃ ⁹ גֹּל אֶל־יְהוָה יְפַלְּטֵהוּ
יַצִּילֵהוּ כִּי חָפֵץ בּוֹ׃ ¹⁰ כִּי־אַתָּה גֹחִי מִבָּטֶן מַבְטִיחִי
עַל־שְׁדֵי אִמִּי׃ ¹¹ עָלֶיךָ הָשְׁלַכְתִּי מֵרָחֶם מִבֶּטֶן אִמִּי
אֵלִי אָתָּה׃ ¹² אַל־תִּרְחַק מִמֶּנִּי כִּי־צָרָה קְרוֹבָה כִּי־
אֵין עוֹזֵר׃ ¹³ סְבָבוּנִי פָּרִים רַבִּים אַבִּירֵי בָשָׁן כִּתְּרוּנִי׃
¹⁴ פָּצוּ עָלַי פִּיהֶם אַרְיֵה טֹרֵף וְשֹׁאֵג׃ ¹⁵ כַּמַּיִם
נִשְׁפַּכְתִּי וְהִתְפָּרְדוּ כָּל־עַצְמוֹתָי הָיָה לִבִּי כַּדּוֹנָג נָמֵס
בְּתוֹךְ מֵעָי׃

16 For dogs have surrounded me; A band of evildoers has encompassed me; They pierced my hands and my feet. 17 I can count all my bones. They look, they stare at me; 18 They divide my garments among them, And for my clothing they cast lots. 19 But You, O LORD, be not far off; O You my help, hasten to my assistance. 20 Deliver my soul from the sword, My only life from the power of the dog. 21 Save me from the lion's mouth; And from the horns of the wild oxen You do answer me. 22 I will tell of Your name to my brethren; In the midst of the assembly I will praise You. 23 You who fear the LORD, praise Him; All you descendants of Jacob, glorify Him, And stand in awe of Him, all you descendants of Israel. 24 For He has not despised nor abhorred the affliction of the afflicted; Neither has He hidden His face from him; But when he cried to Him for help, He heard. 25 From You *comes* my praise in the great assembly; I shall pay my vows before those who fear Him. 26 The afflicted shall eat and be satisfied; Those who seek Him will praise the LORD. Let your heart live forever! 27 All the ends of the earth will remember and turn to the LORD, And all the families of the nations will worship before You. 28 For the kingdom is the Lord's, And He rules over the nations. 29 All the prosperous of the earth will eat and worship, All those who go down to the dust will bow before Him, Even he who cannot keep his soul alive. 30 Posterity will serve Him; It will be told of the LORD to the *coming* generation. 31 They will come and will declare His righteousness To a people who will be born, that He has performed it. (ASV)

יָבֵשׁ כַּחֶרֶשׂ כֹּחִי וּלְשׁוֹנִי מֻדְבָּק מַלְקוֹחָי וְלַעֲפַר־ 16
מָוֶת תִּשְׁפְּתֵנִי: 17 כִּי סְבָבוּנִי כְּלָבִים עֲדַת מְרֵעִים
הִקִּיפוּנִי כָּאֲרִי יָדַי וְרַגְלָי: 18 אֲסַפֵּר כָּל־עַצְמוֹתָי הֵמָּה
יַבִּיטוּ יִרְאוּ־בִי: 19 יְחַלְּקוּ בְגָדַי לָהֶם וְעַל־לְבוּשִׁי יַפִּילוּ
גוֹרָל: 20 וְאַתָּה יְהוָה אַל־תִּרְחָק אֱיָלוּתִי לְעֶזְרָתִי
חוּשָׁה: 21 הַצִּילָה מֵחֶרֶב נַפְשִׁי מִיַּד־כֶּלֶב יְחִידָתִי:
22 הוֹשִׁיעֵנִי מִפִּי אַרְיֵה וּמִקַּרְנֵי רֵמִים עֲנִיתָנִי:
23 אֲסַפְּרָה שִׁמְךָ לְאֶחָי בְּתוֹךְ קָהָל אֲהַלְלֶךָ: 24 יִרְאֵי
יְהוָה הַלְלוּהוּ כָּל־זֶרַע יַעֲקֹב כַּבְּדוּהוּ וְגוּרוּ מִמֶּנּוּ כָּל־
זֶרַע יִשְׂרָאֵל: 25 כִּי לֹא־בָזָה וְלֹא שִׁקַּץ עֱנוּת עָנִי וְלֹא־
הִסְתִּיר פָּנָיו מִמֶּנּוּ וּבְשַׁוְּעוֹ אֵלָיו שָׁמֵעַ: 26 מֵאִתְּךָ
תְהִלָּתִי בְּקָהָל רָב נְדָרַי אֲשַׁלֵּם נֶגֶד יְרֵאָיו: 27 יֹאכְלוּ
עֲנָוִים וְיִשְׂבָּעוּ יְהַלְלוּ יְהוָה דֹּרְשָׁיו יְחִי לְבַבְכֶם לָעַד:
28 יִזְכְּרוּ וְיָשֻׁבוּ אֶל־יְהוָה כָּל־אַפְסֵי־אָרֶץ וְיִשְׁתַּחֲווּ
לְפָנֶיךָ כָּל־מִשְׁפְּחוֹת גּוֹיִם: 29 כִּי לַיהוָה הַמְּלוּכָה
וּמֹשֵׁל בַּגּוֹיִם: 30 אָכְלוּ וַיִּשְׁתַּחֲווּ כָּל־דִּשְׁנֵי־אֶרֶץ לְפָנָיו
יִכְרְעוּ כָּל־יוֹרְדֵי עָפָר וְנַפְשׁוֹ לֹא חִיָּה: 31 זֶרַע יַעַבְדֶנּוּ
יְסֻפַּר לַאדֹנָי לַדּוֹר: 32 יָבֹאוּ וְיַגִּידוּ צִדְקָתוֹ לְעַם נוֹלָד
כִּי עָשָׂה:

Note that the Hebrew verse numbering is different to the English numbering for this passage.

Psalm 22 is the most famous of the Messianic psalms, the entire song being devoted to the events of the first coming and a few aspects of the second. It divides into two main parts, the first dealing with the suffering of Messiah, followed by His exaltation in the second.

The whole psalm could be viewed as a poetic version of Isaiah 53, although it was in fact written before the prophecy of Isaiah.

The Sufferings of the Messiah—Psalm 22:1-21

Messiah's Cry for Help—Psalm 22:1-2

These verses find Messiah crying out in deepest anguish. It is no accident that these are the very words that Yeshua cried out while hanging on the cross. He quoted these words after a period of three hours of intense darkness. During those three hours, the entire wrath of God, due to the sins of Israel and the world, was poured out upon Him. This is the one and only place in the Gospel accounts that Yeshua addresses God as "my God." On every other occasion, and there are over 170 references, Yeshua says "Father" or "my Father." It is made very clear that Yeshua enjoyed a very special, unique relationship with God. On the cross, however, Yeshua was dying for the sins of the world and was experiencing a judicial relationship with God, not a paternal one; hence His cry of "my God, my God" instead of "my Father, my Father."

God's Past Deliverance—Psalm 22:3-5

These verses recount the past deliverances of God. God is fully able to deliver yet is choosing not to do so.

Messiah Despised—Psalm 22:6-8

These verses describe the taunts and jibes of evil men at the suffering of Messiah. The psalmist used words similar to Isaiah 53, and they are indeed very similar to the words of ridicule used by the crowds at the crucifixion of Yeshua. He is reproached, scorned, and taunted.

God is Messiah's Trust—Psalm 22:9-11

These verses state that Messiah has trusted in God from His birth. There are references here to the mother of Messiah but, as in all other Messianic prophecies, there is never any mention of a human father. Messiah would be born of a virgin as prophesied in Isaiah 7:14.

Description of the Agony—Psalm 22:12-18

These verses describe the suffering of Messiah, and some of these words are quoted almost identically in the New Testament.

1. **Surrounded and stared at—Psalm 22:12-13.**

2. **Physical agony—Psalm 22:14-17.**

   i.   *I am poured out like water.*
        This emphasizes excessive sweat.

   ii. *All my bones are out of joint.*
        After the person was nailed to the cross on the ground, the cross would be raised to the vertical and dropped into a deep slot in the ground. The shock of this action would cause dislocations.

   iii. *My heart is like melted wax.*
        A Hebrew phrase meaning "a ruptured heart," evidenced by the pouring out of blood and water.

   iv. *My strength is dried up like a potsherd.*
        His strength is totally gone.

   v.   *My tongue cleaves to my jaws.*
        This emphasizes excessive thirst. After six hours on the cross, three of them in total darkness, Yeshua said, "I thirst." This meant more than physical thirst. During those three hours of intense darkness, Yeshua suffered the outpouring of God's wrath, the pangs of hell itself. He had previously spoken of a rich man who—after only a few moments in hell—had said, "I thirst" (Luke 16). The fact that Yeshua used the same words reflects the extreme suffering of the pain of hell which He experienced while hanging on the cross.

   vi. *They pierced my hands and my feet.*
        The Hebrew word used here for piercing is not the same as that used in Zechariah 12:10. The word used in Zechariah means "to thrust through" and would be consistent with the Roman spear which pierced Yeshua's side. The word in Psalm 22 would be used, for example, of ear piercing and would be consistent with the nailing of Yeshua's hands and feet to the cross.

   vii. *I can count all my bones.*
        His bones are protruding.

3. ***They divide my garments among them—Psalm 22:18.***
   In verse 18, Messiah's clothes are divided amongst His tormentors by the casting of lots. Once again, this was quite literally fulfilled at Yeshua's crucifixion (e.g., Mark 15:24).

Messiah's Prayer for Help—Psalm 22:19-21

Verses 19-21 are again a cry for help from Messiah while still hanging on the cross.

The Exaltation of the Messiah—Psalm 22:22-31

With His suffering complete, verses 22-31 turn and speak of Messiah's exaltation. In verse 22, Messiah will praise God in the midst of the assembly. But how is this possible if He died in verses 1-21? Clearly this can only be possible by resurrection. The rest of the psalm goes on to describe what happens after His resurrection, culminating in His second coming and the establishment of His kingdom.

A Note on Verse 16

Some wish to translate verse 16 as "like a lion, my hands and my feet," instead of, "they pierced my hands and my feet." The former is based on the pointing of the Masoretic text and the latter on the *Septuagint*, a Greek translation of the Hebrew text that preceded the Masoretic text by over one thousand years and hence is closer to the original writing. While it is true that the writer uses several animal motifs in the context, the psalmist *only* uses animalistic terms to describe his enemies and not himself. Hence both the context and the antiquity of the Hebrew text behind the Septuagint favor the rendering of "pierce."

Psalm 22
teaches that:

- ✡ In extreme agony, Messiah would cry out for God's help.
- ✡ Messiah would be a despised and rejected individual.
- ✡ In the agony of death, Messiah would be stared at and mocked.
- ✡ The Messiah's bones would be pulled out of joint.
- ✡ The Messiah's heart would rupture.
- ✡ The Messiah would suffer an extreme degree of thirst.
- ✡ Messiah's hands and feet would be pierced.
- ✡ Messiah's clothing would be divided by the casting of lots.
- ✡ At the point of death, Messiah's trust would be in God the Father.
- ✡ Messiah would be resurrected.

Psalm 80:17

The Man of Your Right Hand

17 Let Your hand be upon the man of Your right hand, Upon the son of man whom You did make strong for Yourself. (ASV)

18 תְּהִי־יָדְךָ עַל־אִישׁ יְמִינֶךָ עַל־בֶּן־אָדָם אִמַּצְתָּ לָּךְ׃

Note that the Hebrew verse numbering is different to the English numbering for this passage.

The whole of Psalm 80 deals with the national salvation of Israel just prior to the second coming. Israel is now pleading for Messiah to return, but within their prayers there is one verse—verse 17—which is relevant to our study of Messiah's first coming. Verse 17 is in fact a development of the teaching of Psalm 110:1, which should be studied first.

Israel is praying to God for deliverance. In verse 17, the One they ask to come and deliver them is the One seated at God's right hand. We are told in Psalm 110 that this is the Messiah who has ascended to the right hand of God following His rejection. Psalm 110 also states that Messiah will remain there until Israel repents and asks for His return. It is this repentance which is being described in Psalm 80.

The title given to Messiah in verse 17 is "the Son of Man." This is a very common Messianic title in the New Testament, particularly in the Gospel of Luke. Since the Son of Man is sitting at the right hand of God, He must be equal with God (see Psalm 110). Thus, we have another verse which affirms that Messiah must be a God-Man.

Psalm 80:17
teaches that:

- ✡ **The Messiah would be seated at the right hand of God the Father.**
- ✡ **Messiah must be equal with God to be seated at His right hand; Messiah must therefore be both God and man.**

Psalm 110:1-7

A Priest after the Order of Melchizedek

A Psalm of David.

[1] The LORD says to my Lord: "Sit at My right hand, Until I make Your enemies a footstool for Your feet." [2] The LORD will stretch forth Your strong scepter from Zion, *saying*, "Rule in the midst of Your enemies." [3] Your people will volunteer freely in the day of Your power; In holy array, from the womb of the dawn, Your youth are to You as the dew. [4] The LORD has sworn and will not change His mind, "You are a priest forever According to the order of Melchizedek." [5] The Lord is at Your right hand; He will shatter kings in the day of His wrath. [6] He will judge among the nations, He will fill *them* with corpses, He will shatter the chief men over a broad country. [7] He will drink from the brook by the wayside; Therefore He will lift up His head. (ASV)

לְדָוִד מִזְמוֹר

[1] נְאֻם יְהוָה לַאדֹנִי שֵׁב לִימִינִי עַד־אָשִׁית אֹיְבֶיךָ הֲדֹם לְרַגְלֶיךָ: [2] מַטֵּה־עֻזְּךָ יִשְׁלַח יְהוָה מִצִּיּוֹן רְדֵה בְּקֶרֶב אֹיְבֶיךָ: [3] עַמְּךָ נְדָבֹת בְּיוֹם חֵילֶךָ בְּהַדְרֵי־קֹדֶשׁ מֵרֶחֶם מִשְׁחָר לְךָ טַל יַלְדֻתֶיךָ: [4] נִשְׁבַּע יְהוָה וְלֹא יִנָּחֵם אַתָּה־כֹהֵן לְעוֹלָם עַל־דִּבְרָתִי מַלְכִּי־צֶדֶק: [5] אֲדֹנָי עַל־יְמִינְךָ מָחַץ בְּיוֹם־אַפּוֹ מְלָכִים: [6] יָדִין בַּגּוֹיִם מָלֵא גְוִיּוֹת מָחַץ רֹאשׁ עַל־אֶרֶץ רַבָּה: [7] מִנַּחַל בַּדֶּרֶךְ יִשְׁתֶּה עַל־כֵּן יָרִים רֹאשׁ:

P salm 110 falls into the fourth category of Messianic prophecy mentioned in the appendices, as it encompasses the entire Messianic program. Within its seven short verses, it includes all four periods of this program: the first coming, the interval, the second coming, and the Messianic kingdom. The psalm divides into three sections or stanzas, a stanza usually being referred to as a "strophe" in Hebrew poetry.

Strophe One—Psalm 110:1-2

We should note first that the psalmist here is David. David was king over all of Israel. He established a Jewish empire by subjugating the surrounding nations and collecting tribute from them. David had no human lord; there was no authority over him except Jehovah Himself. Yet, in verse 1 of this psalm, David speaks of two lords: "The Lord [Jehovah] said to my Lord." Keeping in mind that David had no over-lord, the question arises who the second person is. Who was David's Lord? The only way to understand this verse is to see Jehovah as God the Father and "David's

Lord" as Messiah. It is Messiah, therefore, who is invited to sit at God's right hand. What we have here is a prophecy which was fulfilled at Yeshua's ascension from earth to heaven after His resurrection. He had completed His redemptive work and sat down at His Father's right hand.

Implicit within this prophecy is the concept of the God-Man. We know from 1 Kings 2:19 that anyone who sits at a king's right hand must be equal with the king. When one king made a visit of state to another king, he would sit at his host's right hand. Since Messiah is invited to sit at God's right hand, it follows that Messiah must be equal with God.

As to His humanity, Messiah is to be a descendant of David. Because of His deity, He can sit at the right hand of God. He is to sit there for some period of time, "Until I make Your enemies a footstool." This statement presupposes the first coming and its rejection. The first coming is to be in hostile circumstances. In verse 2, the enemies of verse 1 are said to be in Zion itself. Because the first coming is rejected, Messiah is invited to sit at the right hand of God for a period of time, until His enemies subject themselves to Him. This is further developed in Psalm 80.

Strophe Two—Psalm 110:3-4

Here we find the change of heart looked for in the enemies of Messiah. When Messiah comes a second time, in His day of power, His people will be willing volunteers.

Then, in verse 4, a new and very important statement is introduced concerning Messiah: He will be a priest after the order of Melchizedek. According to Genesis 14, a priest in the order of Melchizedek could be both a priest and a king. This was before the time of Moses, since under the Mosaic Law this would no longer be possible. The Law of Moses laid down that all priests had to be of the tribe of Levi and that kings had to be of the tribe of Judah. For this prophecy to be fulfilled, it is therefore clear that it will be necessary for the Law of Moses and the Levitical order to be removed.

The New Testament clearly teaches that with the death of Yeshua, the Law of Moses was rendered inoperative by His fulfillment of it and was replaced with the law of Messiah (Hebrews 7:11-18). Under the new law, the order of Melchizedek is instituted in place of the Levitical order; therefore, Messiah is indeed a priest and a king. Verse 4 states that Messiah's priesthood and kingship will be eternal.

Strophe Three—Psalm 110:5-7

These verses deal with the second coming and are outside the scope of this study.

Psalm 110:1-7

teaches that:

✡ The Messiah would be both a priest and a king after the order of Melchizedek.

✡ Messiah would have to be both God and man. To be a priest He would have to be a man, but to sit at God's right hand He must be equal with God.

✡ Messiah's first coming would be rejected.

✡ After His rejection, Messiah would ascend into heaven.

✡ After His ascension, Messiah would sit down at God's right hand.

✡ Messiah will return when Israel accepts Him.

✡ Messiah will rule over Israel.

Proverbs 30:4

The Name of God's Son

⁴ Who has gone up to heaven and come down? Who has gathered up the wind in the hollow of his hands? Who has wrapped up the waters in his cloak? Who has established all the ends of the earth? What is his name, and the name of his son? Tell me if you know! (NIV)

⁴ מִי עָלָה־שָׁמַיִם וַיֵּרַד מִי אָסַף־רוּחַ בְּחָפְנָיו מִי צָרַר־מַיִם בַּשִּׂמְלָה מִי הֵקִים כָּל־אַפְסֵי־אָרֶץ מַה־שְּׁמוֹ וּמַה־שֶּׁם־בְּנוֹ כִּי תֵדָע׃

Amongst the sayings of Agur in Proverbs 30 is a riddle. The riddle consists of six questions, the first four of which are rhetorical. The answers to these questions are obvious since only God Himself could accomplish these things. The fifth question is also easy since the name of God was revealed to men long before the book of Proverbs was written. The name of God, YHVH, is often translated *Jehovah*. With the typographic conventions of modern translations, it is usually rendered as "the Lord".

It is the sixth question which is the tricky one: "What is the name of his son?" It has already been shown that the Hebrew Scriptures reveal that God has a son. This was stated twice in Psalm 2. Here it is stated again. What is not revealed, however, is the name of that son, hence the teasing "*if* you know." At this stage of progressive revelation, no one *could* know His name. It is only in the New Testament that His name is revealed as Yeshua—"and no other name is given under heaven whereby you can be saved" (Acts 4:12). His name has now been revealed.

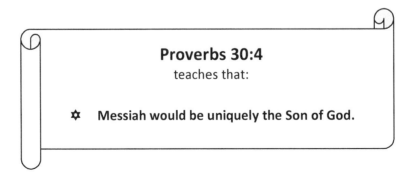

Proverbs 30:4
teaches that:

✡ **Messiah would be uniquely the Son of God.**

Daniel 9:1-27

The Messianic Timetable

[1] In the first year of Darius the son of Ahasuerus, of Median descent, who was made king over the kingdom of the Chaldeans—[2] in the first year of his reign, I, Daniel, observed in the books the number of the years which was *revealed as* the word of the LORD to Jeremiah the prophet for the completion of the desolations of Jerusalem, *namely,* seventy years. [3] So I gave my attention to the Lord God to seek *Him by* prayer and supplications, with fasting, sackcloth and ashes. [4] I prayed to the LORD my God and confessed and said, "Alas, O Lord, the great and awesome God, who keeps His covenant and lovingkindness for those who love Him and keep His commandments, [5] we have sinned, committed iniquity, acted wickedly and rebelled, even turning aside from Your commandments and ordinances. [6] Moreover, we have not listened to Your servants the prophets, who spoke in Your name to our kings, our princes, our fathers and all the people of the land. [7] "Righteousness belongs to You, O Lord, but to us open shame, as it is this day—to the men of Judah, the inhabitants of Jerusalem and all Israel, those who are nearby and those who are far away in all the countries to which You have driven them, because of their unfaithful deeds which they have committed against You. [8] Open shame belongs to us, O Lord, to our kings, our princes and our fathers, because we have sinned against You. [9] To the Lord our God *belong* compassion and forgiveness, for we have rebelled against Him; [10] nor have we obeyed the voice of the LORD our God, to walk in His teachings which He set before us through His servants the prophets.

בִּשְׁנַת אַחַת לְדָרְיָוֶשׁ בֶּן־אֲחַשְׁוֵרוֹשׁ מִזֶּרַע מָדָי ¹
אֲשֶׁר הָמְלַךְ עַל מַלְכוּת כַּשְׂדָּים: ² בִּשְׁנַת אַחַת
לְמָלְכוֹ אֲנִי דָּנִיֵּאל בִּינֹתִי בַּסְּפָרִים מִסְפַּר הַשָּׁנִים
אֲשֶׁר הָיָה דְבַר־יְהֹוָה אֶל־יִרְמִיָה הַנָּבִיא לְמַלֹּאות
לְחָרְבוֹת יְרוּשָׁלַם שִׁבְעִים שָׁנָה: ³ וָאֶתְּנָה אֶת־פָּנַי
אֶל־אֲדֹנָי הָאֱלֹהִים לְבַקֵּשׁ תְּפִלָּה וְתַחֲנוּנִים בְּצוֹם
וְשַׂק וָאֵפֶר: ⁴ וָאֶתְפַּלְלָה לַיהֹוָה אֱלֹהַי וָאֶתְוַדֶּה
וָאֹמְרָה אָנָּא אֲדֹנָי הָאֵל הַגָּדֹל וְהַנּוֹרָא שֹׁמֵר הַבְּרִית
וְהַחֶסֶד לְאֹהֲבָיו וּלְשֹׁמְרֵי מִצְוֹתָיו: ⁵ חָטָאנוּ וְעָוִינוּ
וְהִרְשַׁעְנוּ וּמָרָדְנוּ וְסוֹר מִמִּצְוֹתֶךָ וּמִמִּשְׁפָּטֶיךָ: ⁶ וְלֹא
שָׁמַעְנוּ אֶל־עֲבָדֶיךָ הַנְּבִיאִים אֲשֶׁר דִּבְּרוּ בְּשִׁמְךָ אֶל־
מְלָכֵינוּ שָׂרֵינוּ וַאֲבֹתֵינוּ וְאֶל כָּל־עַם הָאָרֶץ: ⁷ לְךָ
אֲדֹנָי הַצְּדָקָה וְלָנוּ בֹּשֶׁת הַפָּנִים כַּיּוֹם הַזֶּה לְאִישׁ
יְהוּדָה וּלְיוֹשְׁבֵי יְרוּשָׁלַם וּלְכָל־יִשְׂרָאֵל הַקְּרֹבִים
וְהָרְחֹקִים בְּכָל־הָאֲרָצוֹת אֲשֶׁר הִדַּחְתָּם שָׁם
בְּמַעֲלָם אֲשֶׁר מָעֲלוּ־בָךְ: ⁸ יְהֹוָה לָנוּ בֹּשֶׁת הַפָּנִים
לִמְלָכֵינוּ לְשָׂרֵינוּ וְלַאֲבֹתֵינוּ אֲשֶׁר חָטָאנוּ לָךְ: ⁹
לַאדֹנָי אֱלֹהֵינוּ הָרַחֲמִים וְהַסְּלִחוֹת כִּי מָרָדְנוּ בּוֹ: ¹⁰
וְלֹא שָׁמַעְנוּ בְּקוֹל יְהֹוָה אֱלֹהֵינוּ לָלֶכֶת בְּתוֹרֹתָיו
אֲשֶׁר נָתַן לְפָנֵינוּ בְּיַד עֲבָדָיו הַנְּבִיאִים:

[11] Indeed all Israel has transgressed Your law and turned aside, not obeying Your voice; so the curse has been poured out on us, along with the oath which is written in the law of Moses the servant of God, for we have sinned against Him. [12] Thus He has confirmed His words which He had spoken against us and against our rulers who ruled us, to bring on us great calamity; for under the whole heaven there has not been done *anything* like what was done to Jerusalem. [13] As it is written in the law of Moses, all this calamity has come on us; yet we have not sought the favor of the Lord our God by turning from our iniquity and giving attention to Your truth. [14] Therefore the Lord has kept the calamity in store and brought it on us; for the Lord our God is righteous with respect to all His deeds which He has done, but we have not obeyed His voice. [15] "And now, O Lord our God, who have brought Your people out of the land of Egypt with a mighty hand and have made a name for Yourself, as it is this day—we have sinned, we have been wicked. [16] O Lord, in accordance with all Your righteous acts, let now Your anger and Your wrath turn away from Your city Jerusalem, Your holy mountain; for because of our sins and the iniquities of our fathers, Jerusalem and Your people *have become* a reproach to all those around us. [17] So now, our God, listen to the prayer of Your servant and to his supplications, and for Your sake, O Lord, let Your face shine on Your desolate sanctuary. [18] O my God, incline Your ear and hear! Open Your eyes and see our desolations and the city which is called by Your name; for we are not presenting our supplications before You on account of any merits of our own, but on account of Your great compassion. [19] O Lord, hear! O Lord, forgive! O Lord, listen and take action! For Your own sake, O my God, do not delay, because Your city and Your people are called by Your name." [20] Now while I was speaking and praying, and confessing my sin and the sin of my people Israel, and presenting my supplication before the Lord my God in behalf of the holy mountain of

[11] וְכָל־יִשְׂרָאֵל עָבְרוּ אֶת־תּוֹרָתֶךָ וְסוֹר לְבִלְתִּי שְׁמוֹעַ בְּקֹלֶךָ וַתִּתַּךְ עָלֵינוּ הָאָלָה וְהַשְּׁבֻעָה אֲשֶׁר כְּתוּבָה בְּתוֹרַת מֹשֶׁה עֶבֶד־הָאֱלֹהִים כִּי חָטָאנוּ לוֹ: [12] וַיָּקֶם אֶת־דְּבָרָיו אֲשֶׁר־דִּבֶּר עָלֵינוּ וְעַל שֹׁפְטֵינוּ אֲשֶׁר שְׁפָטוּנוּ לְהָבִיא עָלֵינוּ רָעָה גְדֹלָה אֲשֶׁר לֹא־נֶעֶשְׂתָה תַּחַת כָּל־הַשָּׁמַיִם כַּאֲשֶׁר נֶעֶשְׂתָה בִּירוּשָׁלָם: [13] כַּאֲשֶׁר כָּתוּב בְּתוֹרַת מֹשֶׁה אֵת כָּל־הָרָעָה הַזֹּאת בָּאָה עָלֵינוּ וְלֹא־חִלִּינוּ אֶת־פְּנֵי יְהוָה אֱלֹהֵינוּ לָשׁוּב מֵעֲוֺנֵנוּ וּלְהַשְׂכִּיל בַּאֲמִתֶּךָ: [14] וַיִּשְׁקֹד יְהוָה עַל־הָרָעָה וַיְבִיאֶהָ עָלֵינוּ כִּי־צַדִּיק יְהוָה אֱלֹהֵינוּ עַל־כָּל־מַעֲשָׂיו אֲשֶׁר עָשָׂה וְלֹא שָׁמַעְנוּ בְּקֹלוֹ: [15] וְעַתָּה אֲדֹנָי אֱלֹהֵינוּ אֲשֶׁר הוֹצֵאתָ אֶת־עַמְּךָ מֵאֶרֶץ מִצְרַיִם בְּיָד חֲזָקָה וַתַּעַשׂ־לְךָ שֵׁם כַּיּוֹם הַזֶּה חָטָאנוּ רָשָׁעְנוּ: [16] אֲדֹנָי כְּכָל־צִדְקֹתֶךָ יָשָׁב־נָא אַפְּךָ וַחֲמָתְךָ מֵעִירְךָ יְרוּשָׁלַם הַר־קָדְשֶׁךָ כִּי בַחֲטָאֵינוּ וּבַעֲוֺנוֹת אֲבֹתֵינוּ יְרוּשָׁלַם וְעַמְּךָ לְחֶרְפָּה לְכָל־סְבִיבֹתֵינוּ: [17] וְעַתָּה שְׁמַע אֱלֹהֵינוּ אֶל־תְּפִלַּת עַבְדְּךָ וְאֶל־תַּחֲנוּנָיו וְהָאֵר פָּנֶיךָ עַל־מִקְדָּשְׁךָ הַשָּׁמֵם לְמַעַן אֲדֹנָי: [18] הַטֵּה אֱלֹהַי אָזְנְךָ וּשְׁמָע פְּקַח עֵינֶיךָ וּרְאֵה שֹׁמְמֹתֵינוּ וְהָעִיר אֲשֶׁר־נִקְרָא שִׁמְךָ עָלֶיהָ כִּי לֹא עַל־צִדְקֹתֵינוּ אֲנַחְנוּ מַפִּילִים תַּחֲנוּנֵינוּ לְפָנֶיךָ כִּי עַל־רַחֲמֶיךָ הָרַבִּים: [19] אֲדֹנָי שְׁמָעָה אֲדֹנָי סְלָחָה אֲדֹנָי הַקְשִׁיבָה וַעֲשֵׂה אַל־תְּאַחַר לְמַעֲנְךָ אֱלֹהַי כִּי־שִׁמְךָ נִקְרָא עַל־עִירְךָ וְעַל־עַמֶּךָ: [20] וְעוֹד אֲנִי מְדַבֵּר וּמִתְפַּלֵּל וּמִתְוַדֶּה חַטָּאתִי וְחַטַּאת עַמִּי יִשְׂרָאֵל וּמַפִּיל תְּחִנָּתִי לִפְנֵי יְהוָה אֱלֹהַי עַל הַר־קֹדֶשׁ אֱלֹהָי:

my God, ²¹ while I was still speaking in prayer, then the man Gabriel, whom I had seen in the vision previously, came to me in *my* extreme weariness about the time of the evening offering. ²² He gave *me* instruction and talked with me and said, "O Daniel, I have now come forth to give you insight with understanding. ²³ At the beginning of your supplications the command was issued, and I have come to tell *you*, for you are highly esteemed; so give heed to the message and gain understanding of the vision. ²⁴ "Seventy weeks have been decreed for your people and your holy city, to finish the transgression, to make an end of sin, to make atonement for iniquity, to bring in everlasting righteousness, to seal up vision and prophecy and to anoint the most holy *place*. ²⁵ So you are to know and discern *that* from the issuing of a decree to restore and rebuild Jerusalem until Messiah the Prince *there will be* seven weeks and sixty-two weeks; it will be built again, with plaza and moat, even in times of distress. ²⁶ Then after the sixty-two weeks the Messiah will be cut off and have nothing, and the people of the prince who is to come will destroy the city and the sanctuary. And its end *will come* with a flood; even to the end there will be war; desolations are determined. ²⁷ And he will make a firm covenant with the many for one week, but in the middle of the week he will put a stop to sacrifice and grain offering; and on the wing of abominations *will come* one who makes desolate, even until a complete destruction, one that is decreed, is poured out on the one who makes desolate." (NASB)

וְעוֹד אֲנִי מְדַבֵּר בַּתְּפִלָּה וְהָאִישׁ גַּבְרִיאֵל אֲשֶׁר ²¹ רָאִיתִי בֶחָזוֹן בַּתְּחִלָּה מֻעָף בִּיעָף נֹגֵעַ אֵלַי כְּעֵת מִנְחַת־עָרֶב: ²² וַיָּבֶן וַיְדַבֵּר עִמִּי וַיֹּאמַר דָּנִיֵּאל עַתָּה יָצָאתִי לְהַשְׂכִּילְךָ בִינָה: ²³ בִּתְחִלַּת תַּחֲנוּנֶיךָ יָצָא דָבָר וַאֲנִי בָּאתִי לְהַגִּיד כִּי חֲמוּדוֹת אָתָּה וּבִין בַּדָּבָר וְהָבֵן בַּמַּרְאֶה: ²⁴ שָׁבֻעִים שִׁבְעִים נֶחְתַּךְ עַל־עַמְּךָ וְעַל־עִיר קָדְשֶׁךָ לְכַלֵּא הַפֶּשַׁע וּלְחָתֵם חַטָּאוֹת וּלְכַפֵּר עָוֹן וּלְהָבִיא צֶדֶק עֹלָמִים וְלַחְתֹּם חָזוֹן וְנָבִיא וְלִמְשֹׁחַ קֹדֶשׁ קָדָשִׁים: ²⁵ וְתֵדַע וְתַשְׂכֵּל מִן־מֹצָא דָבָר לְהָשִׁיב וְלִבְנוֹת יְרוּשָׁלַ‍ם עַד־מָשִׁיחַ נָגִיד שָׁבֻעִים שִׁבְעָה וְשָׁבֻעִים שִׁשִּׁים וּשְׁנַיִם תָּשׁוּב וְנִבְנְתָה רְחוֹב וְחָרוּץ וּבְצוֹק הָעִתִּים: ²⁶ וְאַחֲרֵי הַשָּׁבֻעִים שִׁשִּׁים וּשְׁנַיִם יִכָּרֵת מָשִׁיחַ וְאֵין לוֹ וְהָעִיר וְהַקֹּדֶשׁ יַשְׁחִית עַם נָגִיד הַבָּא וְקִצּוֹ בַשֶּׁטֶף וְעַד קֵץ מִלְחָמָה נֶחֱרֶצֶת שֹׁמֵמוֹת: ²⁷ וְהִגְבִּיר בְּרִית לָרַבִּים שָׁבוּעַ אֶחָד וַחֲצִי הַשָּׁבוּעַ יַשְׁבִּית זֶבַח וּמִנְחָה וְעַל כְּנַף שִׁקּוּצִים מְשֹׁמֵם וְעַד־כָּלָה וְנֶחֱרָצָה תִּתַּךְ עַל־שֹׁמֵם: פ

More than any other book of the Hebrew Scriptures, the writings of the Prophet Daniel confront us with evidence of the time of Messiah's coming—evidence that many people would rather not see. But it is there and cannot be ignored. That Daniel was indeed a prophet is well substantiated. He accurately prophesied the rise of the Medo-Persian, Greek, and Roman empires, even at a time when the Babylonian Empire, which preceded them all, was at its height. He accurately predicted the fortunes, conflicts, wars, and conspiracies of the two kingdoms of Syria and Egypt between the fracturing of the Greek Empire and the conquest by Rome. He prophesied the role of the Maccabees during this period. It is Daniel's detailed accuracy in his prophecies that has caused many critics to try to give a late date to his book, although no evidence has been discovered that would negate its composition at the time that it claims to have been written. At the very latest, the book was completed around 530 B.C.

The key prophecies which are of interest in our present study are contained in verses 24-27 of Daniel Nine. However, it will be wise to survey the entire chapter in order to see what engendered the prophecy of when Messiah would come.

The Background—Daniel 9:1-2

The date for Daniel's prophecy is "the first year of Darius," which means that it occurred in the year 539 B.C., about 66 or 67 years after the Jews initially went into exile to Babylonia.

It was on this occasion, Daniel stated that he was studying the Scriptures, and from these Scriptures he came to understand that the number of years for the completion of the desolations of Jerusalem was almost over, since the duration was to be 70 years. Daniel mentioned that he was studying "books," and one of them was the writings of Jeremiah; the lives of Jeremiah and Daniel did overlap to some extent. On two occasions, Jeremiah predicted that the captivity and desolation of Jerusalem would last 70 years (Jeremiah 25:10-14; 29:10-14). What other books Daniel may have been studying we cannot know with certainty. But there are some strong possibilities that he also studied the book of Isaiah, because Isaiah named Cyrus as the one who would permit the Jews to return (Isaiah 44:28-45:1). Furthermore, there are other writings in Moses and the Prophets that spelled out some specific conditions for the establishment of the Messianic kingdom, and Daniel may have looked at some of these as well. They are Leviticus 26:40-43, 1 Kings 8:46-53, Jeremiah 3:12-18, and Hosea 5:15-6:3. These passages emphasize that Israel as a nation must repent and confess sin prior to the establishment of the Messianic kingdom.

Reckoning the 70 years from the year 605 B.C., when the first of three deportations into exile took place, would bring the end of the 70 years to 536 B.C. Daniel realized that the captivity had only about three years to go. The city and Temple were not destroyed until 586 B.C., and if the 70 years began then, it would mean the 70 years would not end until 515 B.C. But Daniel's calculation began with 605 B.C., the first deportation—not 597 B.C., the second deportation, or 586 B.C., the destruction and final deportation.

Daniel not only expected the captivity to end after 70 years, he also expected a final termination of any possibility of future desolations for Jerusalem; he acted as if the Messianic kingdom was about to occur. As the kingdom was to be established on the basis of prayer, he prayed; and realizing that the prerequisite was the confession of national sin, he confessed the sins of Israel.

Daniel's Prayer—Daniel 9:3-19

Daniel's detailed prayer can be divided into two portions. The first (verses 3-14) is the confession of sin. Daniel acknowledged both sin and guilt which had been incurred in two ways: first by disobedience to the Law of Moses, and second by disobedience to the prophets who came after Moses. Daniel neither denied the sin of his nation nor his own sin; using the pronoun "we," he fully identified with all Jewish people in their sins. He did not see sin as merely a bad habit, but as something ingrained in the people that had brought on divine judgment. This disobedience to both the law and the Prophets caused Israel, literally, "confusion of face" (v. 7), an idiom which implies a sense of shame. It also resulted in the need for forgiveness. Here Daniel confessed that to God belong forgiveness and mercy, and that forgiveness was needed. Daniel concluded the first part of his prayer by describing the punishment for Israel's sin and guilt. That punishment (the captivity in Babylon) confirmed the words of the prophets who had predicted it and confirmed the Law of Moses which taught that divine judgment would come because of disobedience.

The second part of the prayer (verses 15-19) is a plea for mercy. Daniel made his plea based on God's righteousness. He also pleaded for mercy because of God's grace, for Israel did not merit mercy; but the grace of God was, and is, able to extend mercy anyway. Furthermore, the righteousness of God required Him to fulfill His promises. Therefore, He should do so at the end of the 70-year period.

The conclusion of Daniel's prayer is very dramatic: "O Lord, hear! O Lord, forgive! O Lord, listen and take action! For Your own sake, O my God, do not delay, because Your city and Your people are called by Your name." When Daniel asks God to "not delay," he is asking God to count the 70 years from 605 B.C. and not 597 B.C. or 586 B.C.

The Arrival of Gabriel—Daniel 9:20-23

While Daniel was presenting his supplications, he was interrupted; he apparently had intended to say more when Gabriel arrived. The interruption came "about the time of the evening offering." This refers to the daily, regular evening sacrifice that was offered while the Temple stood. Although it had not been practiced for several decades, Daniel showed his longing for the return from captivity and for the rebuilding of the Temple by remembering the sacrifice.

Gabriel told the prophet that the purpose of his visit was to correct Daniel's misunderstanding concerning when the Messianic kingdom would be set up. Furthermore, the angel was to present God's revelation which contained a timetable for Messiah's first coming.

The Decree of the Seventy Sevens—Daniel 9:24a

Gabriel's prophecy to Daniel began with the words: "Seventy sevens have been decreed for your people and your holy city." Many English versions have translated the phrase to read seventy "weeks." But this translation is not totally accurate and has caused some confusion about the meaning of the passage. Most Jews know the Hebrew for "weeks" because of the observance of the Feast of Weeks, and that Hebrew word is *shavuot*. However, the word that appears here in the Hebrew text is *shavuim*, which means "sevens." This word refers to a "seven" of anything with the context determining the content of the "seven." It is similar to the English word "dozen," which means twelve of anything based upon context.

It is obvious here that Daniel had been thinking in terms of years—specifically the 70 years of captivity. He had assumed that the captivity would end after 70 years and that the kingdom would be established. But here Gabriel was using a play upon words in the Hebrew text, pointing out that insofar as Messiah's kingdom was concerned, it was not 70 years, but 70 sevens of years, or a total of 490 years (70 × 7). This period of 490 years had been decreed for the Jewish people and for the holy city of Jerusalem. The Hebrew word translated "decreed" literally means "to cut off" or "to determine." In chapters 2, 7, and 8, God revealed to Daniel the course of future world history in which Gentiles would have a dominant role over the Jewish people. This lengthy period began with the Babylonian Empire and was to continue until the establishment of Messiah's kingdom. For that reason, it is often referred to as "the times of the Gentiles." Now the prophet was told that a total of 490 years was to be cut out of the times of the Gentiles. This 490-year period had been decreed for the accomplishment of the final restoration of Israel and the establishment of Messiah's kingdom.

The focus of the program of the seventy sevens was "your people and your holy city." The people were Daniel's people, the Jewish people; and the city was Daniel's city, Jerusalem. Although he had spent most his life in Babylon, Jerusalem was still Daniel's city. For Jews, whether they are in the land or outside the land, their city is always Jerusalem—not any other.

It is important to note that the program of the seventy sevens does not concern the Gentiles or the Church; it concerns the Jewish people and the city of Jerusalem. It also concerns both the first coming and the second coming of the Messiah, but it is primarily the first coming that will be our concern here.

The Purpose of the Seventy Sevens—Daniel 9:24b

Next, Gabriel told the prophet that the seventy sevens are to accomplish six purposes. The first three are negative and undesirable elements which will be removed. The second three are positive and desirable elements to be effected.

The first purpose is "to finish the transgression." The Hebrew word translated as "to finish" means "to restrain firmly," "to restrain completely," or "to bring to completion." The Hebrew word translated as "transgression" is a very strong word for sin and more literally means "to rebel." The Hebrew text uses this word with the definite article, so it is, literally, "*the* transgression," or "*the* rebellion." The point is that some specific act of rebellion is finally going to be restrained and brought to an end. It is to come under complete control so that it will no longer flourish. Israel's apostasy is now to be firmly restrained in keeping with a similar prediction in Isaiah 59:20. Specifically, this is the rejection of the Messiah as dealt with in Isaiah 52:13-53:12.

The second purpose of the seventy sevens is "to make an end of sin." The Hebrew word translated as "to make an end" literally means "to seal up" or "to shut up in prison." It means "to be securely kept," "locked up," "not allowed to roam at random." The Hebrew word translated as "sin" literally means "to miss the mark." It refers to sins of daily life, rather than to any specific sin. Even these sins are to be put to an end and taken away. This, too, is quite in keeping with predictions by the prophets who proclaim that in the Messianic kingdom, sinning would cease from Israel (Isaiah 27:9; Ezekiel 36:25-27; 37:23; Jeremiah 31:31-34).

The third purpose is "to make atonement for iniquity." The Hebrew word translated as "to make atonement" is *kaphar*, which has the same root meaning as the word *kippur*, as in *Yom Kippur*, the Day of Atonement. The third purpose then is to make atonement in some way for iniquity. In fact, it is by means of this atonement that the first two purposes will also be accomplished: that of finishing the transgression and making an end of sin. The word translated as "iniquity" refers to inward sin. This has sometimes been referred to as the sin nature. Perhaps a more common term among Jewish people would be *yetzer hara*, "the evil inclination."

The fourth purpose of the seventy sevens is "to bring in everlasting righteousness." This could be more literally translated as "to bring in an age of righteousness" since the Hebrew *olam* is better translated as "age" rather than as "everlasting." This age of righteousness is to be the Messianic kingdom spoken of in the Prophets (Isaiah 1:26; 11:2-5; 32:17; Jeremiah 23:5-6; 33:15-18). It is this very age that Daniel had been expecting to see established after the 70 years of captivity, but now he is told that it will happen after the period of the seventy sevens.

The fifth purpose is "to seal up vision and prophecy." Here, Daniel used a word which means "to shut up." Therefore, "to seal up" means "to cause a cessation" or "to completely fulfill." Thus, vision and prophecy are to be completely fulfilled. "Vision" is a reference to oral prophecy, while "prophecy" refers to that which is written down. Both oral and written prophecy will cease with the final fulfillment of all revelations.

The final purpose of the seventy sevens is "to anoint the most holy place." This is a reference to the Jewish Temple which is to be rebuilt when Messiah comes. It refers to the same Temple that Daniel's contemporary, Ezekiel, described in great detail (Ezekiel 40-48).

The Start of the Seventy Sevens—Daniel 9:25a

Daniel was clearly told when the seventy sevens would begin their countdown. Gabriel said, "know and discern, that from the issuing of a decree to restore and rebuild Jerusalem." Thus, the seventy sevens would begin with a decree involving the rebuilding of Jerusalem. Not everything in Persian chronology is as clear as we would like to have it, and there are still some gaps in our knowledge of history. But from what biblical and historical records we do have, there are four possible answers to the question of which decree the passage refers to.

One is the decree of Cyrus, issued somewhere between 538-536 B.C., which concerned the rebuilding of the Temple (2 Chronicles 36:22-23; Ezra 1:1-4; 6:1-5) and of the city of Jerusalem (Isaiah 44:28; 45:13). Another option is the decree of Darius Hystaspes (Ezra 6:6-12), issued in the year 521 B.C., which was a reaffirmation of the decree of Cyrus. A third possibility is the decree of Artaxerxes to Ezra (Ezra 7:11-26), issued in 458 B.C., which contained permission to proceed with the Temple service. The last option is the decree of Artaxerxes to Nehemiah (Nehemiah 2:1-8), issued in the year 444 B.C. This decree specifically concerned the rebuilding of the walls around Jerusalem. Of these four possibilities, only the first and fourth decrees have any real validity in fulfilling the wording that Gabriel gave to Daniel. It is not necessary for our purpose here to deal with the various arguments of either option, but one thing is certain: by the year 444 B.C., the countdown of the seventy sevens had begun.[11]

The First Sixty-Nine Sevens—Daniel 9:25b

The seventy sevens are divided into three separate units: seven sevens, sixty-two sevens, and one seven. During the first period of seven sevens (49 years), Jerusalem would be "built again, with plaza and moat, even in times of distress." The second block of time (62 sevens, or a total of 434 years) will follow the first for a total of 69 sevens, or 483 years. There is no implication of a gap of time between the first and second subdivision of the seventy sevens.

The ending point of the sixty-nine sevens is "until Messiah the Prince." As clearly as Daniel could have stated it, he taught that Messiah would be on earth 483 years after the decree to rebuild Jerusalem had been issued. The obvious conclusion is this: If Messiah was not on earth 483 years after a decree was issued to rebuild Jerusalem, then Daniel was a false prophet and his book has no business being in the Hebrew Scriptures; but if Daniel was correct and his prophecy was fulfilled, then who was the Messiah of whom he spoke?

The Events between the Sixty-Ninth and the Seventieth Seven— Daniel 9:26

Whereas the second subdivision of the seventy sevens was immediately to follow the first, the third subdivision was not immediately to follow the second. Daniel pointed out in verse 26 that three things would occur in between the intervals. (For the study of this verse, it is helpful to step back in time and look into the future from Daniel's perspective.)

---

[11] The author's opinion is detailed in Appendix 4.

First, "the Messiah will be cut off and have nothing." The Hebrew word translated as "cut off" is a common word used in the Mosaic Law and simply means "to be killed." The implication of the term is that the Messiah would not only be killed, but also that He would die a penal death by execution. The Hebrew expression translated as "and have nothing" has two possible meanings. It may mean "nothingness," emphasizing Messiah's state at death. It can also be translated as "but not for himself," and the meaning would then be that He died for others rather than for Himself—a substitutionary death. The latter meaning would be much more consistent with what the prophets had to say about the reason for Messiah's death (e.g. Isaiah 53:1-12). The first three purposes of the seventy sevens—to finish the transgression, to make an end of sin, to make atonement for iniquity—have all to be accomplished by some means of atonement. The Law of Moses decreed that atonement is made by blood (Leviticus 17:11). It appears that Messiah's death, "not for himself" but for others, would be how Israel's transgression, sin, and iniquity would be atoned for. The point of this phrase is that between the end of the second subdivision, the sixty-ninth seven, and before the start of the seventieth seven, Messiah would be killed and would die a penal, substitutionary death.

Second, during this interim period, "the people of the prince who is to come will destroy the city and the sanctuary. And its end will come with a flood." The city and the Temple which were to be rebuilt because of the decree by which the seventy sevens began, would now be destroyed; some time after the Messiah was cut off, Jerusalem and the Temple would suffer another destruction. Our knowledge of history is extremely clear: The people responsible for this deed were the Romans; Jerusalem and the Temple were destroyed in the year A.D. 70. Based upon this verse, it is also clear that the Messiah should have both come and died prior to the year A.D. 70. If such an event did not take place, then Daniel was a false prophet. If such an event did occur, then the question must be answered: Who was that Messiah who was killed before A.D. 70?

Third, for the remainder of the interval between the sixty-ninth and the seventieth seven, "even to the end there will be war; desolations are determined." Israel would be characterized by war, and its resulting condition would be desolation. All this would set the stage for the final seven.

The Seventieth Seven—Daniel 9:27

From where we stand in time today, the last seven years of Daniel's prophecy are still future, but it is with their conclusion that all six purposes of verse 24 will reach their fulfillment. The main points of Daniel 9:27 are as follows: First, the seventieth seven will begin only with the signing of a 7-year covenant or treaty between Israel and a major Gentile political leader. The pronoun "he" in verse 27 goes back to its nearest antecedent in verse 26, which is not the Messiah but "the prince who is to come." This prince has been a topic of Daniel's earlier prophecies in chapters 7-8. This political leader is better known to Christians as the Antichrist.

Second, in the middle of the seventieth seven, that is, after 3½ years, this Gentile leader will break his treaty with Israel and cause a cessation of the sacrificial system. The implication here is that by this time, there will be a temple in Jerusalem. The sacrificial system of Moses will have been re-instituted, then be stopped by force.

Third, the result of the breaking of this covenant is that the Temple will now be abominated. The term "abomination" refers to an image or an idol. Just as it was in the days of Antiochus Epiphanes, so it will be again in the future when a Gentile ruler will abominate the Temple by means of idolatry.

Fourth, the "abomination" is to be followed by wrath and desolation, persecution and warfare, for the remaining half of the seventieth seven, or the final 3½ years. This is similar to the trials and tribulations the rabbis spoke of as preparation for the establishment of the Messianic kingdom. These terrible days were referred to as "the footsteps of the Messiah," and also as "the birth-pangs of the Messiah." Once those days have run their course, the last three things predicted in verse 24 will occur. The age of righteousness will be brought in; the most holy place will be anointed; and every vision and prophecy will be fulfilled. At this point the Messianic kingdom for which the prophet Daniel yearned will be set up.

Obviously, the Messianic kingdom requires the Messiah to rule as king. This means the Messiah will come after the seventieth seven. Yet, earlier Daniel stated that the Messiah would come and be killed after the sixty-ninth seven. This would appear to be a contradiction unless Daniel was speaking of two comings of the Messiah. The first time was to be after the sixty-ninth seven, when He would die a penal, substitutionary death for the sins of Israel and accomplish the first three purposes listed in verse 24. The second time, still future, was to be after the seventieth seven, when He will establish the Messianic kingdom and fulfill the last three prophecies mentioned in verse 24.

There is also an important implication here that should not be missed: The Messiah would be killed after His first coming, yet He would be alive at His second coming. The implication is that the Messiah would be resurrected from the dead after He was killed.

Conclusions

This dramatic prophecy features certain things in very clear and unmistakable terms. First, the Messiah was to be on earth 483 years after the decree to rebuild Jerusalem. Second, after His appearance on earth, He was to be killed—not for His own sins, but rather for those of others— and the death He would die was to be the death of the penalty of the law. Third, the death of the Messiah had to come sometime before Jerusalem and the Temple were destroyed again; this occurred in the year A.D. 70. Fourth, sometime after the destruction of Jerusalem and the Temple, and following a long period of warfare, the seventieth seven will commence. Once that has run its course, Messiah's kingdom and age of righteousness will be established. For that to occur, the implication is that the Messiah who was killed would return.

But who is this Messiah? Only one man fulfills all that is required in this passage: Yeshua of Nazareth. He was born into the Jewish world and proclaimed His Messiahship 483 years after the decree to rebuild and restore Jerusalem was issued. In the year A.D. 30, Yeshua was executed by crucifixion. Daniel indicated that He would be cut off—not for Himself, but rather for others. Isaiah 53 also prophesied the death of the Messiah, pointing out that He would die a substitutionary death on behalf of His people Israel. The teaching of the New Testament is that Yeshua died a penal death by taking upon Himself the penalty of the law as a substitute for His people. In keeping with Daniel 9:24, He died for the purpose of making an atonement for sins. Three days after His death, He was resurrected. Finally, the New Testament proclaims the fact that He will someday return to set up His kingdom and the age of righteousness.

If Daniel was right, then Messiah came and died prior to the year A.D. 70. If Daniel was right, then there are no other options for who the Messiah is: Yeshua of Nazareth. If Daniel was right, this Yeshua is destined to return and to set up the Messianic kingdom.[12]

Daniel 9:24-27
teaches that:

- ✿ Messiah would be present 483 years after the decree to rebuild Jerusalem.
- ✿ Messiah would be legally executed.
- ✿ Messiah's death would result in the destruction of Jerusalem and the Temple.
- ✿ Messiah's birth and death, therefore, must both have happened prior to A.D. 70.

---

[12] There is a further discussion of this prophecy in Appendix 5.

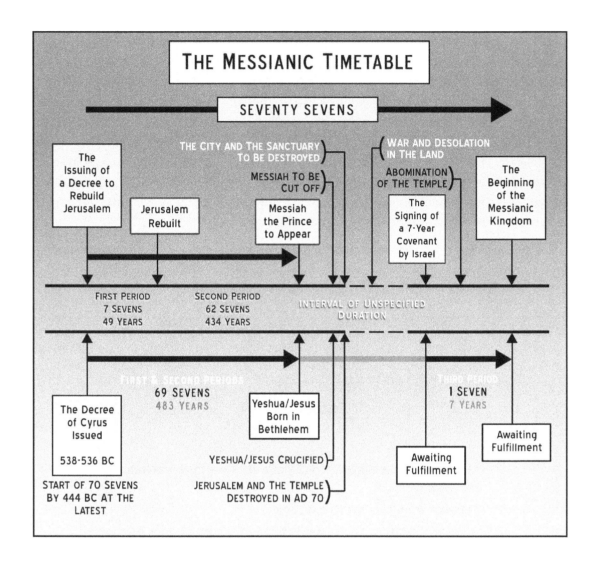

CHAPTER 4:

OTHER LINES OF EVIDENCE

Introduction

The previous three sections of this study have dealt with the prophecies of the Hebrew Scriptures in relation to the first coming of Messiah. It has been shown that Yeshua is the only person who could possibly fulfill these prophecies. Associated with a Christian interpretation of these Scriptures are certain doctrines which are consistently regarded under Judaism as being contrary to Hebrew Scripture and therefore wholly unacceptable to any Jew. These are:

1. The belief that Messiah is God.

2. The belief in God as a Triune Being.

These two doctrines are obviously closely related. It is only possible to believe that Messiah is God if He is considered to be one member of the Godhead. It is commonly stated that these beliefs are thoroughly un-Jewish, being the invention of Christianity and originating in the New Testament. However, having been written entirely by Jewish men, the New Testament is just as Jewish as the Old Testament. One of the chief writers of the New Testament was Rabbi Saul, also known as the Apostle Paul, who studied under Rabban Gamaliel (Philippians 3:5-6; Acts 22:3).

Although it is commonly stated that any concept of plurality in the Godhead is totally alien to Judaism, there is at least one place in Jewish literature where this is not the case. The author of the *Zohar* sensed plurality in the *Tetragrammaton*, the personal name of God, and wrote:

> Come and see the mystery of the word YHVH: there are three steps, each existing by itself: nevertheless they are One, and so united that one cannot be separated from the other. The Ancient Holy One is revealed with three heads, which are united into one, and that head is three exalted. The Ancient One is described as being three: because the other lights emanating from him are included in the three. But how can three names be one? How three can be one can only be known through the revelation of the Holy Spirit.[13]

Of greater importance, however, is the teaching of the Hebrew Scriptures themselves. Several Messianic prophecies have already been studied which clearly teach that Messiah would be both God and man. There are several other lines of evidence which can be explored to justify the belief in God as a triune Being. It can be shown that the doctrine of the Trinity originates in the Hebrew Scriptures and is merely developed and clarified in the New Testament.

---

[13] *Zohar* Vol. III, 288; Vol. II, 43, Hebrew editions. See also *Soncino* Press edition, Vol. III, 134.

The Plurality of the Godhead

The Plural Noun *Elohim*

The word for "God" most commonly used in Hebrew Scripture is *Elohim*. It is generally agreed that Elohim is a plural noun having the masculine plural ending "-im." The very word "Elohim," used of the one true God in Genesis 1:1, is also used of false gods in Exodus 20:3 and Deuteronomy 13:2.[14]

> **Genesis 1:1:** In the beginning God [Elohim] created the heavens and the earth.

> **Exodus 20:3:** You shall have no other gods [Elohim] before Me.

> **Deuteronomy 13:2:** and the sign or the wonder comes true, concerning which he spoke to you, saying, 'Let us go after other gods [Elohim] (whom you have not known) and let us serve them,'

While the use of the plural Elohim does not prove a triunity, it certainly opens the door to a doctrine of plurality in the Godhead since it is the same word that is used for the one true God as for the many false gods. This causes something of a problem for rabbis. In the *Siddur*, the Sabbath prayer book compiled by Rabbi Hertz, it says concerning Genesis 1:1, "The plural is to denote the plentitude of might; God comprehends and unifies all the ends of eternity and infinity." The fact remains, however, that although the word does not of itself prove a plurality within the Godhead, it certainly does open the door to it.

It is sometimes said that Elohim had to be used both for God and gods because there is no alternative in Hebrew. This is not true; the singular form of Elohim is *Eloah* and is used in passages such as Deuteronomy 32:15-17 and Habakkuk 3:3.

> **Deuteronomy 32:15:** "But Jeshurun grew fat and kicked—You are grown fat, thick, and sleek—Then he forsook God who made him, And scorned the Rock of his salvation. "They made Him jealous with strange *gods*; With abominations they provoked Him to anger. "They sacrificed to demons who were not God, To gods whom they have not known, New gods who came lately, Whom your fathers did not dread.

> **Habakkuk 3:3:** God comes from Teman, And the Holy One from Mount Paran. Selah. His splendor covers the heavens, And the earth is full of His praise.

---

[14] All verses on this page are from the NASB.

This singular form could have been used consistently, but it is found in only 250 places, as compared to the 2,500 instances of the plural form. The far greater use of the plural form tends to turn the argument in favor of plurality in the Godhead rather than against it.

Plural Verbs Used with Elohim

It is also said that while Elohim is plural, the verbs used with it are always singular when applied to the true God and plural for false gods. The rules of Hebrew grammar require that verbs agree with the associated nouns in both gender and number. When Elohim is used for pagan gods, these rules are always followed, and a plural verb is always used. When Elohim is used of the one true God, however, these rules are normally broken—the plural noun "Elohim" is usually followed by a singular verb. While it is true that this is most often the case, it is not always the case. The following are a few examples:[15]

1. Genesis 20:13

> and it came about, when God caused me to wander from my father's house, that I said to her, "This is the kindness which you will show to me: everywhere we go, say of me, ´He is my brother.´"

These are the words of Abraham, a worshipper of the one true God. It literally says, "God (Elohim) they caused me to wander."

2.   Genesis 35:7

> And he built an altar there, and called the place El-bethel, because there God had revealed Himself to him, when he fled from his brother.

These are the words of Jacob, who also worshiped the one true God. It literally reads, "the Gods (Elohim) revealed themselves."

3.   2 Samuel 7:23

> "And what one nation on the earth is like Your people Israel, whom God went to redeem for Himself as a people and to make a name for Himself, and to do a great thing for You and awesome things for Your land, before Your people whom You have redeemed for Yourself from Egypt, from nations and their gods?

Literally, "whom the Gods (Elohim) they went to redeem for themselves."

---

[15] All verses on this and the following pages are from the NASB, unless indicated otherwise.

4. Psalm 58:11

> And men will say, "Surely there is a reward for the righteous; Surely there is a God who judges on earth!"

Literally, "the Gods (Elohim) they judge on earth!"

These verses are just four examples of many, and, again, the use of plural verbs in reference to the one true God supports the idea of plurality in the Godhead.

The Word "Elohim" Applied to Two Divine Personalities

As if to make the case for plurality even stronger, there are verses in the Hebrew Scriptures where the term "Elohim" is applied to two personalities.

> One example is Psalm 45:6-7:

> [6] Your throne, O God, is forever and ever; A scepter of uprightness is the scepter of Your kingdom. [7] You have loved righteousness, and hated wickedness; Therefore God, Your God, has anointed You With the oil of joy above Your fellows.

It should be noted that the first Elohim is being addressed, and the second Elohim is the God of the first Elohim. There are two quite distinct personalities here; it is Elohim's Elohim who has set Elohim above His companions and anointed Him with the oil of joy.

> A second example is Hosea 1:2 and 7:

> [1:2] When the Lord first spoke through Hosea, the Lord said to Hosea, "Go, take to yourself a wife of harlotry, and have children of harlotry; for the land commits flagrant harlotry, forsaking the Lord." . . . [1:7] "But I will have compassion on the house of Judah and deliver them by the Lord their God, and will not deliver them by bow, sword, battle, horses, or horsemen."

The speaker is Elohim who says that He will have mercy on the house of Judah and will save the people by the instrumentality of Jehovah, their Elohim. Elohim number 1 is promising to save Israel by means of Elohim number 2. Again, we see the word Elohim used of two distinct personalities within the same passage.

The Name YHVH Applied to Two Divine Personalities

Not only is Elohim applied to two personalities in the same verse, but so is the very name of God, Jehovah (YHVH). One example of this is Genesis 19:24:

> [24] Then Jehovah rained upon Sodom and upon Gomorrah brimstone and fire from Jehovah out of heaven. (ASV)

The first YHVH is on earth and is said to be raining down sulfur from a second YHVH who is in heaven. Two distinct persons are called YHVH in the same text.

A second example is Zechariah 2:8-9:

> [8] For thus says Jehovah of hosts: After glory has he sent me unto the nations which plundered you; for he that touches you touches the apple of his eye. [9] For, behold, I will shake my hand over them, and they shall be a spoil to those that served them; and ye shall know that Jehovah of hosts has sent me. (ASV)

Again, we have one YHVH, the speaker in these verses, who is being sent by another YHVH to perform a specific task.

The Plural Noun *Adonai*

Another word for God in Hebrew is *Adonai*, translated as "Lord" in, for example, Psalm 110:1—"Jehovah said to my Lord." Whenever this word is used of God it is consistently in the plural, never in the singular.

Plural Pronouns

Another case in point regarding Hebrew grammar is God's use of plural pronouns when speaking of Himself. Mostly in Scripture, God uses singular pronouns, but there are several instances of God speaking in the plural:

1. **Genesis 1:26**

   Then God said, "Let Us make man in Our image, according to Our likeness; and let them rule over the fish of the sea and over the birds of the sky and over the cattle and over all the earth, and over every creeping thing that creeps on the earth."

The plurality of the Godhead is very clear here: "let *us* make . . . in *our* image . . . *our* likeness." Jewish theology teaches that the phrase "let us make" in this passage refers to angels, but this cannot be the case. God alone did the work of creation, and angels are not mentioned anywhere in the context. God could not have been consulting with angels or the passage would have said so, as it does in 1 Kings 22:19-23, where we do find God consulting the heavenly court about doing something. That is not the picture presented here. Furthermore, the phrase "in *our* image" could hardly have referred to angels, since man was created in the image of God and not of angels.

Rashi said: "Man was created in the image of angels. Although angels did not help God create, he said 'us' to teach good manners and humility in that the greater person should also ask permission of the smaller." This quotation shows the enormous lengths the rabbis must go to in order to avoid the concept of plurality in the Godhead.

The *Midrash Rabbah* (8:8) on Genesis recognizes the strength of this passage and comments as follows:

Rabbi Samuel Bar Hanman in the name of Rabbi Jonathan said, that at the time when Moses wrote the Torah, writing a portion of it daily, when he came to the verse which says "And Elohim said let us make man in our image, after our likeness," Moses said, "Master of the universe, why do you give herewith an excuse to the sectarians [who believe in the triunity of God]." God answered Moses, "You write and whoever wants to err, let him err."[16]

The "sectarians" or heretics mentioned here are Messianic Jews. It is obvious that the *Midrash Rabbah* is simply trying to get around the problem and fails to adequately explain why God refers to Himself in the plural.

The *Midrash Rabbah* 9:9 says:

The heretics asked Rabbi Simlai how many deities created the world. He replied, 'If you must, enquire of the first day, as it is written "For ask now of the first days [Deuteronomy 4:32] not since the day God created (*baru*)." What is written here but "God created (*bara*)." ' Then they asked him a second time, 'Why is it written in the beginning elohim created.' He answered, " 'In the beginning *baru elohim*" it is not written here but ´*bara elohim* the heavens and the earth.' " Rabbi Simlai said, 'Wherever you find a point supporting the heretics you find the refutation at its side.' They asked him again what is meant by "And God said let us make man." He replied, 'Read what follows. Not "And gods created (*vayir baru*) man" is it written here but "And God created (*vayir bara*)."´

This deals with a discussion between Messianic Jews and a rabbi. The Jewish believers are asking the rabbi, "Why do you have these plural pronouns and nouns?" The rabbi responds that it does not prove plurality because the verb that follows is always singular and not plural.

In *The Torah Anthology* by Rabbi Yaacov Culi (*Maznaim*, New York, 1977) on pages 107 and 108, it says:

This must be explained since the wording is very surprising. Nonbelievers argue that there is a multiple Godhead attempting to use this verse as a proof text for their contention, since it says "Let us make man" . . . Why then did the Torah use the plural expression . . . ? Some say that man resembles the angels so they wished to see him created right away. God announced to them and said "Let us make man. Come and rejoice for I am about to create man."

---

[16] *Midrash Rabbah* on Genesis 1:26 (New York: NOP Press, n.d.)

The text then goes on to quote Rashi as already given above. Finally, on this critical verse, Rabbi Nachmanides said that the plural denotes both God and the earth; the body came from the earth, and the spirit or soul came from God.

2.   Genesis 3:22

And Jehovah God said, Behold, the man is become as one of us, to know good and evil; and now, lest he put forth his hand, and take also of the tree of life, and eat, and live for ever. (ASV)

3.   Genesis 11:6-7

[6] And Jehovah said, Behold, they are one people, and they have all one language. And this is what they begin to do. And now nothing will be withholden from them, which they purpose to do. [7] Come, let us go down, and there confound their language, that they may not under-stand one another's speech. (ASV)

4.   Isaiah 6:8

And I heard the voice of the Lord, saying, Whom shall I send, and who will go for us? Then I said, Here am I; send me. (ASV)

This last passage would appear contradictory with the singular "I" and the plural "us" except as viewed as a plurality (us) in a unity (I).

Plural Descriptions

Another point that comes out of the Hebrew is the fact that often, nouns and their adjectives used in speaking of God are plural. Usually when speaking of the one God, these adjectives are singular. Sometimes, however, they are found in the plural form. Although, in the Hebrew, these appear as adjectives, they do not translate that way into English. Some examples of them being in the plural are as follows:

1.   Joshua 24:19

Then Joshua said to the people, "You will not be able to serve the Lord, for He is a holy God. He is a jealous God; He will not forgive your transgression or your sins.

In the Hebrew, the word for "holy" is a plural adjective; literally it reads "holy Gods."

2.   Psalm 149:2

Let Israel be glad in his Maker; Let the sons of Zion rejoice in their King.

In the Hebrew, the word for "maker" is plural; literally, it reads, "let Israel be glad in his makers." In English, the word "maker" is a noun, but in Hebrew it is an adjective.

3.   Ecclesiastes 12:1

Remember also your Creator in the days of your youth, before the evil days come and the years draw near when you will say, "I have no delight in them";

Again, this would literally read "remember also your Creators," a plural adjective.

4.   Isaiah 54:5

For your Maker is your husband; Jehovah of hosts is his name: and the Holy One of Israel is your Redeemer; the God of the whole earth shall he be called. (ASV)

In this verse, the words for "maker" and "husband" are both plural adjectives in the Hebrew text; literally, "for your makers is your husbands; Jehovah of hosts is his name."

The Unity of the Godhead

Everything which has been said so far rests firmly on the Hebrew language of the Scriptures. If we are to base our doctrine on the Scriptures alone, we must say that on the one hand, they affirm God's unity, while at the same time, they tend towards the concept of a compound unity, allowing for a plurality in the Godhead.

This idea of plurality within the Godhead is consistently rejected by Judaism despite all the evidence discussed so far, and invariably, the argument returns to Deuteronomy 6:4 as final evidence of the singular nature of God.

> *"Sh'ma Yisrael Adonai Eloheinu Adonai Echad."*
>
> **"Hear, O Israel! The Lord is our God, the Lord is one!"** (NASB)

Deuteronomy 6:4, known as the *Shema*, has always been Israel's great confession. It is this verse, more than any other, which is used to affirm the fact that God is one and to contradict the concept of plurality in the Godhead. But is it a valid use of this verse?

In Hebrew, the very words "our God" are in the plural. Hence, the verse literally reads "our Gods." The main argument, however, lies in the word "one," which is the Hebrew word *"echad."* A quick glance through the verses in the Hebrew text where this word is used will show that the word "echad" does not mean an "absolute one," but a "compound one." For example, in Genesis 1:5, the combination of evening and morning comprise one [echad] day. In Genesis 2:24, a man and a woman come together in marriage, "and the two shall become one [echad] flesh." In Ezra 2:64, we are told that the whole assembly was as one [echad], though of course, it was composed of numerous people. Ezekiel 37:17 provides a rather striking example where two sticks are combined to become one [echad]. Thus, the use of the word "echad" in Scripture shows it to be a compound unity, not an absolute unity.

There is a Hebrew word which does mean an absolute unity, and that is the word *"yachid."* This word is used in numerous places with the emphasis being on the meaning of "only one." If Moses had intended to teach God's absolute oneness, this would have been a far more appropriate word to have used. In fact, Maimonides noted the strength of yachid and chose to use it in his "Thirteen Articles of Faith" in place of *echad*. However, the Shema does not use yachid in reference to God.

The Triunity of the Godhead

S o far we have seen from the use of various plural words that there is plurality in the nature of the one true God. We have also looked at several passages where the names of God are applied to two quite distinct divine personalities. The question that therefore arises is: How many personalities exist in the Godhead? A reading of the Hebrew Scriptures shows that three, and only three, distinct personalities are ever considered divine. They are:

1. The Lord YHVH

2. The Angel of YHVH

3. The Spirit of God

We will now consider each of these in turn.

The Lord YHVH

There are numerous places in Scripture where there is reference to the first of the three divine personalities. The usage of "the Lord YHVH" is so frequent that there is no need to devote further space to it; a great many of the Messianic prophecies already discussed serve as examples of this.

The Angel of Jehovah

The Expression *Malach YHVH*

The second divine personality is the Angel of Jehovah—but who is He? The "Angel of Jehovah" is not to be taken as a title; following Hebrew grammar, it always functions as a proper name. This individual is always considered distinct from all other angels and is unique. It never appears in the plural. Nowhere in Scripture are the phrases "the angels of Jehovah" or "the angels of the God," but rather there are three, and only three, different expressions which are used:

1. The Angel of Jehovah—*Malach YHVH*, always singular.

2. The Angel of the God—*Malach Ha-Elohim*, always singular with the definite article.

3. The angels of God—*Malachei Elohim*, plural, and never with a definite article.

The third of these expressions is used in general terms of ordinary angels. The first two expressions are both used to describe a very special and distinct individual—the Angel of Jehovah. We can see this in Judges 6:20-21, where the same Person is described first in verse 20 as "the Angel of the God" and then in verse 21 as "the Angel of Jehovah." This is also brought out in Judges

119

chapter 13; in verse 3, there is a reference to "the Angel of Jehovah," and later in verse 9, this same individual is called "the Angel of the God."

Consistently, throughout the Hebrew text, there is a distinction made between ordinary angels and this unique Person referred to as both "the Angel of YHVH" and "the Angel of the God." The Angel of Jehovah is clearly revealed as being different in stature, nature, person, and essence from ordinary angels.

The Angel of Jehovah is Jehovah

What the Hebrew grammar is trying to show is that this unique individual is in fact God Himself. In virtually every context in which He appears, He is referred to as both the Angel of Jehovah and Jehovah Himself. There are many examples which show this:

1. **Genesis 16:7-14**

    [7] And the angel of Jehovah found her by a fountain of water in the wilderness, by the fountain in the way to Shur. [8] And he said, Hagar, Sarai's handmaid, whence came you? And whither do you go? And she said, I am fleeing from the face of my mistress Sarai. [9] And the angel of Jehovah said unto her, Return to your mistress, and submit yourself under her hands. [10] And the angel of Jehovah said unto her, I will greatly multiply your seed, that it shall not be numbered for multitude. [11] And the angel of Jehovah said unto her, Behold, you are with child, and shall bear a son. And you shall call his name Ishmael, because Jehovah has heard your affliction. [12] And he shall be (as) a wild ass among men. His hand (shall be) against every man, and every man's hand against him. And he shall dwell over against all his brethren. [13] And she called the name of Jehovah that spoke unto her, You are a God that sees. For she said, Have I even here looked after him that sees me? [14] Wherefore the well was called Beer-lahai-roi. Behold, it is between Kadesh and Bered.[17]

There are four references here to the Angel of Jehovah, in verses 7, 9, 10, and 11, but then, in verse 13, the reference is to Jehovah Himself, and so Hagar names the place "You are a God that sees."

2. **Genesis 22:9-16**

    [9] And they came to the place which God had told him of. And Abraham built the altar there, and laid the wood in order, and bound Isaac his son, and laid him on the altar, upon the wood. [10] And Abraham stretched forth his hand, and took the knife to slay his son. [11] And the angel of Jehovah called unto him out of heaven, and said, Abraham, Abraham. And he said, Here I am. [12] And he said, Lay not your hand upon the lad, neither do you anything unto him. For now I

---

[17] The verses in this chapter are all from the ASV.

know that you fear God, seeing you have not withheld your son, your only son, from me. [13] And Abraham lifted up his eyes, and looked, and behold, behind (him) a ram caught in the thicket by his horns. And Abraham went and took the ram, and offered him up for a burnt-offering in the stead of his son. [14] And Abraham called the name of that place Jehovah-jireh. As it is said to this day, In the mount of Jehovah it shall be provided. [15] And the angel of Jehovah called unto Abraham a second time out of heaven, [16] and said, By myself have I sworn, says Jehovah, because you have done this thing, and have not withheld your son, your only son, . . .

Twice here He is called the Angel of Jehovah (verses 11 and 15). In verse 12, He is also referred to as God, and in verse 16, He is called Jehovah.

3.   Genesis 31:11-13

[11] And the angel of God said unto me in the dream, Jacob: and I said, Here am I. [12] And he said, Lift up now your eyes, and see, all the he-goats which leap upon the flock are ringstreaked, speckled, and grizzled: for I have seen all that Laban does unto you. [13] I am the God of Beth-el, where you anointed a pillar, where you vowed a vow unto me: now arise, get you out from this land, and return unto the land of your nativity.

In verse 11, the reference is literally to "the Angel of the God," but when He speaks in verse 13, He says, "I am the God of Bethel."

4.   Genesis 32:24-30

[24] And Jacob was left alone; and there wrestled a man with him until the breaking of the day. [25] And when he saw that he prevailed not against him, he touched the hollow of his thigh; and the hollow of Jacob's thigh was strained, as he wrestled with him. [26] And he said, Let me go, for the day breaks. And he said, I will not let you go, except you bless me. [27] And he said unto him, What is your name? And he said, Jacob. [28] And he said, Your name shall be called no more Jacob, but Israel: for you have striven with God and with men, and have prevailed. [29] And Jacob asked him, and said, Tell me, I pray you, your name. And he said, Wherefore is it that you do ask after my name? And he blessed him there. [30] And Jacob called the name of the place Peniel: for, (said he), I have seen God face to face, and my life is preserved.

This is the very famous passage which describes Jacob wrestling with the Angel of Jehovah. But with whom is he really wrestling? In verse 28, it states, "for you have striven with God." In verse 30, Jacob declares, "I have seen God face to face." The angel that he wrestled with is recognized to be God Himself.

5.   Exodus 3:1-5

[1] Now Moses was keeping the flock of Jethro his father-in-law, the priest of Midian: and he led the flock to the back of the wilderness, and came to the mountain of God, unto Horeb. [2] And

the angel of Jehovah appeared unto him in a flame of fire out of the midst of a bush: and he looked, and, behold, the bush burned with fire, and the bush was not consumed. [3] And Moses said, I will turn aside now, and see this great sight, why the bush is not burnt. [4] And when Jehovah saw that he turned aside to see, God called unto him out of the midst of the bush, and said, Moses, Moses. And he said, Here am I. [5] And he said, Draw not nigh hither: put off your shoes from off your feet, for the place whereon you stand is holy ground.

In verse 2, it is the Angel of Jehovah who is in the burning bush, but verse 4 says that "God called unto him out of the midst of the bush."

6. Judges 2:1

[1] And the angel of Jehovah came up from Gilgal to Bochim. And he said, I made you to go up out of Egypt, and have brought you unto the land which I swore unto your fathers; and I said, I will never break my covenant with you.

In this verse, the Angel of Jehovah claims to be responsible for the Exodus and for making the covenant with Israel. A comparison with Exodus 19:4 clearly shows that it was God Himself who was responsible for both these things; the two are synonymous.

7. Judges 6:11-24

[11] And the angel of Jehovah came, and sat under the oak which was in Ophrah, that pertained unto Joash the Abiezrite: and his son Gideon was beating out wheat in the winepress, to hide it from the Midianites. [12] And the angel of Jehovah appeared unto him, and said unto him, Jehovah is with you, you mighty man of valor. [13] And Gideon said unto him, Oh, my lord, if Jehovah is with us, why then is all this befallen us? and where are all his wondrous works which our fathers told us of, saying, Did not Jehovah bring us up from Egypt? but now Jehovah has cast us off, and delivered us into the hand of Midian. [14] And Jehovah looked upon him, and said, Go in this your might, and save Israel from the hand of Midian: have not I sent you? [15] And he said unto him, Oh, Lord, wherewith shall I save Israel? behold, my family is the poorest in Manasseh, and I am the least in my father's house. [16] And Jehovah said unto him, Surely I will be with you, and you shall smite the Midianites as one man. [17] And he said unto him, If now I have found favor in your sight, then show me a sign that it is you that talks with me. [18] Depart not hence, I pray you, until I come unto you, and bring forth my present, and lay it before you. And he said, I will tarry until you come again. [19] And Gideon went in, and made ready a kid, and unleavened cakes of an ephah of meal: the flesh he put in a basket, and he put the broth in a pot, and brought it out unto him under the oak, and presented it. [20] And the angel of God said unto him, Take the flesh and the unleavened cakes, and lay them upon this rock, and pour out the broth. And he did so. [21] Then the angel of Jehovah put forth the end of the staff that was in his hand, and touched the flesh and the unleavened cakes; and there went up fire out of the rock, and consumed the flesh and the unleavened cakes; and the angel of Jehovah departed out of his sight. [22] And Gideon saw that he was the angel of Jehovah; and Gideon said, Alas, O

Lord Jehovah! forasmuch as I have seen the angel of Jehovah face to face. [23] And Jehovah said unto him, Peace be unto you; fear not: you shall not die. [24] Then Gideon built an altar there unto Jehovah, and called it Jehovah-shalom: unto this day it is yet in Ophrah of the Abiezrites. (ASV)

Four times, in this passage, He is the Angel of Jehovah (verses 11, 12, 20, 21), and four times He is Jehovah Himself (verses 14, 16, 22, 23).

8. Judges 13:2-24

[2] And there was a certain man of Zorah, of the family of the Danites, whose name was Manoah; and his wife was barren, and bare not. [3] And the angel of Jehovah appeared unto the woman, and said unto her, Behold now, you are barren, and bear not; but you shall conceive, and bear a son. [4] Now therefore beware, I pray you, and drink no wine nor strong drink, and eat not any unclean thing: [5] for, lo, you shall conceive, and bear a son; and no razor shall come upon his head; for the child shall be a Nazirite unto God from the womb: and he shall begin to save Israel out of the hand of the Philistines. [6] Then the woman came and told her husband, saying, A man of God came unto me, and his countenance was like the countenance of the angel of God, very terrible; and I asked him not whence he was, neither told he me his name: [7] but he said unto me, Behold, you shall conceive, and bear a son; and now drink no wine nor strong drink, and eat not any unclean thing; for the child shall be a Nazirite unto God from the womb to the day of his death. [8] Then Manoah entreated Jehovah, and said, Oh, Lord, I pray you, let the man of God whom you didst send come again unto us, and teach us what we shall do unto the child that shall be born. [9] And God hearkened to the voice of Manoah; and the angel of God came again unto the woman as she sat in the field: but Manoah her husband was not with her. [10] And the woman made haste, and ran, and told her husband, and said unto him, Behold, the man has appeared unto me, that came unto me the (other) day. [11] And Manoah arose, and went after his wife, and came to the man, and said unto him, Are you the man that spoke unto the woman? And he said, I am. [12] And Manoah said, Now let your words come to pass: what shall be the ordering of the child, and (how) shall we do unto him? [13] And the angel of Jehovah said unto Manoah, Of all that I said unto the woman let her beware. [14] She may not eat of anything that cometh of the vine, neither let her drink wine or strong drink, nor eat any unclean thing; all that I commanded her let her observe. [15] And Manoah said unto the angel of Jehovah, I pray you, let us detain you, that we may make ready a kid for you. [16] And the angel of Jehovah said unto Manoah, Though you detain me, I will not eat of your bread; and if you will make ready a burnt-offering, you must offer it unto Jehovah. For Manoah knew not that he was the angel of Jehovah. [17] And Manoah said unto the angel of Jehovah, What is your name, that, when your words come to pass, we may do you honor? [18] And the angel of Jehovah said unto him, Wherefore do you ask after my name, seeing it is wonderful? [19] So Manoah took the kid with the meal-offering, and offered it upon the rock unto Jehovah: and (the angel) did wondrously, and Manoah and his wife looked on. [20] For it came to pass, when the flame went up toward heaven from off the altar, that the angel of Jehovah ascended in the flame of the altar: and

Manoah and his wife looked on; and they fell on their faces to the ground. [21] But the angel of Jehovah did no more appear to Manoah or to his wife. Then Manoah knew that he was the angel of Jehovah. [22] And Manoah said unto his wife, We shall surely die, because we have seen God. [23] But his wife said unto him, If Jehovah were pleased to kill us, he would not have received a burnt-offering and a meal-offering at our hand, neither would he have showed us all these things, nor would at this time have told such things as these. [24] And the woman bare a son, and called his name Samson: and the child grew, and Jehovah blessed him.

Nine times in this passage He is referred to as the Angel of Jehovah: in verses 3, 9, 13, 15, 16, 17, 18, 20, and 21. But then, in verse 22, He is said to be God Himself. Note also in verse 18 that this Angel's name is "Wonderful." In our study of Isaiah 9:6, it was pointed out that *pele*, the Hebrew word for "wonderful," is only used of God, never of man or an angel. The very fact that He claims this name for Himself shows that He is not a common angel, but God Himself.

Beyond the book of Judges, the Angel of Jehovah virtually disappears from Jewish history. He only appears twice more in the Scriptures. In Isaiah 37:36, He slaughters the Assyrian army, and in the first six chapters of Zechariah, He is the One who gives Zechariah his eight visions.

The Uniqueness of His Person

In Isaiah 42:8, God says of Himself, "I Am Jehovah; that is my name, my glory I will not give to another." When we compare this statement with Exodus 23:21, we are better able to understand the unique nature of the Angel of Jehovah. In Exodus 23:20-23, it is God who is speaking, and He says:

> [20] Behold, I send an angel before you, to keep you by the way, and to bring you into the place which I have prepared. [21] Take ye heed before him, and hearken unto his voice; provoke him not; for he will not pardon your transgression: for my name is in him. [22] But if you shall indeed hearken unto his voice, and do all that I speak; then I will be an enemy unto your enemies, and an adversary unto your adversaries. [23] For mine angel shall go before you, and bring you in unto the Amorite, and the Hittite, and the Perizzite, and the Canaanite, the Hivite, and the Jebusite: and I will cut them off.

In Exodus 23:20, God says that this Angel will lead the Jewish people throughout the Exodus, until they arrive in the promised land. This is consistent with Judges 2:1, which we have already looked at. In verse 21, several commands are given. Israel is commanded to be obedient to this Angel and not to provoke Him to anger. Why? Because "my Name is in him."

This Angel is very special for several reasons:

1. ***He will not pardon your transgression*** (v. 21).
   He has the power to forgive sins, a prerogative that only God has.

2. ***My name is in him*** (v. 21).

    The name is Jehovah, a name given only to members of the Godhead; this Angel has that name. Hosea 12:3-5 also says that this Angel has the very name of God in Him. The fact that He has all four letters of God's name within His Name indicates that He is actually God Himself.

3. **There are blessings for obeying Him** (v. 22).

4. **He is the Angel of the Exodus** (v. 23).

    In Exodus 32:34-35, we read that despite the warnings, the people did indeed rebel against this Angel and were punished for it.

When Isaiah 63:7-14 describes Him as the Angel of God's presence, He is in fact the second Person of the Trinity.

The Spirit of God

The third personality, who is evident in the Hebrew Scriptures, is the Spirit of God. In Hebrew, He is often simply referred to as the *Ruach Ha-Kodesh*. There are many references to the Spirit of God, among which are:

1. **Genesis 1:2**

    And the earth was formless and void, and darkness was over the surface of the deep; and the Spirit of God was moving over the surface of the waters. (NASB)

2. **Genesis 6:3**

    Then the Lord said, "My Spirit shall not strive with man forever, because he also is flesh; nevertheless his days shall be one hundred and twenty years." (NASB)

3. **Job 33:4**

    "The Spirit of God has made me, And the breath of the Almighty gives me life. (NASB)

4. **Psalm 51:11**

    Do not cast me away from Your presence, And do not take Your Holy Spirit from me. (NASB)

5. **Psalm 139:7**

    Where can I go from Your Spirit? Or where can I flee from Your presence? (NASB)

6. **Isaiah 11:2**

And the Spirit of the Lord will rest on Him, The spirit of wisdom and understanding, The spirit of counsel and strength, The spirit of knowledge and the fear of the Lord . . . (NASB)

7. **Isaiah 63:10**

But they rebelled And grieved His Holy Spirit; Therefore, He turned Himself to become their enemy, He fought against them. (NASB)

8. **Isaiah 63:14**

As the cattle which go down into the valley, The Spirit of the Lord gave them rest. So didst You lead Your people, To make for Yourself a glorious name. (NASB)

The Holy Spirit cannot be a mere emanation because, as can be seen in these quotations, He has all the characteristics of personality—intellect, emotion, and will—and is considered divine.

The Three Personalities in the Same Passage

So then, from various sections of the Hebrew Scriptures, there is a clear demonstration that three personalities are referred to as divine and as being God: the Lord YHVH, the Angel of YHVH, and the Spirit of God.

Furthermore, there are places in the Hebrew Scriptures where all three personalities of the Godhead are referred to in a single passage. This can be seen in Isaiah 42:1 and 61:1, but the two clearest examples are Isaiah 48:12-16 and Isaiah 63:7-14.

Isaiah 48:12-16

[12] Hearken unto me, O Jacob, and Israel my called: I am he; I am the first, I also am the last. [13] Yea, my hand has laid the foundation of the earth, and my right hand has spread out the heavens: when I call unto them, they stand up together. [14] Assemble yourselves, all ye, and hear; who among them has declared these things? He whom Jehovah loves shall perform his pleasure on Babylon, and his arm (shall be on) the Chaldeans. [15] I, even I, have spoken; yea, I have called him; I have brought him, and he shall make his way prosperous. [16] Come ye near unto me, hear ye this; from the beginning I have not spoken in secret; from the time that it was, there am I: and now the Lord Jehovah has sent me, and his Spirit.

In verse 12, it is God, the Creator of the earth, who is speaking. It is still God, the "I Am," who is speaking in verse 16 where He says that He has been sent by another Person, Jehovah, together with a third Person—the Spirit of Jehovah. Here is the Triunity of God as clearly defined as the Hebrew Scriptures can make it.

Isaiah 63:7-14

[7] I will make mention of the lovingkindness of Jehovah, (and) the praises of Jehovah, according to all that Jehovah has bestowed on us, and the great goodness toward the house of Israel, which he has bestowed on them according to his mercies, and according to the multitude of his lovingkindness. [8] For he said, Surely, they are my people, children that will not deal falsely: so he was their Savior. [9] In all their affliction he was afflicted, and the angel of his presence saved them: in his love and in his pity he redeemed them; and he bare them, and carried them all the days of old. [10] But they rebelled, and grieved his holy Spirit: therefore he was turned to be their enemy, (and) himself fought against them. [11] Then he remembered the days of old, Moses (and) his people, (saying), Where is he that brought them up out of the sea with the shepherds of his flock? where is he that put his holy Spirit in the midst of them? [12] that caused his glorious arm to go at the right hand of Moses? that divided the waters before them, to make himself an everlasting name? [13] that led them through the depths, as a horse in the wilderness, so that they stumbled not? [14] As the cattle that go down into the valley, the Spirit of Jehovah caused them to rest; so didst you lead your people, to make yourself a glorious name.

In this passage, Isaiah is recounting the experiences of Israel in the Exodus and the Wilderness Wanderings. In the course of these seven verses, he mentions three distinct divine personalities. These are as follows:

1. In verse 7, Isaiah mentions the Lord Jehovah—the first Person.

2. In verse 9, he mentions the Angel of His presence—the second Person.

3. The third Person is the Holy Spirit, mentioned three times, in verses 10, 11, and 14.

While often throughout the Hebrew Scriptures God refers to Himself as being the One solely responsible for Israel's redemption from Egypt, in this passage three personalities are given credit for it. There is, however, no contradiction seen here since all three comprise the unity of the one Godhead.

Conclusions

The teaching of the Hebrew Scriptures, then, is that there is a plurality of the Godhead. The first Person is consistently called YHVH, while the second Person is given the names of YHVH, the Angel of YHVH, and the Servant of YHVH. Consistently and without fail, the second Person is sent by the first Person. The third Person is referred to as the Spirit of YHVH or the Spirit of God or the Holy Spirit. He, too, is sent by the first Person but is continually related to the ministry of the second Person.

If the concept of the Triunity of God is not Jewish, then neither are the Hebrew Scriptures. Jewish believers cannot be accused of having slipped into paganism when they hold to the fact that Yeshua is the divine Son of God. He is the One of whom God said in Exodus 23:20-23:

> [20] Behold, I send an angel before you, to keep you by the way, and to bring you into the place which I have prepared. [21] Take ye heed before him, and hearken unto his voice; provoke him not; for he will not pardon your transgression: for my name is in him. [22] But if you shall indeed hearken unto his voice, and do all that I speak; then I will be an enemy unto your enemies, and an adversary unto your adversaries. [23] For mine angel shall go before you, and bring you in unto the Amorite, and the Hittite, and the Perizzite, and the Canaanite, the Hivite, and the Jebusite: and I will cut them off.

New Testament Light

In keeping with the teaching of the Hebrew Scriptures, the New Testament clearly recognizes that there are three Persons in the Godhead, although it becomes quite a bit more specific. The first Person is called the Father, while the second is called the Son. With this, the New Testament answers the question of Proverbs 30:4: "What is his name, and what is his son's name, if you know?" His son's name is Yeshua, Jesus. In accordance with the Hebrew Scriptures, He is sent by God to be the Messiah, but this time as a man, not as an angel. Furthermore, He is sent for a specific purpose: to die for our sins. In order to accomplish this work of atonement, God became a man.

The New Testament calls the third Person of the Godhead the Holy Spirit. Throughout the New Testament, He is related to the work of the second Person, in keeping with the teaching of the Hebrew Scriptures. We see, then, that there is a continuous body of teaching in both the Hebrew Scriptures and the New Testament relating to the Triunity of God.

CHAPTER 5:

APPENDICES

Appendix 1

How the *Brit Chadasha* Quotes the *Tanach*

n reading through the *Brit Chadasha* or New Testament, it is soon realized that it frequently quotes the *Tanach* or Old Testament and quotes it in various ways. Because sometimes the context of the Tanach quotation does not seem to fit the Brit Chadasha context, some have questioned the validity of the Brit Chadasha's use of the Tanach. This will be a study to examine exactly how the Brit Chadasha does quote the Tanach.

When the Brit Chadasha quotes the Tanach, it does so in four different ways. [18] Every Tanach quotation found within the Brit Chadasha will always fit into one of these four categories. There is one example of each of the four ways in Matthew Two, so this will be used as the basis for explaining them.

Literal Prophecy Plus Literal Fulfillment

The first category of quotes is known as "literal prophecy plus literal fulfillment." The example of this first category is found in Matthew 2:5-6:[19]

> [5] And they said unto him, In Bethlehem of Judaea: for thus it is written through the prophet,
> [6] And you Bethlehem, land of Judah, are in no wise least among the princes of Judah: For out of you shall come forth a governor, who shall be shepherd of my people Israel.

This passage in the Brit Chadasha quotes Micah 5:2. If we go back to the context of Micah 5:2 to see what the Tanach was talking about, we discover that it is dealing with the birth of the Messiah. The point of Micah 5:2 is that when the Messiah is born, He will be born in the town of Bethlehem in the region of Judah and nowhere else; not the Bethlehem of Galilee, and not any other town in Judah. That is the literal meaning, the literal interpretation of Micah 5:2; the Messiah, when He is born, will be born in the town of Bethlehem, within the tribal territory of Judah.

In the Brit Chadasha, there is a literal fulfillment of that literal prophecy. Yeshua, when He was born as the Messiah, was born in the town of Bethlehem. Furthermore, He was born in

---

[18] David L. Cooper, *Messiah: His Historical Appearance* (Los Angeles: Bible Research Society, 1958), pages 174-177.

[19] All Scripture quotations in this appendix are from the ASV of 1901.

Bethlehem of Judah and not Bethlehem of Galilee. This was a literal fulfillment of Micah 5:2, by which the Brit Chadasha quotes the Tanach—literal prophecy plus literal fulfillment. The prophecy makes only one point. When it is fulfilled in the Brit Chadasha in a perfect way, the Brit Chadasha quotes the Tanach.

Another example of this first category is Matthew 1:22-23:

[22] Now all this is come to pass, that it might be fulfilled which was spoken by the Lord through the prophet, saying, [23] Behold, the virgin shall be with child, and shall bring forth a son, And they shall call his name Immanuel; which is, being interpreted, God with us.

This is a quotation of Isaiah 7:14. The context of Isaiah 7:14 is predicting that when the Messiah is born, He will be born of a virgin. That is the literal meaning of Isaiah 7:14. In the Brit Chadasha (or the New Testament, a term we will now use interchangeably), there is a literal fulfillment of the literal prophecy, and so the passage is quoted by the New Testament.

Two other examples of the first category are found in Matthew 3:3, which quotes Isaiah 40:3, and in Mark 1:2, which quotes Malachi 3:1. Both the Isaiah and Malachi passages predict that before the Messiah is made known, He will be preceded by a forerunner. A forerunner will announce the soon coming of the King. This prophecy was fulfilled in a literal way by John the Baptist, and for that reason, the verses in Isaiah and Malachi were quoted by Matthew, Mark, and Luke.

Another example is Luke 4:18-19, which quotes Isaiah 61:1-2. The context in the Isaiah account is speaking of the kind of ministry the Messiah was to have at His first coming, the nature and style of His ministry. In Luke, Yeshua was literally fulfilling that prophecy, so it is quoted.

Another example is Matthew 4:13-16, which quotes Isaiah 8:22-9:2. The context of that prophecy is speaking of where the ministry of the Messiah will primarily take place and specifies that the area will be within the tribal territories of Zebulun and Naphtali. In the New Testament, Yeshua ministered primarily in these two tribal territories. Nazareth, where He grew up, was within the tribal territory of Zebulun, and Capernaum, where He set up His headquarters, was within the tribal territory of Naphtali. In this way, the prophecy was literally fulfilled.

Another example of this first category is Matthew 21:5, which quotes Zechariah 9:9. The context of Zechariah 9:9 speaks about the Messiah riding into Jerusalem upon a donkey. When Yeshua, in His triumphal entry, rode into Jerusalem on that type of an animal, then that prophecy was literally fulfilled. Therefore, it is quoted by the New Testament.

Another example is John 12:38, which quotes Isaiah 53:1. Isaiah 53:1 clearly prophesies that when the Messiah comes, He is going to be rejected by His own people. When Yeshua was rejected by Israel, that was a literal fulfillment of that particular prophecy.

Another example of this first category of prophecy is to be found within the context of the death of the Messiah. In the context of the crucifixion, John 19:24 states:

²⁴ They said therefore one to another, Let us not rend it, but cast lots for it, whose it shall be: that the scripture might be fulfilled, which says, They parted my garments among them, And upon my vesture did they cast lots.

John quoted Psalm 22:18, and the context of that verse speaks of the death of the Messiah. Part of the death scene is that His clothing will be taken away from Him and the tormentors will gamble for His clothes. That is the literal meaning of the prophecy of Psalm 22:18. In the New Testament, there is a literal fulfillment of this particular prophecy. When the Roman soldiers gambled for the clothing of Yeshua, they fulfilled the prophecy. For that reason, John quoted that prophecy in this particular passage.

Closely related is another quotation found in Matthew 27:46:

⁴⁶ And about the ninth hour Yeshua cried with a loud voice, saying, Eli, Eli, lama sabachthani? that is My God, my God, why have you forsaken me?

Here, Matthew recorded Yeshua quoting Psalm 22:1. The context of Psalm 22:1 is speaking about the sufferings of the Messiah and the death of the Messiah. During His sufferings, He was to cry, "My God, my God, why have you forsaken me?" When Yeshua cried this, it was a direct fulfillment of the Tanach prophecy, and for that reason, it was quoted in this New Testament passage.

This is the first category of New Testament quotations of the Tanach: literal prophecy plus literal fulfillment. In these cases, the Tanach literally speaks of a specific event in the future. When that specific event is literally fulfilled in the context of the New Testament, the New Testament quotes that particular prophecy as a point-by-point fulfillment. Many of the quotations of the Tanach in the New Testament fall into this category.

Literal Plus Typical (Typology)

The second category of quotations can be labeled "literal plus typical." An example of this category is found in Matthew 2:15:

¹⁵ and was there until the death of Herod: that it might be fulfilled which was spoken by the Lord through the prophet, saying, Out of Egypt did I call my son.

If we go back to the context of Hosea 11:1, which is what this passage is quoting, we discover that it is not even a prophecy; it is speaking of a literal historical event. The background to Hosea 11:1 is Exodus 4:22-23. Israel, as a nation, is the son of God: *Israel is my son, my firstborn*. When God brought Israel out of Egypt, it is pictured by Hosea 11:1 as God bringing His son out of the land of Egypt. That is the literal meaning of Hosea 11:1. It is an historical verse dealing with an historical event, the Exodus. However, the literal Old Testament event becomes a type of a New Testament event. Now there is a more ideal Son of God, the Messianic Son of God, the Messiah Himself. When Yeshua was brought out of the land of Egypt, God was again bringing His Son out of Egypt.

This is a type and anti-type. The type was Israel, the national son, coming out of Egypt. The anti-type is the Messianic Son of God also coming out of Egypt. This is an example of the second category—literal plus typical.

Another example of this category is Matthew 15:7-9:

[7] Ye hypocrites, well did Isaiah prophesy of you, saying, [8] This people honors me with their lips; But their heart is far from me. [9] But in vain do they worship me, Teaching (as their) doctrines the precepts of men.

These verses contain a quotation of Isaiah 29:13. The context of Isaiah 29:13 is speaking of an historical event when the people were rejecting the prophetic word of Isaiah the prophet. The literal meaning of Isaiah 29:13 deals with Israel's rejection of the prophet. Israel's rejection of the prophetic word of the prophet becomes a type of Israel's rejection of the prophetic word of the Messiah, and so the Tanach is quoted.

Another example is John 12:39-40:

[39] For this cause they could not believe, for that Isaiah said again, [40] He has blinded their eyes, and he hardened their heart; Lest they should see with their eyes, and perceive with their heart, And should turn, And I should heal them.

Here, John quoted Isaiah 6:10, which in context states that the prophetic message of Isaiah will be rejected by his own people. And that is the literal meaning of this passage. Again, Israel's rejection of the prophetic word of Isaiah the Prophet becomes a type of the rejection of the prophetic word of the Messiah. For that reason, the Tanach verse is quoted in this particular situation.

Another example in this category is found in Matthew 21:42:

[42] Yeshua says unto them, Did ye never read in the scriptures, The stone which the builders rejected, The same was made the head of the corner; This was from the Lord, And it is marvelous in our eyes?

This passage quotes Psalm 118:22-23. The Psalm makes the point that a stone which the builders did not know what to do with was rejected or set aside. Later, when they finished the building, they realized that it was the top stone, the chief stone, that was the head of the corner. That is the literal meaning of Psalm 118:22-23. The rejection of the stone and the acceptance of the stone become a type of Israel's rejection and later acceptance of the Messiahship of Yeshua.

One more example of the second category is in John 19:36:

> [36] For these things came to pass, that the scripture might be fulfilled, A bone of him shall not be broken.

Here, John quoted Exodus 12:46. In the context of Exodus 12:46, Moses was dealing with an historical event which would save the Jews from the last plague. In the process of slaughtering the Passover lamb, then roasting and eating it, the instruction was that not a bone of the sacrificial animal was to be broken. That is the literal meaning of this command. The Passover lamb is a type of the Messiah, who is *our Passover* (1 Corinthians 5:7, NASB). During His crucifixion, His bones were not broken while the bones of the other men crucified left and right of Him were broken. This was a fulfillment in a typical sense, not in a literal, prophetic sense.

To summarize this category, the literal meaning of the passage from the Hebrew Scriptures deals with an historical event and not a prophetic event. However, that historical event becomes a type of a New Testament event, and therefore, it is quoted in that way. The book of Hebrews uses this category frequently (the sin of Kadesh Barnea, the Tabernacle, the sacrificial system, the Aaronic priesthood, the Melchizedekian priesthood, etc.).

Literal Plus Application

The third category is "literal plus application." The example of this category is in Matthew 2:17-18:

> [17] Then was fulfilled that which was spoken through Jeremiah the prophet, saying, [18] A voice was heard in Ramah, Weeping and great mourning, Rachel weeping for her children; And she would not be comforted, because they are not.

This time, Matthew quotes Jeremiah 31:15. In the original context, Jeremiah is speaking of an event at the beginning of the Babylonian Captivity. As the Jewish young men were being taken away into captivity, they went by the town of Ramah. Not too far from Ramah is where Rachel was buried, and she was the symbol of Jewish motherhood in the Tanach. As the young Jewish men were marched toward Babylon, the Jewish mothers of Ramah came out weeping for the sons they would never see again. Jeremiah pictured this as "Rachel weeping for her children; And she would not be comforted, because they are not." Rachel weeping symbolized Jewish mothers weeping. That is the literal meaning of Jeremiah 31:15. Because of one point of similarity, the verse is quoted in the New Testament. It is not a literal fulfillment, nor a full-scale typology, but simply an application because of one point of similarity. In the New Testament case, the one point of similarity was this: Jewish mothers were weeping for sons they would never see again because Herod had slaughtered all the males of Bethlehem from the age of two years and under. Jewish mothers were again weeping for their sons. Everything else is different. In Jeremiah, the event takes place at Ramah, north of Jerusalem; in Matthew, it takes place in Bethlehem, south of Jerusalem. In Jeremiah, the sons are still alive but are going into captivity; in Matthew, the sons are dead. Because of one point of similarity, the New Testament quotes the Tanach as an application only.

Another example of this same type of quotation is found in Acts 2:16-21:

[16] but this is that which has been spoken through the prophet Joel: [17] And it shall be in the last days, says God, I will pour forth of My Spirit upon all flesh: And your sons and your daughters shall prophesy, And your young men shall see visions, And your old men shall dream dreams: [18] Yea and on My servants and on My handmaidens in those days Will I pour forth of My Spirit; and they shall prophesy. [19] And I will show wonders in the heaven above, And signs on the earth beneath; Blood, and fire, and vapor of smoke: [20] The sun shall be turned into darkness. And the moon into blood, Before the day of the Lord come, That great and notable (day). [21] And it shall be, that whosoever shall call on the name of the Lord shall be saved.

In this passage, Peter quoted Joel 2:28-32. The context of Joel is speaking of the outpouring of the Holy Spirit upon Israel, resulting in supernatural manifestations and causing the whole nation to be saved, in preparation for the establishment of the Messianic kingdom spoken of in the next chapter, Joel 3. Hence, the literal meaning of the Joel passage is the outpouring of the Holy Spirit upon the whole nation of Israel, resulting in supernatural manifestations. Nothing predicted by Joel 2 happened in Acts 2. For example, Joel spoke about the pouring out of the Spirit upon all Jewish flesh. However, in Acts 2, the Spirit was poured out upon twelve or, at the most, 120 people. Joel spoke about the sons and daughters of Israel prophesying, the young men seeing visions, and the old men dreaming. None of that happened in Acts 2. No one did any prophesying; the young men did not see visions; and old men did not dream dreams. Furthermore, according to Joel, the servants of the Jewish people were to experience these same things, and there were no servants involved in the context of Acts 2. Finally, Joel spoke of climactic events in the heavens and on earth: blood, fire, pillars of smoke, the sun turning into darkness and the moon into blood, yet none of these things happened in Acts 2.

Nothing predicted by Joel 2 happened in Acts 2, and what did happen in Acts 2 is not even mentioned in Joel 2. What did happen in Acts 2 was a manifestation of the Spirit, resulting in the speaking of tongues. Joel did not mention the gift of tongues at all. What we have here is the third category of quotation—literal plus application. The literal meaning of the Joel passage speaks of Israel's national salvation when the Holy Spirit will be poured out on all Jewish people, in preparation for the Messianic kingdom. Of course, that did not happen in the book of Acts, but there was one point of similarity. That one point of similarity was an outpouring of the Holy Spirit, resulting in a unique manifestation, the speaking in tongues. Because of one point of similarity— the outpouring of the Holy Spirit—the Tanach was quoted by the New Testament as an application.

This can be compared to English idiomatic expressions, such as "He met his Waterloo." The term alludes to an actual, historical event, Napoleon Bonaparte's defeat at Waterloo, Belgium, in 1815. When we say that someone met their Waterloo, do we mean that they were defeated in battle? No. We mean that they experienced a decisive defeat of their ambitions. When Napoleon lost the battle of Waterloo, he also lost his whole empire; it was there that his imperial ambitions were decisively defeated. Therefore, when we say that someone met his Waterloo, we mean that he has one thing in common with Napoleon Bonaparte: Some climactic event in his life has caused him to suffer a decisive defeat of an ambition. In the same manner, the New Testament will often quote the Old Testament because of one point of similarity.

Summation

The fourth category is "summation" or "summary." An example of the fourth category is found in Matthew 2:23.

> [23] and came and dwelt in a city called Nazareth; that it might be fulfilled which was spoken through the prophets, that he should be called a Nazarene.

The apparent quotation is "he should be called a Nazarene," but no such statement is to be found anywhere in the Tanach. Some have tried to connect this with Isaiah 11:1, but that connection is far-fetched and based on a similarity of sound between the Hebrew word for "branch" (*netzer*) and the Hebrew name for "Nazareth" (*Natzeret* or *Natzrat*). In verse 23, Matthew uses the plural term *prophets*, so at least two references might be expected, but there is not even one. The reason is that this is not a direct quote from the Old Testament. Instead it is a summation of what the Old Testament taught about the Messiah. This is the difference between the first three categories and the fourth. The clue is that the word *prophet* is used in the plural, as it is in Matthew 2:23. In the first three categories, the word *prophet* is, in most cases, used in the singular. In the fourth category, it is used in the plural, "spoken through the *prophets*." The author is not quoting any specific prophet, but summarizing what the Old Testament prophets said. In this case, they stated that *he should be called a Nazarene*. What was a Nazarene? In the first century, Nazarenes were a despised people. The term was used to reproach and to shame. This attitude is reflected in John 1:45-46::

> [45] Philip finds Nathanael, and says unto him, We have found him, of whom Moses in the law, and the prophets, wrote, Yeshua of Nazareth, the son of Joseph. [46] And Nathanael said unto him, Can any good thing come out of Nazareth? Philip says unto him, Come and see.

Nathanael's question, "Can any good thing come out of Nazareth?" is a reflection of the low opinion people had of Nazarenes. Nazarenes were despised and rejected. And what did the prophets say about the Messiah? They did predict that He would be a despised and rejected individual. The specific term "Nazarene" is a convenient way of summarizing this teaching; it is not a quotation as such, but a summary.

Another example of this category is Luke 18:31-33:

> [31] And he took unto him the twelve, and said unto them, Behold, we go up to Jerusalem, and all the things that are written through the prophets shall be accomplished unto the Son of man. [32] For he shall be delivered up unto the Gentiles, and shall be mocked, and shamefully treated, and spit upon: [33] and they shall scourge and kill him: and the third day he shall rise again.

Again, note the use of the plural term *prophets*. What the prophets said about the Messiah included nine things:

1. The Messiah will go up to Jerusalem;

2. He will fall into the hands of the priests and scribes;

3. The Jewish people will condemn Him to death;

4. They will turn Him over to the Gentiles;

5. The Gentiles will mock Him;

6. They will spit on Him;

7. They will scourge Him;

8. They will kill Him;

9. He will be resurrected on the third day.

No individual prophet said *all* of this, and no such quotation exists anywhere in the section of the Hebrew Scriptures called "The Prophets." However, the prophets taken together did say all of these things, so this is not a direct quotation, but a summary.

One more example of this fourth category is Matthew 26:54-56:

> [54] How then should the scriptures be fulfilled, that thus it must be? [55] In that hour said Yeshua to the multitudes, Are ye come out as against a robber with swords and staves to seize me? I sat daily in the Temple teaching, and ye took me not. [56] But all this is come to pass, that the scriptures of the prophets might be fulfilled. Then all the disciples left him, and fled.

Although Yeshua had taught the people in clear language, they rejected Him. This rejection became obvious when they were ready to arrest Him. He said that all this had to come to pass *that the scriptures of the prophets might be fulfilled.* No single prophet prophesied what was happening in the garden of Gethsemane using the words of Yeshua. But the prophets together did say that the Messiah would be rejected. He would be arrested and undergo a trial. Just one passage alone, Isaiah 53, is a good example of this. But here, Yeshua is not quoting a specific prophecy; rather, He is summarizing what the prophets said. In summary, they certainly taught what Yeshua is saying here. Again, this is the fourth category: summation.

An example of summation in rabbinic literature can be seen in the *Midrash Rabbah* 63:11 where it reads: "Hence it is written as in the verse, 'And I will no more make you a reproach of famine among the nations.'" Nowhere in the Tanach is there any such verse. Nowhere can you find the words, "And I will no more make you a reproach of famine among the nations." What we have here is a summarization of two passages, Joel 2:19 and Ezekiel 36:30.

Joel 2:19 says:

¹⁹ And Jehovah answered and said unto his people, Behold, I will send you grain, and new wine, and oil, and ye shall be satisfied therewith; and I will no more make you a reproach among the nations . . .

Ezekiel 36:30 says:

³⁰ And I will multiply the fruit of the tree, and the increase of the field, that ye may receive no more the reproach of famine among the nations.

What the *Midrash Rabbah* is doing is summarizing the teaching of these two passages.

Conclusion

There are four categories by which the Brit Chadasha quotes the Tanach. To determine into which category a quotation falls, the procedure is first to go back to the Hebrew Scriptures to see the context of the original quotation. Once that is determined, then it can also be determined to which of the four categories the quotation belongs. If it is a point-for-point literal fulfillment, then it is **literal prophecy plus literal fulfillment**. If it is using a historical account of the Tanach as a type, then it is **literal plus typical**. If there is only one point of similarity between what is happening in the Tanach context and what is happening in the Brit Chadasha context, then it is **literal plus application**. If there is no direct quotation in the Tanach, then it can be assumed to be merely a **summary**. Every quotation of the Tanach in the Brit Chadasha will always fit into one of these four categories. The New Testament is very consistent in the way it quotes the Old.

Appendix 2

The Sons of God

In discussing Genesis 6:1-4, one of the early echoes of the promise of Genesis 3:15, it has been stated that these verses describe the intermarriage of fallen angels with human women. Because this view is contested by some, it will be necessary to study these verses in some detail and provide a justification of the interpretation which has been given.

The Multiplication of Humanity—Genesis 6:1

[1] Now it came about, when men began to multiply on the face of the land, and daughters were born to them,[20]

Verse 1 emphasizes the multiplication of humanity before the Flood. The Hebrew word for "men" used here is generic and refers to humanity in general, including male and female. The word, as such, cannot be limited to the sons of Cain. It included both Sethites and Cainites, and both of these groups died in the Flood.

Another key word found in verse 1 is "daughter," a Hebrew word that means "females." The emphasis in the second part of verse 1, "daughters were born unto them," is on the female portion of humanity. Again, the expression cannot be limited to the female descendants of Cain, as some teach. It simply is a word that means "the female portion of the population."

Verse 1 can read: "Humanity multiplied, and females were born unto them." The distinction in verse 1 is not between male Sethites and female Cainites, but the emphasis is on the female portion of humanity in general which would include both Cainites and Sethites.

The Intermarriage—Genesis 6:2

[2] that the sons of God saw that the daughters of men were beautiful; and they took wives for themselves, whomever they chose.

Verse 2 describes an intermarriage. The first key phrase is "sons of God," which is a general term meaning "to be brought into existence by God's creative act." Because the term carries this

---

[20] All Scripture quotations in this appendix are from the NASB.

meaning, it is used very selectively, and throughout the Tanach, it always refers to angels (see, for example, Job 1:6; 2:1; 38:7). No one debates this. Still, some want to make Genesis 6:1-4 the one exception, and there is simply no warrant for this. In the New Testament, the term "sons of God" is expanded. Adam is called "the son of God" (Luke 3:38) because he was brought into existence by creation. Believers are called "sons of God" (John 1:12) because they are considered to be a new creation (Galatians 6:15). But in Genesis, the text is dealing with a specific Hebrew expression, *bnei ha-Elohim*. As it is used in the Hebrew Old Testament, it is a term that always refers to angels. The distinction in this passage, then, is not between Sethites and Cainites, but between humanity and angels. The word "men" here emphasizes humanity. The term "sons of God" emphasizes angels.

The second key expression in verse 2 is "daughters of men." This is again a generic term for women, which includes female descendants of both Sethites and Cainites. What the verse is saying is, "the sons of God saw the daughters of men." There is no justification for this verse to be interpreted to mean "godly males" intermarried with "ungodly females." Would truly godly men marry ungodly females? The expression "daughters of men" simply means womankind, and the term "sons of God" refers to angels. If the meaning is kept consistent with its usage elsewhere in the Tanach, the passage is clearly speaking of fallen angels intermarrying with human women. This is obvious in two ways.

First, the verse speaks of a one-way intermarriage; the sons of God married the daughters of men. There is no record of daughters of God marrying sons of men. If the distinction was between Sethites and Cainites, it simply would not happen this way. In human society, intermarriage occurs both ways. Today, saved males sometimes marry unsaved females, and sometimes saved females marry unsaved males. If the other claim was true, it would mean that male Sethites married female Cainites, but male Cainites never married female Sethites, which is entirely unlikely. Intermarriage would thus be confined to godly men with ungodly women, but not godly women with ungodly men. In Genesis 6, however, there is only a one-way intermarriage, the sons of God intermarrying with the daughters of men.

Second, the context clearly speaks of a cohabitation that is unusual and unnatural and causes the worldwide Flood. Verses 1-4 deal with the angelic cause of the worldwide Flood, while verses 5-6 deal with the human cause. Cohabitation between Sethites and Cainites would not be unusual or unnatural, while cohabitation between angels and humans would be.

Those who do not like this teaching object to it by quoting Matthew 22:30, claiming that this verse clearly teaches that angels are sexless:

[30] For in the resurrection they neither marry, nor are given in marriage, but are like angels in heaven.

What Yeshua said is that human beings *in the resurrection* do not *marry, nor are given in marriage*. The angels He was speaking of are *angels in heaven*. The comparison is not with angels in general, but with angels "in heaven." The emphasis is that in heaven, good angels neither marry nor are given in marriage. Matthew 22:30 makes the same point about human beings. Humans in heaven do not marry, nor are they given in marriage. What about humans here on earth? Humans on earth certainly do marry and are given in marriage. This is a contrast between what happens in heaven as compared to what happens here on earth. Genesis 6, however, is speaking of angels on earth and discusses things happening on earth. Matthew 22:30 teaches that angels do not procreate after their kind, meaning that angels do not give birth to other angels. Still, angels are never declared to be sexless. On the contrary, angels are always described in the masculine gender, not in the feminine, nor in the neuter. This is true for the Old and New Testaments. Whenever angels became visible, they always appeared as young men, never as women (Genesis 18:1-19:22; Mark 16:5-7; Luke 24:4-7; Acts 1:10-11). Matthew 22:30 cannot be used as an argument against the angelic interpretation of Genesis 6:1-4, because it is dealing with a situation on earth, not in heaven; nor does Matthew 22:30 teach that angels are sexless.

Another question is: Why did Satan have some of his fallen angels intermarry with human women? Why bother? The reason for this can be understood by investigating the greater context of Genesis. Three chapters earlier (Genesis 3:15), the first Messianic prophecy is recorded. This prophecy declared that the Messiah would be the seed of the woman, and this Seed would crush the head of Satan. What is happening in Genesis 6:1-4 is Satan's attempt to corrupt the seed of the woman by having some of his angels take on human form and intermarry with the daughters of men. Therefore, the events of Genesis 6:1-4 were a Satanic attempt to cancel out the prophecy of Genesis 3:15.

The Result of the Intermarriage—Genesis 6:3

The result of this intermarriage was the judgment of God:

> [3] Then the Lord said, "My Spirit shall not strive with man forever, because he also is flesh; nevertheless his days shall be one hundred and twenty years."

In verse 3, God pronounced the judgment: The Holy Spirit would not continue to strive with this kind of evil forever, and God decreed the destruction of humanity to be fulfilled 120 years later. The means of the destruction would be a flood, the purpose of which was to destroy the product of the union of angels and women discussed in the next verse.

The Product of the Intermarriage—Genesis 6:4

> [4] The Nephilim were on the earth in those days, and also afterward, when the sons of God came in to the daughters of men, and they bore *children* to them. Those were the mighty men who *were* of old, men of renown.

To get a clearer understanding of what this verse is saying as a whole, the individual parts need to be discussed first.

First is the name *Nephilim*. In some translations, this Hebrew word has been translated by the word "giant." People reading it picture huge human beings. But *Nephilim* does not mean "giants"; rather, it means "fallen ones." The reason it was translated as "giants" is because in the Septuagint, the Greek translation of the Tanach made around 250 B.C., the Jewish scholars translated verse 4 by the Greek word *gigantes*. This term was used in Greek mythology to describe the Titans, and our English word "giant" comes from it. The Titans were part man and part god, because they were products of gods and men. When the Jewish scholars translated the word *Nephilim*, they used the Greek word for Titans because they recognized Genesis 6,4 to be a union not of two human beings, but of angels and humans which produced a being that was neither angelic nor human. So at least the Jewish scholars of 250 B.C., who lived much closer to the time when Moses originally wrote this passage, clearly understood this to be a marriage between angels and human women. This union resulted in a new race of creatures called the *Nephilim*. It was a race of fallen ones. They were *gigantes*, they were superhuman, but not necessarily in size. They had human characteristics, but at the same time, they had mental and physical capacities that superseded those of regular men and women. Still, they may not have been any larger than normal human beings.

It is from the events of Genesis 6:1-4 that the source of Greek and Roman mythologies were derived. These mythologies record how gods from Mount Olympus married human beings on earth and produced children who had superhuman characteristics, who were greater than men, but less than the gods. The book of Genesis gives the true history of what really happened, while Greek and Roman mythologies give the corrupted account. In Greek and Roman mythologies, the human perspective is given, and what happened is elevated to something special and glorified, but God called it sin.

The second word to note in this verse is *giborim*, which is translated as "the mighty men," "the men of renown." Again, because this was a product of fallen angels and human women, they were unique. They were the *giborim*. Notice that there is no mention of mighty women, which would be strange if this were a product of a normal union. After all, a normal union produces both males and females. If this were a natural union, then the product should have been mighty men and mighty women. But there are only mighty men because this is a new race of beings that is neither human nor angelic. The only way to explain the origin of the *giborim* is that they were the product of this unholy union, the point of verse 4.

Only by the angelic explanation of chapter 6 do other areas of biblical teaching make sense. It provides the only adequate explanation for certain statements in II Peter and Jude which will be studied next. The union described in Genesis 6 is a peculiar sin. It is connected to the Flood, and it is different from the original fall of the angels.

2 Peter 2:4-5

> 2:4 For if God did not spare angels when they sinned, but cast them into hell and committed them to pits of darkness, reserved for judgment; 5 and did not spare the ancient world, but preserved Noah, a preacher of righteousness, with seven others, when He brought a flood upon the world of the ungodly;

This passage talks about a confinement of a select group of angels. Verse 4 mentions the place of confinement as being "hell." In the Greek text, the word is *tartaróō*, a verb meaning "send to *Tartarus*." Tartarus must be distinguished from the abyss. The abyss is a section of *Sheol* or *Hades*, which is a temporary place of confinement for fallen angels. Tartarus is another section of Sheol, which is a permanent place of confinement for fallen angels. Tartarus is described as being *pits of darkness,* and they are *reserved unto judgment*. These angels confined in Tartarus are reserved unto the Great White Throne judgment (Rev. 20:11). Unlike the demons in the abyss that do get released after the course of time, those in the Tartarus will never be freed. They will go directly from Tartarus to the Lake of Fire, by means of the Great White Throne judgment. It was necessary to confine these angels permanently to assure that they would not repeat the sin of Genesis 6 after the Flood.

Verse 5 reveals the timing of their confinement: it was in conjunction with the Flood. This agrees well with the events of Genesis 6:1-4, which are also connected with the Flood. The purpose of the Flood was to destroy this product of fallen angels and human women. So, by comparing the II Peter passage with the Genesis passage, there is good evidence to show that Genesis is not speaking about Sethites intermarrying with Cainites, but fallen angels intermarrying with human women. This is a valid conclusion just from a study of the Tanach passages themselves. However, the New Testament also supports this interpretation.

Jude 6-7

> 6 And angels who did not keep their own domain, but abandoned their proper abode, He has kept in eternal bonds under darkness for the judgment of the great day. 7 Just as Sodom and Gomorrah and the cities around them, since they in the same way as these indulged in gross immorality and went after strange flesh, are exhibited as an example, in undergoing the punishment of eternal fire.

Verse 6 emphasizes the fall of a select group of angels and describes it in four statements. First, they kept not *their own domain*. The word "domain" is frequently used of the angelic realm and is one of the various ranks within that realm. It means that they did not remain in their position and place of rank within the Satanic cosmos. Second, they *abandoned their proper abode*. They left the demonic-angelic sphere of operation and entered the human sphere by taking on the form of young men and intermarrying with human women. Third, they are now *kept in eternal bonds under darkness*. Here Jude mentioned the same thing as Peter, that these angels are now permanently confined. Fourth, they are to be kept in Tartarus until *the judgment of the great day*. Again, Jude reaffirms Peter's statement that they are being kept in bondage until the Great White Throne judgment. When the time comes, they will be taken out of Tartarus in order to be judged, and then they will be cast into the Lake of Fire.

Verse 7 deals with the nature of the angels' sin. The key phrase is *in the same way*. In the same way as Sodom and Gomorrah, the angels went after *strange flesh*. The sin they committed is similar to the sin of Sodom and Gomorrah, and it is the sexual sin of going after strange flesh. "Strange flesh" refers to a sexual union that goes contrary to nature. In the case of Sodom and Gomorrah, the strange flesh was homosexuality; in the case of these angels, the strange flesh was female flesh. Instead of remaining in their proper abode, they invaded a new sphere, one of alien flesh, to commit sexual immorality. Therefore, Sodom, Gomorrah, and these angels have one thing in common: they are guilty of sexual sins.

By comparing the Genesis passage with the passages in II Peter and Jude, it is clear that these are angels who intermarried with human women and not simply Sethites who intermarried with Cainites.

Why Did Messiah Have to Die?

Since the whole concept of a dying Messiah is so foreign to modern Judaism, although it was once part of Judaism, there is a question that must be answered: Why did the Messiah have to die? In the course of answering this question, a second one arises: What is the means of redemption? If there is one theme that seems to go throughout the entire Scriptures, it is the theme of redemption by blood.

According to the Tanach

Redemption became necessary when sin entered the human sphere and separated man from God. When Adam and Eve committed that first act of disobedience, sin entered and separated them from God. From that point on, the means of bridging the separation of man from God was the means of blood. This bridging of the gap is called redemption. In the history of God's dealing with His people, the means of redemption was always by blood.

The redemptive element of blood begins to come into the theme of Scripture at the same time that sin does, for until sin came, no blood was necessary. We read that just as soon as man is expelled from the Garden of Eden, "Jehovah God made for Adam and for his wife coats of skins, and clothed them" (Genesis 3:21). The skins were animal skins. The nakedness, that the element of sin now revealed, needed to be covered. But the covering required the death of several animals, and so, for the first time in history, blood was shed. This provides the root meaning of the Hebrew word for atonement, which is "a covering."

The necessity of blood was a lesson soon learned by the sons of the first human couple. The time came for both Abel and Cain to bring their sacrifices before God. Cain offered for sacrifice the fruit of his labors in the field. The offering was vegetable, and it was bloodless. Abel brought a blood offering taken from his flock. When God passed judgment on the two types of offerings, He rejected Cain's sacrifice and accepted that of Abel. So, a lesson was taught: One cannot approach God by whatever means one chooses. It is man who sinned and offended the holy God; it is God who must do the forgiving. Therefore, it is not for man to choose the means of forgiveness but for God, and God has chosen the means to be blood. Cain had chosen to approach God in his own way, but he was rejected. Abel chose the way God demanded and was accepted.

As biblical history develops in the book of Genesis, we find that all those with whom God was pleased came to Him by means of blood. Noah offered up blood sacrifices the moment he left the ark. He was followed by other great men in Jewish history—Abraham, Isaac, Jacob—all of whom were careful to approach God by means of blood.

When Moses received the law at Mount Sinai, the redemptive element of blood ran through all of the 613 commandments. A great summary statement for the entire law is to be found in the third book of Moses, Leviticus 17:11:[21]

> For the life of the flesh is in the blood; and I have given it to you upon the altar to make atonement for your souls: for it is the blood that makes atonement by reason of the life.

It can easily be said that the whole law revolves around this one statement. There are commandments which God gave in the law that were to be obeyed. Disobedience was sin. If disobedience did take place, the means of atonement for the sin was blood. The book of Leviticus opens by giving great detail to the different types of blood sacrifices. All these different sacrifices had the same purpose: that the Jew might be rightly related to God. All seven feasts of Israel—Passover, Unleavened Bread, Firstfruits, Pentecost, Trumpets, *Yom Kippur* (Day of Atonement), and Tabernacles—required the shedding of blood. The Yom Kippur ceremony was greatly detailed in Leviticus 16, where careful instructions were given for the shedding of blood to atone for the sins of the Jewish nation. The tabernacle and the Temple both were built to expedite and to make efficient the required shedding of blood for the atonement of the people's sins. The Holy of Holies, which contained the *Shechinah* glory,[22] the visible manifestation of the presence of God, could only be entered once a year, by only one man, the high priest. In order for him to enter, he had to have the blood of the Yom Kippur sacrifice with him, and this blood had to be sprinkled on the Ark of the Covenant, which contained the tablets of the law itself:

> [15] Then shall he kill the goat of the sin—offering, that is for the people, and bring his blood within the veil, and do with his blood as he did with the blood of the bullock, and sprinkle it upon the mercy—seat, and before the mercy—seat: [16] and he shall make atonement for the holy place, because of the uncleannesses of the children of Israel, and because of their transgressions, even all their sins: and so shall he do for the tent of meeting, that dwells with them in the midst of their uncleannesses. [17] And there shall be no man in the tent of meeting when he goes in to make atonement in the holy place, until he come out, and have made atonement for himself, and for his household, and for all the assembly of Israel.

Leviticus 16:15-17

The principle of the sacrificial system stood throughout the remainder of Old Testament history, but it was a burden to the individual. These blood sacrifices had to be repeated year in, and year out, and they had to be done in the Temple at Jerusalem. For the Jews living elsewhere in the country, miles from Jerusalem, it was a burden to come regularly—a minimum of three times a

---

[21] All Scripture quotations in this appendix are from the ASV of 1901.

[22] See p. 160 ff. for a detailed explanation of this term.

year—to offer their sacrifices to the Lord for the atonement of their sins. Only the faithful few, those whom the prophets referred to as the remnant, loved God and His law enough to do so in spite of the burden it created. Others built their own altars on mountains and hills closer to home and offered their sacrifices there. But no atonement was granted at these rival altars, and the prophets of God railed against and condemned this deviation from the law of God. Many had failed to learn the lesson of Cain—that one cannot come to God for forgiveness in any way one may choose, but one must come in the way God Himself has chosen.

It was Isaiah the Prophet who first provided the hope that the day would come when the burden will be lifted. In Isaiah 53:10-11, God declared that the Suffering Servant, the Messiah, would be the sacrifice for sin:

> [10] Yet it pleased Jehovah to bruise him; he has put him to grief: when you shall make his soul an offering for sin, he shall see his seed, he shall prolong his days, and the pleasure of Jehovah shall prosper in his hand. [11] He shall see of the travail of his soul, and shall be satisfied: by the knowledge of himself shall my righteous servant justify many; and he shall bear their iniquities.

Isaiah 53:10-11

The point of Isaiah 53 is basically this: The animal sacrifices under the Mosaic Law were intended to be of temporary duration, a temporary measure only. There would be one final blood sacrifice, and that would be the sacrifice of the Messiah Himself. That is why Isaiah 53 uses the same type of wording, figures, and emphasis found in the book of Leviticus. For example, the expression "you shall make his soul an offering for sin" is a sacrificial concept. These are words that come out of the Mosaic Law itself. Also, the righteous servant "shall bear their iniquities." Not only are these words of sacrifice used generally in the Old Testament Law, but, more specifically, we read of these very terms in Leviticus 16, which is the chapter that expounds and explains all of the details regarding the Yom Kippur sacrifice.

This, then, was the reason Messiah had to die: to provide the blood sacrifice for sin once and for all. No longer would the Jews be burdened with the yearly sacrifices. All a person would need to do is to accept the Messiah's death on his behalf, and his sins would be forgiven. Messiah had to die to provide that atonement, for blood was the means of redemption.

Isaiah 53:10-11 contains another statement that is somewhat confusing. It reads: "by the knowledge of himself shall my righteous servant justify many." A more literal translation from the Hebrew text would read like this: "by the knowledge of him shall my righteous justify many." The word for "knowledge" is a Hebrew term that emphasizes experiential knowledge (a knowledge of the heart, a knowledge of faith), not mere head knowledge. Those, who have a faith knowledge of the Servant (by the knowledge of Him, not by the knowledge of Himself) and believe that He died for their sins, He will justify. Justification means to be declared righteous. We cannot be declared righteous unless our sins have been atoned for. Our sins can only be atoned for by the shedding of blood; the Messiah's blood was the final blood that had to be sacrificed.

According to the New Testament

The book of Hebrews in the New Testament is the counterpart of the book of Leviticus in the Tanach. To understand Hebrews, one must first understand Leviticus. Just as Leviticus had a central verse in 17:11 around which the entire book and the law revolved, the book of Hebrews also makes the very same point in its central verse, 9:22:

> [22] And according to the law, I may almost say, all things are cleansed with blood, and apart from shedding of blood there is no remission.

In Leviticus 17:11, the principle was this: The blood made atonement for the soul. In the New Testament, using different words but giving the same message, it says, "apart from shedding of blood there is no remission." All things are cleansed with blood.

The book of Hebrews was written by a Messianic Jew to a group of Messianic Jewish assemblies in Israel. It picks up the theme of Leviticus and the prophecy of Isaiah to show the superiority of the sacrifice of the Messiah. A number of passages bring these things out. One of them is Hebrews 2:16-18:

> [16] For verily not to angels doth he give help, but he giveth help to the seed of Abraham. [17] Wherefore it behooved him in all things to be made like unto his brethren, that he might become a merciful and faithful high priest in things pertaining to God, to make propitiation for the sins of the people. [18] For in that he himself has suffered being tempted, he is able to succor them that are tempted.

This passage makes the point that Messiah came as a Jew and underwent all the problems that a Jew had to go through in order that He might become a merciful and sympathetic high priest. The reason Messiah came as a Jew was so that He would live under the law and take upon Himself the burden of the law. Therefore, He could clearly sympathize with the Jewish state under the law.

Another central passage is Hebrews 4:14-15:

> [14] Having then a great high priest, who has passed through the heavens, Yeshua the Son of God, let us hold fast our confession. [15] For we have not a high priest that cannot be touched with the feeling of our infirmities; but one that has been in all points tempted like as we are, yet without sin.

This passage further develops the point that Yeshua is the sympathetic high priest for He understands what human beings have to go through since He experienced the same.

Another passage is Hebrews 7:22-25:

> [22] By so much also has Yeshua become the surety of a better covenant. [23] And they indeed have been made priests many in number, because that by death they are hindered from continuing: [24] but he, because he abides for ever, has his priesthood unchangeable. [25] Wherefore also he is

able to save to the uttermost them that draw near unto God through him, seeing he ever lives to make intercession for them.

The superiority of the priesthood of Messiah is seen in the fact that all other priests are mortal. One high priest would serve, but sooner or later he would die; a new priest would need to be chosen to begin the cycle all over again. The life-and-death cycle proved to be a disadvantage to the old priesthood. The superiority of the priesthood of Messiah is shown in that it abides eternally. By virtue of His resurrection, Yeshua remains a high priest forever.

Another shortcoming of the Levitical system of priesthood is found in Hebrews 7:26-27:

[26] For such a high priest became us, holy, guileless, undefiled, separated from sinners, and made higher than the heavens; [27] who needs not daily, like those high priests, to offer up sacrifices, first for his own sins, and then for the sins of the people: for this he did once for all, when he offered up himself.

This passage indicates that under the Mosaic Law, the sacrifices had to be repeated day in and day out, year in and year out. The Messiah was to be the "once for all" sacrifice for sin. This is what happened when Yeshua came and offered up His own blood as the atonement for sin. Also, in the old order of priesthood, the high priest had to sacrifice and shed blood for his own sins first before he could sacrifice and shed blood to make atonement for the sins of the people. Since Yeshua was sinless, He did not need to first atone for His own sins, but with His own blood made atonement for all who would accept it. He made atonement for the whole world, of course, but the atonement is only applied to those who would believe.

In summary, we can say that there were at least three disadvantages in the Levitical system: The first disadvantage was that the priests would eventually die. The second disadvantage was that sacrifices had to be repeated year in and year out. The third disadvantage was that the earthly priest had to atone for his own sins before he could atone for the sins of anyone else. As we were able to see above, the priesthood of Yeshua the Messiah rectified all three of these disadvantages.

In the book of Hebrews, the answer to the question of why the Messiah had to die is kept in strict conformity with what was demanded in Leviticus and by the hope of Isaiah 53. That which the Tanach hoped for was found in the New Testament in total fulfillment by the death of the Messiah.

The superiority of Messiah over all other sacrifices is pointed out in Hebrews 9:11-15:

[11] But Messiah having come a high priest of the good things to come, through the greater and more perfect tabernacle, not made with hands, that is to say, not of this creation, [12] nor yet through the blood of goats and calves, but through his own blood, entered in once for all into the holy place, having obtained eternal redemption. [13] For if the blood of goats and bulls, and the ashes of a heifer sprinkling them that have been defiled, sanctify unto the cleanness of the flesh: [14] how much more shall the blood of Messiah, who through the eternal Spirit offered himself without blemish unto God, cleanse your conscience from dead works to serve the living

God? [15] And for this cause he is the mediator of a new covenant, that a death having taken place for the redemption of the transgressions that were under the first covenant, they that have been called may receive the promise of the eternal inheritance.

Unlike the animal sacrifices, the sacrifice of Yeshua was to bring eternal redemption rather than temporary atonement. This is the fourth distinction between the two systems. Furthermore, even after the animal sacrifice, the Jew was still conscious of his sins. Faith in the sacrifice of Yeshua, however, brings a complete cleansing of the conscience of sins. This is the fifth contrast.

Another passage is found in Hebrews 9:28:

[28] So Messiah also, having been once offered to bear the sins of many, shall appear a second time, apart from sin, to them that wait for him, unto salvation.

Here the twofold aspect of Messiah's ministry is pointed out. Yeshua first came to be the sin offering for the people, just as the Suffering Servant of Isaiah 53 needed to be. Also, just as the Suffering Servant was the One who bore the sins of many, Yeshua did so through His death. Now, the verse states that Yeshua will come "a second time" for a different purpose. The purpose of the first coming was to die for sin. The purpose of the second coming will be to establish the Messianic kingdom.

Once again, a contrast is drawn between the animal sacrifices and the blood sacrifice of Yeshua in Hebrews 10:1-4:

[1] For the law having a shadow of the good things to come, not the very image of the things, can never with the same sacrifices year by year, which they offer continually, make perfect them that draw nigh. [2] Else would they not have ceased to be offered? Because the worshippers, having been once cleansed, would have had no more consciousness of sins. [3] But in those sacrifices there is a remembrance made of sins year by year. [4] For it is impossible that the blood of bulls and goats should take away sins.

Under the Mosaic Law, the animal sacrifices had to be repeated year in and year out. While these sacrifices provided temporary atonement, they never provided permanent forgiveness of sins. Rather, the yearly sacrifices served to remind the Jewish people of their sins; they knew they would have to bring another sacrifice the next year as well. The consciousness of sin was still there. But the sacrifice of Yeshua was once for all and never needed to be repeated. Acceptance of the sacrifice of Yeshua does not bring temporary atonement, but permanent forgiveness. By accepting the substitutionary death of Yeshua for our sins, we are not continually reminded of those sins, but receive a complete cleansing. That is why the sacrifice of Yeshua is so superior to the animal sacrifices of the old system.

The last passage is found in Hebrews 10:10-14:

[10] By which will we have been sanctified through the offering of the body of Yeshua Messiah once for all. [11] And every priest indeed stands day by day ministering and offering often times

the same sacrifices, for which can never take away sins: [12] but he, when he had offered one sacrifice for sins for ever, sat down on the right hand of God; [13] henceforth electing till his enemies be made the footstool of his feet. [14] For by one offering he has perfected for ever them that are sanctified.

This passage again points out how the high priest had to sacrifice day in and day out, and his work was never done. To indicate this unfinished ministry, the high priest is viewed as standing. But Yeshua, who offered Himself as a sacrifice once for all, is viewed as sitting at the right hand of God, thus showing that His work is complete. Furthermore, the animal sacrifices provided a yearly atonement, but never permanently took away sins. But those who accept the sacrifice of Yeshua are perfected forever; their sins are permanently removed.

Conclusion

The conclusion of both the Old and New Testaments is that the means of redemption was by blood, and the permanent blood sacrifice was to be the Messiah Himself. That is why the Messiah *had to die* according to the Tanach. That is why Yeshua *did die* according to the New Testament. Who killed Yeshua was never the issue as far as the New Testament was concerned, for the Messiah had to die. It only became an issue years later because of anti-Semites seeking excuses to persecute the Jews. The only issue in the New Testament itself is whether one will accept the substitutionary sacrifice of Yeshua or not.

The Starting Point of the Seventy Sevens

Daniel 9:24-25 gives the clearest possible prophecy of exactly when Messiah would appear: "Seventy weeks have been decreed for your people and your holy city . . . So you are to know and discern that from the issuing of a decree to restore and rebuild Jerusalem until Messiah the Prince."

The starting point of the seventy sevens is given in the phrase "know and discern that from the issuing of a decree to restore and rebuild Jerusalem." Verse 24 stated that the seventy sevens concern not only Jerusalem but also the Jewish people. Now, in verse 25, it is learned that the seventy sevens will begin with a decree, and this decree involves the rebuilding of Jerusalem.

The question is which decree the verse is speaking about. Usually, there are four options given. First is **the decree of Cyrus**, which was passed in 538-537 B.C. It is a decree found in 2 Chronicles 36:22-23; Ezra 1:1-4, and 6:1-5. Insofar as these three passages speak of it, it concerns the rebuilding of the Temple, but does not actually mention the rebuilding of Jerusalem.

The second possibility is **the decree of Darius Hystaspes** passed in 521 B.C. and spoken of in Ezra 6:6-12. This one is a reaffirmation of the Cyrus decree and concerns the Temple rebuilding.

The third possibility is **the decree of Artaxerxes to Ezra** given in 458 B.C. and mentioned in Ezra 7:11-26. In this decree, there is permission given to proceed with the Temple service, and it concerns only the Temple service.

The fourth possibility is **the decree of Artaxerxes to Nehemiah** that was passed in 444-443 B.C., spoken of in Nehemiah 2:1-8. In its context, it is speaking about the rebuilding of the walls.

Of these four possibilities, only two are valid options: the first and the fourth, though all of them in some way or another did contribute to the building of Jerusalem. Most evangelical scholars today believe that the decree Daniel is speaking of is the decree of Artaxerxes to Nehemiah. This was first popularized by Sir Robert Anderson in his book *The Coming Prince*. He began with the decree of Artaxerxes to Nehemiah and carefully counted off the number of years through a formula, terminating the 483 years to the coming of the Messiah with the triumphal entry in the year A.D. 32. According to Sir Robert Anderson, this period began on March 14, 445 B.C. and ended on April 6, A.D. 32. However, he did make a few miscalculations. In light of the time of the Passover occurrences, it was impossible for the crucifixion to have occurred in the year A.D. 32.

Insofar as when the Passover occurred, there are only two options in that time span, and they are the years A.D. 30 and 33. Dr. Harold Horner wrote a book which corrected Sir Robert Anderson's miscalculations; he, too, begins with the decree of Artaxerxes to Nehemiah but calculated that it was signed on March 4, 444 B.C. He terminates the period also with the triumphal entry on March 29, 33.

The problem with these calculations is that nothing in Daniel's text requires the first sixty-nine sevens to end with the triumphal entry. It only requires it to end with the arrival of the Messiah at the first coming. It would be preferable to terminate the first sixty-nine sevens with the birth of the Messiah rather than the triumphal entry. The second problem with the Artaxerxes/Nehemiah decree is that this is not a decree. If Nehemiah 2:1-8 is read, it becomes clear that there is no decree. Instead, all that Nehemiah receives is the permission to rebuild the walls. Building on the second point, the third one is that rebuilding the wall is not the same as rebuilding the city.

This author's own view is that the decree of which Daniel is speaking is the decree of Cyrus. There are five reasons to believe this. First, this is a real decree; it is in the actual form of a decree.

Second, the year Daniel received the vision of the seventy sevens was the same year Cyrus passed his decree.

Third, this is the decree that is emphasized in Scripture. It was spoken of prophetically by Isaiah in 44:28, 45:1, and 13, about 150 years before it happened. In fact, Isaiah named the one who would issue the decree, Cyrus, before he even lived. The fulfillment of Isaiah's prophecy is recorded four times, in 2 Chronicles 36:22-23, Ezra 1:1-4, 6:1-5, and 6:6-12. This is clearly the decree that is emphasized in Scripture.

The fourth reason is that Cyrus's decree did include the rebuilding of the city. It is understood that the four passages mentioned earlier did not actually mention the rebuilding of the city, but only the rebuilding of the Temple. However, if Isaiah's prophecies are taken literally, it would have included the rebuilding of the city. For example, Isaiah 44:28 and 45:13 clearly mention that Cyrus would not only allow the Temple to be rebuilt, he would also allow the city to be rebuilt. Of course, it is silly to think Cyrus would allow a temple to be rebuilt and then forbid anyone to live anywhere near it by not allowing the city to be rebuilt as well.

The fifth reason is that several parallel passages report that the Jews did rebuild Jerusalem. In fact, they rebuilt the city before Nehemiah ever came to rebuild the walls. In Haggai 1:2-4, seventy years before Nehemiah arrived, the Jews were already living in private homes in Jerusalem although the Temple itself had not as yet been rebuilt. Certainly, they would not dare to rebuild Jerusalem if they did not have permission to do so. According to Ezra 4:12, the city was being built even in Ezra's day, and Ezra preceded the time of Nehemiah.

These are the reasons why it is entirely possible that the decree of which Daniel spoke was the decree of Cyrus. When our own system of chronology is compared to the Persian system of chronology, it produces an apparent 52-year gap, and this author is aware of this discrepancy, but this has been explained by Dr. David L. Cooper in his book *Messiah: His First Coming Scheduled*. The details of the explanation are complex and technical and will, therefore, not be discussed here. But it can be said that the seventy sevens began with the issuing of the decree of Cyrus, and the first 483 years, that is the first sixty-nine sevens, terminated with the birth of Yeshua.

Appendix 5

How Did the Wise Men Know?

There is in the New Testament the account of the wise men's visit to the infant Yeshua, recorded in the Gospel of Matthew 2:1-12 (NASB):

> [1] Now after Yeshua was born in Bethlehem of Judea in the days of Herod the king, behold, magi from the east arrived in Jerusalem, saying, [2] "Where is He who has been born King of the Jews? For we saw His star in the east, and have come to worship Him." [3] And when Herod the king heard it, he was troubled, and all Jerusalem with him. [4] And gathering together all the chief priests and scribes of the people, he began to inquire of them where the Messiah was to be born. [5] And they said to him, "In Bethlehem of Judea, for so it has been written by the prophet, [6] 'AND YOU, BETHLEHEM, LAND OF JUDAH, ARE BY NO MEANS LEAST AMONG THE LEADERS OF JUDAH; FOR OUT OF YOU SHALL COME FORTH A RULER, WHO WILL SHEPHERD MY PEOPLE ISRAEL.' " [7] Then Herod secretly called the magi, and ascertained from them the time the star appeared. [8] And he sent them to Bethlehem, and said, "Go and make careful search for the Child; and when you have found Him, report to me, that I too may come and worship Him." [9] And having heard the king, they went their way; and lo, the star, which they had seen in the east, went on before them, until it came and stood over where the Child was. [10] And when they saw the star, they rejoiced exceedingly with great joy. [11] And they came into the house and saw the Child with Mary His mother; and they fell down and worshiped Him; and opening their treasures they presented to Him gifts of gold and frankincense and myrrh. [12] And having been warned by God in a dream not to return to Herod, they departed for their own country by another way.

This passage contains the record of the visit of the magi from the east who were led to Israel by a star. Because of this, even some believers have stated that there is some validity to astrology, and some have even attempted to develop a doctrine of biblical astrology.

Around Christmas time each year, nativity sets are erected. These nativity sets all tend to look alike. There is a baby Yeshua in some type of manger or in the lap of his mother Mary (*Miriam* in Hebrew); with Mary stands Joseph. On one side of the family of three, we have shepherds, and on the other side, we have three kings. This scene does not reflect biblical teaching for four reasons.

First, the story of the shepherds and the story of the wise men are separated by approximately two years. The shepherds were there when Yeshua was first born. They found him in a stable, lying in a manger. The wise men only saw the star when Yeshua was first born, and it took them some time to get to Jerusalem. The wise men and the shepherds never even met. The Matthew account makes it rather clear that Yeshua was approximately two years old by the time these wise men appear (Matthew 2:7, 16).

Second, when the wise men did find Yeshua, they found Him in a home, not in a stable.

Third, it is commonly said that there were three kings. A famous Christmas carol starts out with the words, "We three kings of orient are." However, we are not told how many there were. We know there had to be at least two because the word "magi" is in the plural. There may have been two, or there may have been two thousand; the Bible does not specifically say. There is no clear evidence as to exactly how many men there were. The reason why people think that there were three is that they gave Yeshua three different types of gifts: gold, frankincense, and myrrh. This is no evidence at all. There could have been ten people who gave gold and twenty who gave frankincense and thirty who gave myrrh; the number of gifts does not indicate the number of givers.

Fourth, Matthew never says that these men were kings. While we do not know how many there were, we do know for certain that they were *not* kings because the specific title they are given in the Greek text is *magoy*, which means "wise men" or, more specifically, "astrologers."

What the Matthew account states is that an unknown number of astrologers from the east arrived in Jerusalem. In the Bible, the east is always the area of Mesopotamia, so there are at least two astrologers from Babylonia, who arrived in Jerusalem and asked, "Where is he that is born King of the Jews?" This incident raises several questions. First, how did these men know anything about the birth of a Jewish king? Second, even knowing about the birth of a Jewish king, why would Babylonian astrologers want to come and worship him? After all, Babylonian astrologers did not worship other Jewish kings. Why would they want to worship this particular king? These are important questions, and it will be necessary to study the account together with other passages of Scripture, in order to understand and explain the events which Matthew records.

The Star

First, we will discuss the issue of the star. The basic rule of interpretation is this:

> When the plain sense of Scripture makes common sense, seek no other sense. Therefore take every word at its primary, ordinary, usual, literal meaning unless the facts of the immediate context studied in the light of related passages and axiomatic and fundamental truths indicate clearly otherwise.[23]

We should take the Bible exactly as it is written unless there is some indication in the text and in the context that tells us we cannot take it literally. Five things indicate that this is not a literal star.

---

[23] This rule was formulated by Dr. David L. Cooper, the late founder and director of the Biblical Research Society.

To begin with, that this was no ordinary star is evident by the "actions" that this star took. The star is referred to as "*His*" star, the King of the Jews' star, in a way that the other stars simply cannot be. This star appears and disappears. This star moves from east to west. This star moves from north to south. This star hovers over one single house in Bethlehem and points to where the Messiah is. Any literal star, as we know it, that will hover over just one house in Bethlehem would destroy this entire planet. These five observations make it clear that this cannot be a physical star, and in summary, we note:

1. It is the personal star of the King of the Jews.

2. It appears and disappears.

3. It moves from east to west.

4. It moves from north to south.

5. It literally hovers over one single house in Bethlehem.

Obviously, it must be something different—but what is it? The root meaning of the Greek word for "star" simply means "radiance" or "brilliance." By this star coming in the form of a light, what we actually have is the appearance of the *Shechinah* glory rather than an astrologer's star. What is the Shechinah glory? The Shechinah glory is the visible manifestation of God's presence. Whenever God became visible in the Old Testament, this is referred to as the Shechinah glory. In most cases, the Shechinah glory came in the form of a light, fire, cloud, or some combination of these three things. Over Babylonia, a light appeared, a brilliance, a radiance, that may have looked like a star from a distance and yet had actions and did things which no star can do or does do. What these wise men actually saw was the Shechinah glory. When they saw this unusual brilliance, they deduced from it that it was a signal that the King of the Jews, the Messiah, had finally been born.[24] Keeping in mind that in ancient times the two disciplines of astronomy and astrology were not separate sciences, if anyone would recognize a new light in the heavens, it would be them.

How Did the Wise Men Know about a Messianic King?

Having determined that this star was not a literal star but the Shechinah glory still does not answer all the questions. The question remains, how did the wise men, these Gentile astrologers from Babylon know anything about the birth of a Jewish king? And even if they did know something about births of Jewish kings, why would they want to come and worship this particular one? To explain this, we must look to the Tanach.

To begin with, we must note that the only place in the entire Tanach that dates Messiah's first coming is the famous "seventy sevens of Daniel" found in Daniel 9:24-27. Unlike many of the other books of the Old Testament, the book of Daniel was not written in Israel, but in Babylon. In

---

[24] A study of the Shechinah glory can be found in Appendix 4 of the author's *The Footsteps of the Messiah*.

fact, half of the book is not written in Hebrew but in Aramaic, the language of the Babylonians. When Daniel was taken to Babylon, he and his three friends were chosen to be instructed at the school of the wise men. Then a day came when Daniel was able to save the lives of all the Babylonian wise men. These astrologers were unable to interpret one of Nebuchadnezzar's dreams. Therefore, the king sentenced every one of them to death. Daniel and his three friends were among those arrested because, from the Babylonian frame of reference, he was considered to be one of the incompetent astrologers. However, Daniel requested and received an audience with the king. He interpreted the dream and, by so doing, saved his life and the lives of all the Babylonian astrologers. No doubt, because of that experience, many of these astrologers turned away from the worship of the stars and became believers in the God of Israel, Daniel's God, the God of Abraham, Isaac, and Jacob.

According to the book of Daniel, Nebuchadnezzar, the king, must not have been a man with great spiritual insight. When he saw that Daniel had some unique abilities, he assumed that he must be a superior astrologer. As a result, Nebuchadnezzar appointed him as head of the Babylonian school of astrology. However, Daniel never received his information and revelation from the stars, but from the Creator of those stars, the God of Israel.

Hence, a line of Babylonian astrologers from generation to generation worshipped the true God and, having Daniel's prophecy, looked forward to the coming of the King of the Jews. However, the book of Daniel did not provide them with information regarding a star that would in some way announce Messiah's birth. How, then, did the astrologers know anything about a star?

For this question, we must go back even earlier in the Tanach to the prophecies of Balaam (these were studied earlier, in chapter 2, "The Law"). Balaam was hired by the king of Moab to curse the Jews. Four times he tried to do so, and each time God took control of his mouth: Instead of cursing the Jews, he found himself blessing them. In the course of his blessings, he gave four key Messianic prophecies, one of which is found in Numbers 24:17:

> [17] I see him, but not now; I behold him, but not near; A star shall come forth from Jacob, And a scepter shall rise from Israel, And shall crush through the forehead of Moab, And tear down all the sons of Sheth. (NASB)

Balaam, with much reluctance and regret, was forced by God to prophesy of the coming of the Jewish Messiah, and he related that to a "star." This is not a literal star, because it then says concerning this star, "And a scepter shall rise from Israel." The star and the scepter are one and the same. Remember that the term "scepter" is a symbol of royalty, of kingship. This star which would rise out of Jacob is himself a king.

Furthermore, Balaam came from the city of Pethor, a city on the banks of the Euphrates River in Babylonia (Numbers 22:5; Deuteronomy 23:4). As an astrologer, he would have been part of the Babylonian school of astrology. Hence, the revelation of a star in relation to Messiah's birth came by way of a Babylonian astrologer who, no doubt, passed the information down to his colleagues. Centuries later, Daniel was able to expound to the Babylonian astrologers as to the time that "the star of Jacob" would come.

Conclusions

How, then, did the wise men know? Not by gazing at the stars in the pseudo-science of astrology, but by the revelation of God as contained in the Scriptures, by means of the prophecies of Balaam and Daniel. Hence, the story of the wise men gives no validity to astrology.

The wise men gave to Yeshua three types of gifts: gold, frankincense, and myrrh. All of these are full of Old Testament symbolism: gold is the symbol of royalty, emphasizing that Yeshua is a king; frankincense is the symbol of deity because frankincense was part of the special scent burned on the altar of incense within the Holy Place, and the smoke penetrated into God's presence in the Holy of Holies itself; thus, frankincense emphasizes Yeshua is God; myrrh was associated in the Tanach with death and embalming.

While the first line of that famous Christmas carol "We three kings of orient are" is not biblically accurate, the last line certainly is. It says, "God and king and sacrifice." These gifts to the family of Joseph, Mary, and Yeshua provided them with the finances they needed in order to escape to Egypt, live there for approximately two years, and then return to Nazareth after the death of Herod the Great.

Appendix 6

Messiah's Right to David's Throne

The question is often raised what right Yeshua has to sit on David's throne since He was not the real son of Joseph but only the son of Mary (*Miriam* in Hebrew). Related to the issue are the two genealogies found in Matthew 1:1-17 and Luke 3:23-38. If Yeshua was only the son of Mary and not Joseph, why was it necessary to give Joseph's genealogy? How do we know that Luke's genealogy is that of Mary? After all, she is not named in that genealogy, but Joseph is. These are questions that need to be answered satisfactorily in order to provide a basis for the understanding of why Yeshua could claim the throne of David.

As an introductory statement, we might note the purpose of Joseph's genealogy in Matthew, which was to show that if Yeshua really was his son, He could not be king. The purpose of Mary's genealogy in Luke, on the other hand, shows why He could claim the throne of David.

Of the four Gospels, only two give a genealogy. Mark and John do not cover Yeshua's birth or His early life, but Matthew and Luke do; so it is natural that only these two would bother giving us a genealogy. However, they tell the story from two different perspectives. Matthew tells the story from Joseph's viewpoint. He reports what Joseph is thinking and what is going on in his mind. We are told nothing of what Mary is thinking. We read of how angels appeared to Joseph, but there is no record of angels appearing to Mary. On the other hand, when we go to Luke's Gospel, we see this same story told from Mary's perspective. It is Mary who plays the active role, while Joseph plays the passive role. We find the angels appearing to Mary, but no angels appearing to Joseph. We are told several times what goes on in the mind of Mary, but we are never told anything about what Joseph is thinking. From these observations alone, it should be very evident that Matthew provides the genealogy of Joseph, since he writes from Joseph's perspective, whereas the genealogy in Luke is that of Mary, since Luke writes from Mary's perspective.

The question still arises, why do we need these two genealogies, especially since Yeshua was not the real son of Joseph? A very popular and common answer is this: In Matthew's Gospel, we have the royal line, whereas in Luke's Gospel, we have the real line. From that statement, another one is developed. Some teachers say that according to Matthew 1, Joseph was the heir apparent to David's throne. Since Yeshua was the adopted son of Joseph, He could have claimed the right to sit on David's throne because of this adoption. On the other hand, in Luke's Gospel, we are given the real line, so that we could know that Yeshua Himself was a descendant of David. Through Mary He was a member of the House of David, but He claims the right to sit on David's throne through Joseph since he was the heir apparent. We will try to show in this study that, actually, the exact opposite is true.

Messiah's Genealogy According to Matthew

[1] The book of the genealogy of Yeshua Messiah, the son of David, the son of Abraham. [2] To Abraham was born Isaac; and to Isaac, Jacob; and to Jacob, Judah and his brothers; [3] and to Judah were born Perez and Zerah by Tamar; and to Perez was born Hezron; and to Hezron, Ram; [4] and to Ram was born Amminadab; and to Amminadab, Nahshon; and to Nahshon, Salmon; [5] and to Salmon was born Boaz by Rahab; and to Boaz was born Obed by Ruth; and to Obed, Jesse; [6] and to Jesse was born David the king. And to David was born Solomon by her *who had been the wife* of Uriah; [7] and to Solomon was born Rehoboam; and to Rehoboam, Abijah; and to Abijah, Asa; [8] and to Asa was born Jehoshaphat; and to Jehoshaphat, Joram; and to Joram, Uzziah; [9] and to Uzziah was born Jotham; and to Jotham, Ahaz; and to Ahaz, Hezekiah; [10] and to Hezekiah was born Manasseh; and to Manasseh, Amon; and to Amon, Josiah; [11] and to Josiah were born Jeconiah and his brothers, at the time of the deportation to Babylon. [12] And after the deportation to Babylon, to Jeconiah was born Shealtiel; and to Shealtiel, Zerubbabel; [13] and to Zerubbabel was born Abihud; and to Abihud, Eliakim; and to Eliakim, Azor; [14] and to Azor was born Zadok; and to Zadok, Achim; and to Achim, Eliud; [15] and to Eliud was born Eleazar; and to Eleazar, Matthan; and to Matthan, Jacob; [16] and to Jacob was born Joseph the husband of Mary, by whom was born Yeshua, who is called Messiah. [17] Therefore all the generations from Abraham to David are fourteen generations; and from David to the deportation to Babylon fourteen generations; and from the deportation to Babylon *to the time* of Messiah fourteen generations.

Matthew 1:1-17 (NASB)

In his account of Joseph's line, Matthew omitted some names and included four women, and this was not the traditional way a Jewish genealogy would be rendered. As to the women, he mentioned Rahab, Ruth, Bathsheba, and Tamar. The question arises why he included these four when there were so many other prominent Jewish women he could have mentioned in the genealogy of Yeshua. One thing all four women had in common was that they were Gentiles. By naming them, Matthew pointed out that while one of the purposes of Yeshua´s coming was to save the lost sheep of the House of Israel, Gentiles also benefitted from it. Three of these women were guilty of specific sexual sins: one was guilty of adultery; one was guilty of prostitution; and one was guilty of incest. Ruth was not herself guilty of sexual sin, but she was a Moabitess. The Moabites originated from the commission of a sexual sin, as they were the product of an incestuous relationship Lot had with one of his daughters (Genesis 19:36-37). The point Matthew hinted at here was that Yeshua came for the purpose of saving sinners.

With this background, the question remains: Why do we have Matthew's genealogy of Joseph anyway? Everyone agrees that Joseph was not the real father of Yeshua. After the division of the kingdom at the death of Solomon, there were two basic requirements for kingship: one was applicable to the throne of Judah in Jerusalem, while the other was applicable to the throne of Israel in Samaria. The requirement for the throne of Judah was that of Davidic descent. No one was allowed to sit on David's throne unless he was a member of the House of David. For that reason, any conspiracy to do away with the House of David was doomed to failure (Isaiah 7-8). The requirement to sit upon the throne of Israel in Samaria was one of prophetic sanction or divine appointment. No one was able to sit on that throne unless he was divinely appointed through prophetic sanction. Anyone who attempted to rule without prophetic sanction was assassinated (1 Kings 11:26-39, 15:28-30, 16:1-4, 11-15, 21:21-29; 2 Kings 9:6-10, 10:29-31, 15:8-12).

With the background of these two Old Testament requirements for kingship and what is stated in the two genealogies, the question of Messiah's right to the throne of David can be resolved. Matthew's genealogy traces the line of Joseph, the step-father of Yeshua. The line is traced from Abraham (verse 2) to David and Solomon (verse 6) and then to King Jeconiah (verse 11), one of the last kings before the Babylonian Captivity. It is the person of Jeconiah, also called Coniah, or Jehoiachin, that is significant in dealing with the genealogy of Matthew because of the special curse pronounced on him:

> [24] "As I live," declares the Lord, "even though Coniah the son of Jehoiakim king of Judah were a signet *ring* on My right hand, yet I would pull you off; [25] and I shall give you over into the hand of those who are seeking your life, yes, into the hand of those whom you dread, even into the hand of Nebuchadnezzar king of Babylon, and into the hand of the Chaldeans. [26] "I shall hurl you and your mother who bore you into another country where you were not born, and there you will die. [27] "But as for the land to which they desire to return, they will not return to it. [28] "Is this man Coniah a despised, shattered jar? Or is he an undesirable vessel? Why have he and his descendants been hurled out And cast into a land that they had not known? [29] "O land, land, land, Hear the word of the Lord! [30] "Thus says the Lord, 'Write this man down childless, A man who will not prosper in his days; For no man of his descendants will prosper Sitting on the throne of David Or ruling again in Judah." '

> Jeremiah 22:24-30 (NASB)

Because of the kind of man Jeconiah was, God pronounced a curse upon him. The content of this curse was that no descendant of his would have any rights to the throne of David. According to the genealogy in Matthew, Joseph was a direct descendant of Jeconiah (verse 16). This means that Joseph, having the blood of Jeconiah in his veins, was not qualified to sit on David's throne. It also means that no son of Joseph would have the right to claim the throne of David. If Yeshua really was the son of Joseph, this would have disqualified Him from sitting upon David's throne.

The point of Matthew's genealogy then is to show why Yeshua could not be king if He was really Joseph's son. For this reason, Matthew starts out with the genealogy and then proceeds with the account of the virgin birth, which from Matthew's viewpoint resolves the Jeconiah problem. So, in essence, Matthew's point is this: If Yeshua was really Joseph's son, He could not claim to sit on David's throne because of the Jeconiah curse. Then Matthew proceeds to show that Yeshua was not truly Joseph's son, for He was born of the virgin Mary (Matthew 1:18-25).

Messiah's Genealogy According to Luke

[23] And when He began His ministry, Yeshua Himself was about thirty years of age, being supposedly *the* son of Joseph, the *son* of Eli, [24] the *son* of Matthat, the *son* of Levi, the *son* of Melchi, the *son* of Jannai, the *son* of Joseph, [25] the *son* of Mattathias, the *son* of Amos, the *son* of Nahum, the *son* of Hesli, the *son* of Naggai, [26] the *son* of Maath, the *son* of Mattathias, the *son* of Semein, the *son* of Josech, the *son* of Joda, [27] the *son* of Joanan, the *son* of Rhesa, the *son* of Zerubbabel, the *son* of Shealtiel, the *son* of Neri, [28] the *son* of Melchi, the *son* of Addi, the *son* of Cosam, the *son* of Elmadam, the *son* of Er, [29] the *son* of Joshua, the *son* of Eliezer, the *son* of Jorim, the *son* of Matthat, the *son* of Levi, [30] the *son* of Simeon, the *son* of Judah, the *son* of Joseph, the *son* of Jonam, the *son* of Eliakim, [31] the *son* of Melea, the *son* of Menna, the *son* of Mattatha, the *son* of Nathan, the *son* of David, [32] the *son* of Jesse, the *son* of Obed, the *son* of Boaz, the *son* of Salmon, the *son* of Nahshon, [33] the *son* of Amminadab, the *son* of Admin, the *son* of Ram, the *son* of Hezron, the *son* of Perez, the *son* of Judah, [34] the *son* of Jacob, the *son* of Isaac, the *son* of Abraham, the *son* of Terah, the *son* of Nahor, [35] the *son* of Serug, the *son* of Reu, the *son* of Peleg, the *son* of Heber, the *son* of Shelah, [36] the *son* of Cainan, the *son* of Arphaxad, the *son* of Shem, the *son* of Noah, the *son* of Lamech, [37] the *son* of Methuselah, the *son* of Enoch, the *son* of Jared, the *son* of Mahalaleel, the *son* of Cainan, [38] the *son* of Enosh, the *son* of Seth, the *son* of Adam, the *son* of God.

Luke 3:23-38 (NASB)

In writing his genealogy, Luke strictly followed Jewish custom and procedure: He did not mention women and did not skip names. The rule against naming women in a Jewish genealogy would raise a question: If you wished to trace a woman's line, how would you do so without using her name? The answer is that you would use the name of her husband. However, this answer presents a problem: How then would you know if the genealogy is that of the wife or the husband? If someone like Luke was doing research and came across a genealogy, how could he tell by looking at the genealogy whether it was that of Mary or that of Joseph, since Joseph's name would be found in both? The answer is quite simple if you are reading the genealogy from a first-century document written in Greek, yet it poses a problem when the New Testament is translated into English. It is not grammatically correct to use the definite article before a proper name in English, yet it was in Greek grammar. Therefore, it was quite allowable to speak of **the** Mary or **the** Joseph. Every single name in Luke's genealogy is preceded by the definite article except one, the name of Joseph, and this allows for how it is rendered into English, *being supposedly* the son *of Joseph, the* son *of Eli* (Lk. 3:23). Someone reading the original language could tell by the missing article that this is not really Joseph's line; it is the line of his wife, Mary. In the Old Testament, there were two cases where a woman's line was traced by the name of her husband: Ezra 2:61 and Nehemiah

7:63. Therefore, Luke's genealogy traces the line of Mary and portrays how Yeshua could claim the throne of David.

Luke begins his genealogy in the reverse order of Matthew, going back from the present into the past. As the line is traced, it returns to the family of David (verses 31-32). However, the son of David involved in this genealogy is not Solomon, but Nathan. The important point here is that Mary was a member of the House of David, totally apart from Jeconiah. Since Yeshua was Mary's son, He too was a member of the House of David, apart from the curse of Jeconiah. Because Luke does not have to deal with the Jeconiah problem, he can begin his account of the life of Yeshua with the virgin birth. Only later does he record the genealogy.

As previously mentioned, one Old Testament requirement for kingship was that of being a member of the House of David apart from Jeconiah. In the case of Yeshua, through Mary, He was a member of the House of David, totally apart from Jeconiah. In this manner, He fulfilled the first requirement of the Old Testament kingship.

However, Yeshua was not the only member of the House of David apart from Jeconiah. There were several other descendants who could claim equality with Yeshua to the throne of David, for they, too, did not have Jeconiah's blood in their veins. At this point, it is important to note the second Old Testament requirement for kingship: divine appointment. Of all the members of the House of David apart from Jeconiah, only one received divine appointment. We read in Luke 1:30-33:

> [30] And the angel said to her, "Do not be afraid, Mary; for you have found favor with God. [31] "And behold, you will conceive in your womb, and bear a son, and you shall name Him Yeshua. [32] "He will be great, and will be called the Son of the Most High; and the Lord God will give Him the throne of His father David; [33] and He will reign over the house of Jacob forever; and His kingdom will have no end." (NASB)

These verses show that Yeshua was divinely appointed to the throne of David. He therefore fulfilled both Old Testament prerequisites to be the legitimate heir to David's throne: He was a member of the House of David, apart from Jeconiah, and He alone received divine appointment to David's throne.

The final question is: On what further grounds can it be said that Luke's account is actually Mary's genealogy? While there is much evidence to support this, it will be necessary to limit it to only two lines of argument.

First, the Talmud itself refers to Yeshua's mother Mary as the daughter of Heli.[25] It is obvious then that in longstanding Jewish tradition, Mary was recognized to be the daughter of Heli.

Second, most Bible translations render Luke 3:23 as follows: "Being the son (as was supposed) of Joseph, the son of Heli . . ." While all the names in Luke's genealogy are preceded

---

[25] *Jerusalem Talmud, Chagigah* 2:4; *Sanhedrin* 23:3; *Babylonian Talmud, Sanhedrin* 44:2.

with the Greek definite article, the name of Joseph is not. Because of this grammatical point, the Greek verse could be translated as follows: "Being the son (as was supposed of Joseph), the son of Heli . . ." In other words, the final parenthesis could be expanded so that the verse reads that, although Yeshua was assumed to be the descendant of Joseph, He was really the descendant of Heli, the father of Mary. As pointed out before, the absence of Mary's name is quite in keeping with the Jewish practices on genealogies, and it was not unusual for a son-in-law to be listed in his wife's genealogy.

The Death of Judas Iscariot

The death of Judas Iscariot is described in two places in the New Testament. The first is Matthew 27:3-10:[26]

> [3] Then Judas, who betrayed him, when he saw that he was condemned, repented himself, and brought back the thirty pieces of silver to the chief priests and elders, [4] saying, I have sinned in that I betrayed innocent blood. But they said, What is that to us? see you (to it). [5] And he cast down the pieces of silver into the sanctuary, and departed; and he went away and hanged himself. [6] And the chief priests took the pieces of silver, and said, It is not lawful to put them into the treasury, since it is the price of blood. [7] And they took counsel, and bought with them the potter's field, to bury strangers in. [8] Wherefore that field was called, the field of blood, unto this day. [9] Then was fulfilled that which was spoken through Jeremiah the prophet, saying, And they took the thirty pieces of silver, the price of him that was priced, whom (certain) of the children of Israel did price; [10] and they gave them for the potter's field, as the Lord appointed me.

The second is Acts 1:18-19:

> [18] (Now this man obtained a field with the reward of his iniquity; and falling headlong, he burst asunder in the midst, and all his bowels gushed out. [19] And it became known to all the dwellers at Jerusalem; insomuch that in their language that field was called Akeldama, that is, The field of blood.)

These verses in Matthew 27 and Acts 1 are frequently quoted by critics of the Bible as being contradictory. Both passages will therefore be discussed in full. However, this is not the only problem which needs to be explained. Of relevance to the subject of Messianic prophecy in the Hebrew Bible is Matthew 27:9-10. These verses create an apparent problem since the book of Jeremiah has nothing to say about thirty pieces of silver. The event is, however, prophesied in Zechariah 11:1-17, a passage which has already been studied.

---

[26] All Scripture quotations are from the ASV of 1901.

Judas' Suicide

In Matthew 27:3, we are told that Judas "repented himself." The Greek word used in the New Testament for salvation repentance is *metanoia*. The Greek word used in Matthew 27:3 is *metamelomai*, which means "remorse" or "regret." Judas is not exercising the *metanoia* repentance that leads to salvation but *metamelomai* repentance which is simply remorse. He returns the thirty pieces of silver, which he was paid for betraying Yeshua, and says, "I have sinned in that I betrayed innocent blood." The chief priests refuse to take the money with the words: "What is that to us? See to it yourself!" Judas then throws the coins into the Temple sanctuary and leaves.

There now arises an apparent contradiction between Matthew 27:5 and Acts 1:18. The former states, "and he went away and hanged himself," while the latter says, "falling headlong he burst asunder." So how did Judas die? By hanging or by falling with his bowels gushing out?

A specific point of rabbinic law clarifies the statement of the book of Acts. By Jewish reckoning of time, a day begins at sundown. Therefore, the first night of an event always comes before the first day of an event. For example, the first night of Passover always comes before the first day of Passover. Jewish families ate their Seder on the first night of Passover. Then at nine o'clock in the morning on the first day of Passover, only the priesthood ate a special Passover sacrifice called the *chagigah.* If, between the first night and the first day of Passover, a dead body was found within the walls of Jerusalem, the city was reckoned as ceremonially unclean. As long as the body was within the walls, the priests could not proceed with the special sacrifice of the first day. If the corpse was thrown over the wall facing the Valley of Hinnom, the city would be reckoned as cleansed. The priesthood could then proceed with the morning Passover sacrifice. When Judas hanged himself, he defiled the city. As long as his body was within the walls, the priests could not proceed with the chagigah sacrifice, so they took it and threw it over the wall facing the Valley of Hinnom. In that fall, Judas's guts gushed out. Therefore, no contradiction exists; Matthew recorded how Judas died, while the book of Acts described what happened to his body after it was found.

What, then, were the chief priests to do with the thirty pieces of silver? By Jewish law, money wrongfully gained could not be put into the Temple treasury: "It is not lawful to put them into the treasury, since it is the price of blood" (Mt. 27:6). The priesthood was legally obligated to either return "the price of blood" to the donor or use it for the public good. In this situation, the first option was impossible since Judas was now dead, so the priests had no choice but to spend the thirty pieces of silver in some way that would benefit the whole community. They purchased a field in the Valley of Hinnom—the same place where Judas had "burst asunder"—for the purpose of burying strangers. The first person to be buried there was Judas himself.

The Matthew account says that the potter's field was bought by the chief priests, but Acts says that "this man," meaning Judas, "obtained a field with the reward of his iniquity." There is no contradiction here. In accordance with the requirements of the law, the field had to be bought posthumously in the name of Judas Iscariot. It is in that sense that Judas obtained a field. Legally, the chief priests were merely viewed as purchasing agents. Matthew states the actual case while the account in Acts deals with the legal ramifications. Therefore, the statements of Matthew and Acts are both true.

Jeremiah's Curse

Another point of confusion arises in Matthew 27:9-10. It is this point which is of importance to our present study of Messianic prophecies in the Hebrew Scriptures. Matthew says:

> [9] Then was fulfilled that which was spoken through Jeremiah the prophet, saying, And they took the thirty pieces of silver, the price of him that was priced, whom (certain) of the children of Israel did price; [10] and they gave them for the potter's field, as the Lord appointed me.

Matthew seems to ascribe these words to Jeremiah, yet this quotation cannot be found anywhere in his book. Rather, as has already been seen, it comes from Zechariah 11. In what sense, then, do the events surrounding Judas' death accord with the prophecy of Jeremiah? The standard conservative response to this is to concede that this might be a scribal error. Others assume that the name "Jeremiah" stood for the whole prophetic section, but there is simply no evidence for this. There is, however, a better explanation.

To understand this, it is necessary to understand both the history of the Valley of Hinnom and Matthew's concern with the divine judgment resulting from the rejection of Yeshua as the Messiah. The historical background is found in two passages of Jeremiah. The first is Jeremiah 7:31-34:

> [31] And they have built the high places of Topheth, which is in the valley of the son of Hinnom, to burn their sons and their daughters in the fire; which I commanded not, neither came it into my mind. [32] Therefore, behold, the days come, says Jehovah, that it shall no more be called Topheth, nor The valley of the son of Hinnom, but The valley of Slaughter: for they shall bury in Topheth, till there be no place (to bury). [33] And the dead bodies of this people shall be food for the birds of the heavens, and for the beasts of the earth; and none shall frighten them away. [34] Then will I cause to cease from the cities of Judah, and from the streets of Jerusalem, the voice of mirth and the voice of gladness, the voice of the bridegroom and the voice of the bride; for the land shall become a waste.

The second is Jeremiah 19:1-15:

> [1] Thus said Jehovah, Go, and buy a potter's earthen bottle, and (take) of the elders of the people, and of the elders of the priests; [2] and go forth unto the valley of the son of Hinnom, which is by the entry of the gate Harsith, and proclaim there the words that I shall tell you; [3] and say, Hear ye the word of Jehovah, O kings of Judah, and inhabitants of Jerusalem: thus says Jehovah of hosts, the God of Israel, Behold, I will bring evil upon this place, which

whosoever hears, his ears shall tingle. [4] Because they have forsaken me, and have estranged this place, and have burned incense in it unto other gods, that they knew not, they and their fathers and the kings of Judah; and have filled this place with the blood of innocents, [5] and have built the high places of Baal, to burn their sons in the fire for burnt-offerings unto Baal; which I commanded not, nor spoke it, neither came it into my mind: [6] therefore, behold, the days come, says Jehovah, that this place shall no more be called Topheth, nor The valley of the son of Hinnom, but The valley of Slaughter. [7] And I will make void the counsel of Judah and Jerusalem in this place; and I will cause them to fall by the sword before their enemies, and by the hand of them that seek their life: and their dead bodies will I give to be food for the birds of the heavens, and for the beasts of the earth. [8] And I will make this city an astonishment, and a hissing; every one that passes thereby shall be astonished and hiss because of all the plagues thereof. [9] And I will cause them to eat the flesh of their sons and the flesh of their daughters; and they shall eat every one the flesh of his friend, in the siege and in the distress, wherewith their enemies, and they that seek their life, shall distress them. [10] Then shall you break the bottle in the sight of the men that go with you, [11] and shall say unto them, Thus says Jehovah of hosts: Even so will I break this people and this city, as one breaks a potter's vessel, that cannot be made whole again; and they shall bury in Topheth, till there be no place to bury. [12] Thus will I do unto this place, says Jehovah, and to the inhabitants thereof, even making this city as Topheth: [13] and the houses of Jerusalem, and the houses of the kings of Judah, which are defiled, shall be as the place of Topheth, even all the houses upon whose roofs they have burned incense unto all the host of heaven, and have poured out drink-offerings unto other gods. [14] Then came Jeremiah from Topheth, whither Jehovah had sent him to prophesy; and he stood in the court of Jehovah's house, and said to all the people: [15] Thus says Jehovah of hosts, the God of Israel, Behold, I will bring upon this city and upon all its towns all the evil that I have pronounced against it; because they have made their neck stiff, that they may not hear my words.

In Jeremiah 19:2, the ASV refers to "the gate Harsith," while most versions translate this as the "Potsherd Gate." Today, it is known as the Dung Gate. It was through this gate that waste material was taken and dumped outside the city. Included in this waste material was the broken and defiled pottery from the Temple. Items of pottery were required for many ceremonial purposes in the Temple. The use of such items was governed by many laws regarding ceremonial purity. This may be what Paul had in mind when he talked about "vessels of honor" as opposed to "vessels of dishonor" in 2 Timothy 2:20-21. All items of pottery required for ritual use were made within the Temple compound so that they could be kept under scrutiny from the time of manufacture to the time of use. Thus, their purity was clearly established. Any items of pottery which were imperfect or broken or unacceptable for any ceremonial reason were removed from the Temple and dumped outside, beyond the city walls. The Potsherd Gate is situated on the south wall of Jerusalem and faces into the Valley of Hinnom at the point where it runs into the Kidron Valley. The juncture of these two valleys is called *Topheth* in the Jeremiah passage and *Akeldama* in Acts. This is the area where rubbish was dumped.

In the days of Jeremiah, the Valley of Hinnom was used by the kings of Judah as a place for burning human sacrifices. Because of the sins of Israel, the Prophet Jeremiah was sent to Topheth to pronounce a curse upon it. He declared that this specific location would become a "valley of Slaughter" (Jer. 19:6) where they would bury and bury "till there be no place to bury" (Jer. 19:11). Centuries later, the leaders of Israel bought a field in the Valley of Hinnom with thirty pieces of silver. They happened to buy the very area of Topheth. When they bought this particular piece of land, they also purchased the curse of Jeremiah that came with it.

The curse was finally fulfilled in A.D. 70 with the massive slaughter of the residents of Jerusalem by the Roman armies, who had been waiting for two years to break through the walls of the city. Suddenly the pent-up frustrations of two years were vented upon the city, and as Jeremiah had predicted, the soldiers slaughtered and slaughtered and buried and buried until there was no more room in the Valley of Hinnom for any more burials.

Of the four Gospel writers, it is Matthew in particular who deals with the impending judgment of A.D. 70. It is in Matthew 12 that we read of the final rejection of Yeshua as the Messiah by the religious leaders. In the subsequent chapters of his Gospel, Matthew records the repeated proclamations of judgment by Yeshua upon "this generation" for their rejection of Him. When Matthew 27:9 refers to Jeremiah, it is not by mistake; it is entirely consistent with the recurring theme of coming judgment. What Matthew is doing here is indicating that the Jewish leaders had purchased for themselves and for the people of Jerusalem the curse which Jeremiah had pronounced upon the Valley of Hinnom and the area of Topheth. Zechariah is quoted as the prophecy of the actual purchase price: thirty pieces of silver.

Appendix 8

Rabbinic Views of Messiah and Isaiah 53

Anyone who sets himself to the task of seeking to know what the Tanach or Old Testament has to say about the coming of the Messiah soon finds himself involved with a seeming paradox. At times one even seems to be faced with an outright contradiction, for the Jewish prophets gave a twofold picture of the Messiah who was to come.

On the one hand, the inquirer will find numerous predictions regarding the Messiah which portray Him as One who is going to suffer humiliation, physical harm, and finally death in a violent manner. This death was stated by the Jewish prophets to be a substitutionary death for the sins of the Jewish people. On the other hand, he will find that the Jewish prophets also spoke of the Messiah coming as a conquering king who will destroy the enemies of Israel and set up the Messianic kingdom of peace and prosperity.

This is the twofold picture the Jewish prophets gave of the Messiah. For centuries past, during the formulation of the *Talmud*, our rabbis made serious studies of Messianic prophecies. They came up with this conclusion: *The prophets spoke of two different Messiahs.*

The Messiah who was to come, suffer, and die was termed Messiah, the Son of Joseph, *Mashiach ben Yoseph*. The second Messiah, who would then come following the first, was termed Messiah, the Son of David, *Mashiach ben David*. This one would raise the first Messiah back to life and establish the Messianic kingdom of peace on earth. That the *Tanach* presents these two lines of Messianic prophecy was something all the early rabbis recognized. The *Tanach* never clearly states that there will be two Messiahs. In fact, many of the paradoxical descriptions are found side by side in the same passages in which, it seems, only one person is meant. But for the early rabbis, the theory of the two Messiahs seemed to be the best answer.

For centuries, Orthodox Judaism held the concept of two Messiahs. Since the Talmudic period, however, in the history of the Jewish people, the Son of David alone was played up in the imaginations of Jewish hearts and minds. The other Messianic figure, Messiah, the Son of Joseph, the suffering one, was ignored. He was there in Jewish theology when needed to explain the suffering Messiah passages contained in the *Tanach*. His existence provided an escape clause when thorny questions were raised. Otherwise, this Messianic figure was largely ignored. Today, few Jews have heard of Him or know of His existence in Jewish theology of days gone by. The One that Jews today know of is the One who is to conquer: Messiah, the Son of David.

The Source of the Paradox

One of the major sources from which the rabbis developed their concept of the suffering Messiah, the Son of Joseph, was Isaiah 53. The present-day bone of contention regarding what the *Tanach* says about the Messiah centers on this chapter. The passage speaks of a servant, the Servant of Jehovah. This Servant undergoes a great deal of suffering, ending in death. The chapter goes on to state that this suffering is a vicarious suffering, that the death is a substitutionary death for sin; He is suffering and dying for the sins of others. The passage goes on to indicate that this Servant is resurrected. The bone of contention is not so much over *what* the passage says, but of *whom* it speaks. Did Isaiah prophesy concerning the Messiah here? Rabbis say that this is the *Christian* interpretation of this passage and not the *Jewish* one. The *Jewish* interpretation, they would say, is that Isaiah is speaking about the people of Israel, the Jewish people suffering in the Gentile world. This is *the* Jewish interpretation the rabbis would say—and it does not speak of the Messiah at all.

But to make the passage speak of the collective body of Israel seems almost to force an interpretation. Taken by itself, the passage seems to have only one individual in mind.

Rabbinic Interpretations of Isaiah 53

But is this conflict merely between the Jewish interpretation and the Christian one? The history of Judaism shows otherwise. The interpretation that Isaiah 53 is referring to the Jewish people is really a recent one. The original interpretation of Isaiah 53 by Jewish rabbis has been that it is speaking of an individual—the Messiah Himself. In fact, the concept of Messiah, the Son of Joseph, comes from this passage. But for a clearer idea of what the old Jewish view of Isaiah 53 was, it would be good to turn to history.

Among the earliest *Targums* are those of Jonathan ben Uzziel dating from the first century A.D. His *Targums* on this passage of Isaiah begin with these words: "Behold my servant Messiah shall prosper . . ."[27] The *Targums* of Jonathan ben Uzziel were heavily quoted by the early rabbis, and he was certainly considered an authority on the Jewish view of Scripture. He definitely considered the Isaiah passage to speak of Messiah. Jonathan ben Uzziel could hardly be accused of adopting the *Christian* interpretation. That he was not alone in this interpretation becomes clear from a quotation from Rabbi Don Yitzchak Abarbanel from about 1500. While he himself did not accept the view that the Isaiah passage referred to the Messiah, he makes a dramatic admission:

> The first question is to ascertain to whom (this Scripture) refers: for the learned among the Nazarenes expound it of the man who was crucified in Jerusalem at the end of the second Temple and who, according to them, was the Son of God and took flesh in the virgin's womb, as is stated in their writings. But Yonathan ben Uzziel interprets it in the

---

[27] *The Fifty–Third Chapter of Isaiah According to the Jewish Interpreters* (New York, Ktav Publishing House, Inc. 1969), p. 5.

Thargum of the future Messiah; *and this is also the opinion of our own learned men in the majority of their Midrashim* . . . (italics added).[28]

In spite of Abarbanel's personal view regarding this passage, he freely admits that the majority of the rabbis of the *Midrashim* took the passage to speak of the Messiah. He thus points out that Jonathan ben Uzziel was not alone in his opinion, but rather this was *the* Jewish view of the period of the *Targumim* and the *Midrashim*.

The *Zohar*, thought to have been written either by Simon bar Yochai in the second century or by a Spanish rabbi in the thirteenth century, makes certain statements which have obvious references to the Isaiah passage:

> There is in the garden of Eden a palace called the Palace of the sons of sickness: this palace the Messiah then enters, and summons every sickness, every pain, and every chastisement of Israel; they all come and rest upon him. And were it not that he had thus lightened them off Israel and taken them upon himself, there had been no man able to bear Israel's chastisements for transgression of the law: and this is that which is written, "Surely our sicknesses he has carried." [29]

The *Zohar* in this quotation quotes from Isaiah 53:4 and referred the passage to the Messiah Himself. The passage further makes Israel distinct from the One referred to in the Isaiah passage. Furthermore, the *Zohar* recognizes the vicariousness and substitutional element in the passage—the Messiah is taking upon Himself the suffering due to Israel for their sins.

More evidence from within the same period is provided by the *Babylonian Talmud*:

> "The Messiah—what is his name? . . . those of the house of Rabbi Yuda the Saint say, 'The sick one,' as it is said, 'Surely he has borne our sicknesses'" (*Sanhedrin* 98b). [30]

Like the *Zohar*, the *Babylonian Talmud* also took the Isaiah passage to refer to the Messiah. Verse 4 is specifically applied to the person of the Messiah Himself.

In *Midrash Thanhumi,* we find:

> Rabbi Nahman says, The word "man" in the passage . . . refers to the Messiah, the son of David, as it is written, "Behold the man whose name is Zemah"; where Yonathan

---

[28] Ibid., p. 153.

[29] Ibid., pp. 14-15

[30] Ibid., p. 7.

interprets, Behold the man Messiah; and so it is said, "A man of pains and known to sickness."[31]

The *Sepher Ha-Gilgalim* sees Isaiah 52:13 as referring to "King Messiah" and says of Him:

"He shall be high and exalted etc.," or, as our Rabbis say, "He shall be higher than Abraham, exceedingly above Adam!" [32]

The *Midrash Cohen*, when dealing with Isaiah 53:5, puts the following words in the mouth of Elijah the prophet:

Elijah says to Messiah: "Bear you the sufferings and wounds wherewith the Almighty doth chastise you for Israel's sin;" and so it is written, 'He was wounded for our transgressions, bruised for our iniquities' until the time when the end should come. [33]

Another *Midrash* on this same passage states:

"All the sufferings are divided into three parts. One part goes to David and the Patriarchs, another to the generation of the rebellion [rebellious Israel] and the third to King Messiah." [34]

Another volume that takes the Isaiah passage to refer to the Messiah is the *Mahsor* or the Prayer Book for the Day of Atonement. One of the many prayers found in this volume is called the *Musaf* Prayer. It was written by Rabbi Eliezer Kalir around the seventh century A.D. Part of the prayer reads as follows:

Messiah our righteousness is departed from us: horror has seized us, and we have none to justify us. He has borne the yoke of our iniquities, and our transgression, and is wounded because of our transgression. He beareth our sins on his shoulder, that he may find pardon for our iniquities. We shall be healed by his wound, at the time that the Eternal will create him (the Messiah) as a new creature. O bring him up from the circle of the earth. Raise him up from Seir, to assemble us the second time on Mount Lebanon, by the hand of Yinnon.[35]

The more this *Yom Kippur* prayer is studied, the more interesting it becomes. The prayer voices fear that the Messiah has departed from the people, which assumes that Messiah had already

---

[31] Ibid., p. 11.

[32] Ibid., p. 395.

[33] Ibid., p. 394.

[34] *Midrash Tehillim* on Psalm 2:7 and *Midrash Samuel* 19.

[35] *Prayer Book for the Day of Atonement* (New York: Hebrew Publishing Company, 1931), p. 239.

come to them and has left them. Furthermore, the Messiah who has departed has suffered vicariously for the people because their sins were placed on Him. Now, after suffering, the Messiah has departed from them; this is the cause of their consternation. Now, the people pray for the Messiah to come back a second time. Much of this prayer is a direct quotation from the Isaiah passage. This shows, therefore, that even as late as the seventh century, the Jewish view was still that this passage had reference to the Messiah.

That this view was still the dominant one among Jewry in the tenth century is seen from the commentary of Yepheth ben 'Ali:

> As to myself, I am inclined, with Benjamin of Nehawend, to regard it as alluding to the Messiah . . . He (the prophet) thus gives us to understand two things: In the first instance, that the Messiah will only reach his highest degree of honor after long and severe trials; and secondly, that these trials will be sent upon him as a kind of sign, so that, if he finds himself under the yoke of misfortunes while remaining pious in his actions, he may know that he is the designated one. . . . The expression "my servant" is applied to the Messiah as it is applied to his ancestor in the verse, "I have sworn to David my servant."[36]

This rabbi, too, recognized the passage to be in reference to the Messiah. He makes the point in accordance with the passage that the Messiah will reach His high state of glory by means of suffering.

Jews in the eleventh century also considered the passage to speak of the Messiah. The *Bereshith Rabbah* of Rabbi Moshe Hadarshan states that the Holy One gave Messiah the opportunity to save souls, but to be severely chastised. We then find these words:

> . . . and forthwith the Messiah accepted the chastisements of love, as it is written, "He was oppressed, and he was afflicted.". . . And when Israel is sinful, the Messiah seeks for mercy upon them, as it is written, "By his stripes we were healed," and, "He carried the sin of many, and made intercession for the transgressors." [37]

By quoting from Isaiah 53, verses 7, 5, and 12 respectively, the *Bereshith Rabbah* draws certain conclusions. One is that the Messiah will save many, but that this salvation of the many is accomplished by means of His suffering. Second, the Messiah's sufferings are viewed to be vicarious in nature, for He is seen as suffering for the sins of Israel.

Another rabbi from the eleventh century, Rabbi Tobiyyah ben Eliezer, in his *Lechah Tova,* has this to say about Isaiah 52:13:

---

[36] *The Fifty –Third Chapter of Isaiah According to the Jewish Interpreters* (New York, Ktav Publishing House, Inc. 1969), pp. 19-20.

[37] Ibid., p. 35.

"And let his kingdom be exalted," in the days of the Messiah, of whom it is said, "Behold my servant shall prosper; he will be high and *exalted*, and lofty exceedingly."[38]

Among the most famous rabbis of this period was Moses ben Maimon, better known as Maimonides or the Rambam. In his writings, he, too, makes the Isaiah passage refer to the Messiah:

What is to be the manner of Messiah's advent, . . . there shall rise up one of whom none have known before, and the signs and wonders which they shall see performed by him will be the proofs of his true origin. . . . And Isaiah speaks . . . of the time when he will appear, without his father or mother or family being known "He came up as a sucker before him, and as a root out of the dry earth, etc." But the unique phenomenon attending his manifestation is, that all the kings of the earth will be thrown into terror at the fame of him . . . that they will lay their hands upon their mouth; in the words of Isaiah, when describing the manner in which the kings will hearken to him, "At him kings will shut their mouth; for that which had not been told them have they seen, and that which they had not heard they have perceived."[39]

The Rambam quotes from Isaiah 53:2 and 52:15 respectively and refers these passages to the Messiah's person. This is his view regarding the entire passage.

Also from the eleventh century, an ancient Jewish writing states concerning the Messiah:

. . . and Messiah, the son of Ephraim, will die there, and Israel will mourn for him. And afterwards the Holy One will reveal to them Messiah, the son of David, whom Israel will desire to stone, saying, You speakest falsely; already is the Messiah slain . . . and so they will despise him, as it is written, "Despised and forlorn of men . . ." [40]

The writer presents the Two-Messiahs theory which was the common Jewish view of his day. One Messiah, the Son of Ephraim or Joseph, will die. After his death will come the Messiah, the Son of David, whom, the rabbi says, Israel will reject. He quotes from Isaiah 53:3 to prove his point.

During this time, we have for the first time in the history of Jewish theology, the idea that this passage was not in reference to the Messiah but in reference to the people of Israel. It was first propounded by Rabbi Shlomo Yitzchaki, better known as Rashi.[41] But since he went contrary to the traditional Jewish view concerning this passage, there was an immediate reaction by other Jewish authorities.

---

[38] Ibid., p. 36.

[39] Ibid., pp. 374-375.

[40] Ibid., p. 32.

[41] Ibid., pp. 37-39.

One rabbi who reacted against the new view propounded by Rashi was Rabbi Moshe Kohen Ibn Crispin of Cordova and Toledo in Spain at about 1350:

. . . I am pleased to interpret it, in accordance with the teaching of our Rabbis, of the King Messiah, and will be careful, so far as I am able, to adhere to the literal sense: thus, possibly, I shall be free from the forced and far-fetched interpretations of which others have been guilty.

. . . This prophecy was delivered by Isaiah at the divine command for the purpose of making known to us something about the nature of the future Messiah, who is to come and deliver Israel, and his life for the day when he arrives at discretion until his advent as a redeemer, in order that if any one should arise claiming to be himself the Messiah, we may reflect, and look to see whether we can observe in him any resemblance to the traits described here: if there is any such resemblance, then we may believe that he is the Messiah our righteousness; but if not, we cannot do so.[42]

The "forced and far-fetched" interpretation that Rabbi Crispin referred to is the interpretation of Rashi that this does not refer to the Messiah but to the people of Israel. This rabbi reacts against this interpretation and insists that this Isaiah passage refers to Messiah and that it was written for the purpose of helping identify the Messiah so that He can be recognized when He comes.

In the sixteenth century, we have the words of Rabbi Saadyah Ibn Danan of Grenada, c. 1500:

One of these, Rabbi Joseph ben Kaspi, was led so far as to say that those who expounded it of the Messiah, who is shortly to be revealed, gave occasion to the heretics to interpret it of Jesus. May God, however, forgive him for not having spoken the truth! Our Rabbis, the doctors of the Thalmud, deliver their opinions by the power of prophecy, possessing a tradition concerning the principles of interpretation . . . alludes covertly to the King Messiah. [43]

This Rabbi also reacts against the interpretation that the Isaiah passage refers to the people of Israel. He demands that Jewish interpreters return to the Talmudic interpretation that this refers to the Messiah. He also helps to shed some light as to the reason why many were switching over to the new view. It was during this period that many debates broke out between rabbis and Christians, and the latter used Isaiah 53 to show that Yeshua was the Messiah. Because of the force of their arguments, as a defense, rabbis began to refer the passage to Israel.

Also from the second half of the sixteenth century are the writings of Rabbi Moshe Le Sheich, or Al Shech, who was a disciple of Joseph Caro, author of the *Shulchan Aruch*. He, too, demanded that all Jewish interpreters return to the more traditional interpretation when he wrote:

---

[42] Ibid., pp. 99-102.

[43] Ibid., p. 203.

"... our Rabbis with one voice accept and affirm the opinion that the prophet is speaking of the King Messiah, and we shall ourselves also adhere to the same view ..." [44]

The writings of Rabbi Eliyyah de Vidas are from about the same time. He wrote the following c. 1575 concerning Isaiah 53:5:

"But he was wounded for our transgressions, bruised for our iniquities," the meaning of which is that since the Messiah bears our iniquities which produce the effect of his being bruised, it follows that whoso will not admit that the Messiah thus suffers for our iniquities, must endure and suffer for them himself. [45]

This rabbi, too, refers the passage to the Messiah and states that the Messiah will suffer vicariously, for He suffers for the sins of the people. The Rabbi goes on to say that those who refuse to believe and accept the vicarious suffering for sin which the Messiah bore are doomed, according to the passage, to suffer for their own sins.

Even in the seventeenth century, there was still reaction against Rashi's interpretation of the Isaiah passage, as the writing of Rabbi Naphtali ben Asher Altschuler (c. 1650) shows:

"I will now proceed to explain these verses of our own Messiah, who, God willing, will come speedily in our days! I am surprised that Rashi and Rabbi David Kimchi have not, with the Targum, applied them to the Messiah likewise." [46]

By the nineteenth century, the new view propounded by Rashi and followed by Rabbi David Kimchi had won over the older view of the rabbis. But the victory was not total, for there was still a reaction against it. Herz Homburg, in his *Korem*, written in 1818, wrote:

"The fact is, that it refers to the King Messiah, who will come in the latter days, when it will be the Lord's good pleasure to redeem Israel from among the different nations of the earth." [47]

To interpret Isaiah 53 as speaking of Messiah is not non-Jewish. In fact, if we are to speak of the *traditional* Jewish interpretation, it would be that the passage speaks of the Messiah. The first one to expound the view that this referred to Israel rather than the Messiah was Shlomo Yizchaki, better known as Rashi (c. 1040-1105). He was followed by David Kimchi (1160-1235). But this was to go contrary to all rabbinic teaching of that day and of the preceding one thousand years. Today, Rashi's view has become dominant in Jewish and rabbinic theology. But that is not *the* Jewish

---

[44] Ibid., p. 258.

[45] Ibid., p. 386.

[46] Ibid., p. 319.

[47] Ibid., p. 400.

view. Nor is it the *traditional* Jewish view. Those closer to the time of the original writings and who had less contact with the Christian apologists interpreted it as speaking of the Messiah.

Appendix 9

Brit Chadasha Usage

The Gospels in the *Brit Chadasha* (New Testament) make it very clear that Yeshua's death took the apostles by surprise. Their confusion arose largely because of their lack of knowledge concerning the full program of the Messiah. They had expected Yeshua to overthrow their enemies and establish His kingdom on earth. They were very familiar with the prophecies concerning this aspect of the Messianic program. What they had failed to grasp was that Messiah had to come twice: first to suffer, and then later in victory. The purpose of His first coming was quite different from the purpose of His second coming.

In order to substantiate the purpose of His first coming, Yeshua does not ask His disciples to simply believe, but refers them back to the authority of their own Hebrew Scriptures—what is now called the Old Testament. One example of this is Luke 24:25-27, 44-48 (NASB):

> [25] And He said to them, "O foolish men and slow of heart to believe in all that the prophets have spoken! [26] "Was it not necessary for the Messiah to suffer these things and to enter into His glory?" [27] And beginning with Moses and with all the prophets, He explained to them the things concerning Himself in all the Scriptures.

> [44] Now He said to them, "These are My words which I spoke to you while I was still with you, that all things which are written about Me in the Law of Moses and the Prophets and the Psalms must be fulfilled." [45] Then He opened their minds to understand the Scriptures, [46] and He said to them, "Thus it is written, that the Messiah should suffer and rise again from the dead the third day; [47] and that repentance for forgiveness of sins should be proclaimed in His name to all the nations, beginning from Jerusalem. [48] "You are witnesses of these things."

Here, on the Emmaus Road, in one of His resurrection appearances, Yeshua reproaches His disciples for not knowing *all* that the Prophets spoke—including the prophecies concerning His suffering and death. They had no difficulty believing the prophecies which presented Messiah as a reigning king who would restore Israel to her former glory. They had great difficulty in accepting those prophecies which foretold of Messiah's suffering and death. The fact that the disciples were so distraught by Yeshua's arrest and execution shows that they were in a state of unbelief. We are told that Yeshua began with the Law of Moses, moved on to the Prophets, and went through all of the Hebrew Scriptures, showing the disciples all of the things concerning Messiah. He was, then, able to prove that His death and resurrection were perfectly in accordance with Scripture and essential to His work—proving His Messiahship.

From the most ancient sources to modern rabbis, Jewish teachers have always divided the Scriptures into three sections: the Law, the Prophets, and the Writings. We see here (particularly in verse 44) that Yeshua does the same. The Writings are sometimes referred to only as "the Psalms," Psalms being the first book in the Writings. Yeshua systematically covers all Scripture, revealing to His disciples all things concerning Himself. "All things" include prophecies of the second coming (which are still to be fulfilled), as well as prophecies concerning the first coming (which were being fulfilled at the time that Yeshua was speaking). By bringing together prophecies from all three sections of Jewish Scripture, Yeshua was able to prove that it was necessary for Him to be killed, buried, and raised again on the third day.

Yeshua's followers learned their lesson well. Later on in the New Testament, after Yeshua's ascension, we see that the disciples repeatedly justified and authenticated Yeshua's Messiahship to Gentiles as well as Jews using only the Hebrew Scriptures. The first example is Acts 8:26-39:

> [26] But an angel of the Lord spoke to Philip saying, "Arise and go south to the road that descends from Jerusalem to Gaza." (This is a desert road.) [27] And he arose and went; and behold, there was an Ethiopian eunuch, a court official of Candace, queen of the Ethiopians, who was in charge of all her treasure; and he had come to Jerusalem to worship. [28] And he was returning and sitting in his chariot, and was reading the prophet Isaiah. [29] And the Spirit said to Philip, "Go up and join this chariot." [30] And when Philip had run up, he heard him reading Isaiah the prophet, and said, "Do you understand what you are reading?" [31] And he said, "Well, how could I, unless someone guides me?" And he invited Philip to come up and sit with him. [32] Now the passage of Scripture which he was reading was this:
>
> > "HE WAS LED AS A SHEEP TO SLAUGHTER; AND AS A LAMB BEFORE ITS SHEARER IS SILENT, SO HE DOES NOT OPEN HIS MOUTH. [33] "IN HUMILIATION HIS JUDGMENT WAS TAKEN AWAY; WHO SHALL RELATE HIS GENERATION? FOR HIS LIFE IS REMOVED FROM THE EARTH."
>
> [34] And the eunuch answered Philip and said, "Please tell me, of whom does the prophet say this? Of himself, or of someone else?" [35] And Philip opened his mouth, and beginning from this Scripture he preached Yeshua to him. [36] And as they went along the road they came to some water; and the eunuch said, "Look! Water! What prevents me from being baptized?" [37] [And Philip said, "If you believe with all your heart, you may." And he answered and said, "I believe that Yeshua Messiah is the Son of God."] [38] And he ordered the chariot to stop; and they both went down into the water, Philip as well as the eunuch; and he baptized him. [39] And when they came up out of the water, the Spirit of the Lord snatched Philip away; and the eunuch saw him no more, but went on his way rejoicing. (NASB)

This is the famous story of the Ethiopian eunuch who is reading the prophecy of Isaiah 53. Philip is sent to him to explain the meaning of the prophecy. We read in verse 35 that "beginning from this Scripture" Philip "preached Yeshua to him." Beginning with Isaiah 53, Philip is able to present the Messiahship of Yeshua. The Ethiopian eunuch is so impressed by the way in which Yeshua's suffering and death fits Isaiah's description of the Messianic Person that he is convinced and immediately becomes a believer.

The second example is Acts 17:1-4:

[1] Now when they had traveled through Amphipolis and Apollonia, they came to Thessalonica, where there was a synagogue of the Jews. [2] And according to Paul's custom, he went to them, and for three Sabbaths reasoned with them from the Scriptures, [3] explaining and giving evidence that the Messiah had to suffer and rise again from the dead, and saying, "This Yeshua whom I am proclaiming to you is the Messiah." [4] And some of them were persuaded and joined Paul and Silas, along with a great multitude of the God—fearing Greeks and a number of the leading women. (NASB)

Here, we see that Paul's procedure in the synagogue was to expound on the Scriptures, meaning the *Torah*, the *Nevi'im*, and the *K'tuvim*, and specifically the Messianic prophecies. Having portrayed the kind of Messiah these Scriptures demanded, he was then able to show how Yeshua perfectly fits the Messianic mold of the Tanach.

The third example is Acts 18:27-28:

[27] And when he wanted to go across to Achaia, the brethren encouraged him and wrote to the disciples to welcome him; and when he had arrived, he helped greatly those who had believed through grace; [28] for he powerfully refuted the Jews in public, demonstrating by the Scriptures that Yeshua was the Messiah. (NASB)

Here, we see that Apollos employed the same method of debating with the Jewish leaders. He went back to the Scriptures and proved how Yeshua satisfied the requirements of Hebrew prophecy.

One final example of this can be seen in Acts 28:23:

[23] And when they had set a day for him, they came to him at his lodging in large numbers; and he was explaining to them by solemnly testifying about the kingdom of God, and trying to persuade them concerning Yeshua, from both the Law of Moses and from the Prophets, from morning until evening. (NASB)

As Paul debated here with the Jewish leaders in Rome, his evidence once again does not rest on Matthew, Mark, Luke, or John but rather the Hebrew Scriptures. There is, in fact, no mention of the Gospels as they had not yet been written. In this particular situation, Paul rests his case exclusively on the Torah and the Prophets. He excludes the Writings probably because of Jewish beliefs concerning the inspiration of Scripture: Judaism teaches that all of Scripture is inspired by God, but that there are three levels of inspiration. The Law is said to be of greatest authority, as it is the very words of God dictated directly to a human scribe. The Prophets are of lesser authority, being God's messages spoken through the mouths of men. The Writings are considered to be of least authority, as they are reckoned to be the words of men whose thinking was guided by God. Judaism holds a very high view of the Law and the Prophets, but does not have a very high view of the inspiration of the Writings. Paul, therefore, restricts himself to using the words of God given in the Law and the Prophets. Yeshua used all three sections of the Tanach because as far as He and the apostles were concerned, all of the Hebrew Scriptures were of equal validity.

Sadly, there are very few people today who can do what the apostles did and present the entire Messianic program exclusively from the Hebrew Scriptures. It is necessary to show the kind of Messiah the Hebrew Scriptures demanded before moving on to the New Testament to prove how Yeshua perfectly fulfilled all of the scriptural requirements.

The Four Types of Messianic Prophecy

When dealing with Messianic prophecy it is very important to understand that there are four categories of Messianic prophecy, and these distinctions are essential. The four categories are:

1. First coming only (e.g., Micah 5:2)

2. Second coming only (e.g., Isaiah 63:1-6)

3. Both first and second coming (e.g., Zechariah 9:9-10)

4. The entire redemptive career (e.g., Psalm 110)

Some prophecies are very straightforward and deal exclusively with either the first coming (category 1) or the second coming (category 2). Other prophecies are more complicated. The third category of prophecies includes verses that blend the first and second comings together in such a way as to negate or conceal the period of time in between. It becomes necessary to study other parallel Scriptures in order to see the distinction. Zechariah 9:9-10 is a good example of this: Verse nine deals with the first coming, and verse 10 deals with the second. These verses alone do not distinguish between the two, but this is clarified by other passages as we were able to see in this study. The fourth category refers to passages which cover the entire Messianic program and include four elements: first coming, interval of time, second coming, and the Messianic kingdom.

In this study, we covered the first category in its entirety. The second category is a subject in its own right and is therefore fully covered in the author's *The Footsteps of the Messiah: A Study of the Sequence of Prophetic Events*. The third and fourth categories of prophecy were touched on only insofar as they relate to the first coming of Messiah.

Importance

A study of this kind has two main benefits: It prevents over-simplifications and helps us understand second coming prophecies.

The relationship between the Old and New Testaments and the nature of Old Testament faith are often over-simplified. For example, a frequently-used cliché is that "Old Testament saints looked forward to the death of Messiah while New Testament saints look back to the death of Messiah." If that were true, then why were the disciples so astounded at Yeshua's death? We tend to read back into the Old Testament a level of New Testament understanding which did not exist in those days. As we follow the progressive revelation of Scripture, we become more aware of the limitations on understanding at various stages of Israel's history. In particular, there would be no way of knowing from the five books of the Law alone that Messiah was to die. This was not revealed until circa 700 B.C. by the Prophet Isaiah. The Law presents Messiah mainly in terms of a king and redeemer but not as a dying savior. It is not true that Old Testament saints looked forward to the death of Messiah; for most of Old Testament history, they did not know that such an event was to happen. We should be careful not to over-simplify the content of faith for Old Testament believers.

Another example is the common saying that "Yeshua fulfilled more than 300 prophecies at His first coming." Those who make this claim never produce a list of such 300 prophecies. This study covered every first coming prophecy, and they numbered well below 300. However, more than enough prophecies were fulfilled to fully authenticate the Messiahship of Yeshua.

Understanding the first coming prophecies and the ways in which they were fulfilled helps us to understand and correctly interpret the second coming prophecies. Because all first coming prophecies were fulfilled in a literal way and not "allegorically" or "spiritually," we should expect the second coming prophecies to be fulfilled in the same way.

Jewish Objections to Yeshua

The more recent articles written by rabbis stating their objections to Yeshua all judge Him on the basis of His conformity, or lack of it, to modern Judaism. Yeshua is all too often judged by twentieth-century Judaism rather than first-century Judaism or Biblical Judaism. The question, however, can never be, "Is Yeshua the Messiah in accordance with Judaism today?" Judaism today is too fragmented with Messianic views ranging from "He will come" to "What Messiah? There will be no Messiah!" The fact is that most Jews today do not believe in any Messiah at all. The real issue is, "Is Yeshua the Messiah of Old Testament Judaism?"

Judaism today is very different from the Judaism of the Old Testament or even the Judaism of Yeshua's day. Modern Judaism is certainly not the "father of Christianity." At best, it is its brother, with Biblical Judaism being the father of both. If one were to read the books of the Old Testament and compare their teachings with the Judaism of today, one could almost conclude that modern Judaism is a completely new religion! Certainly, there are similarities between Judaism then and now. Yet similarities exist between various religions, and they are, nevertheless, distinct one from another. The real issue is whether Yeshua is the Messiah of the Old Testament. The Messiahship of Yeshua must stand or fall on no other criterion than His fulfillment of the Messianic prophecies of the Scriptures.

What Kind of God Do You Have?

Some Jewish objections to the Messiahship of Yeshua rest on questioning the virgin birth and His resurrection from the dead. Objections to these two matters are, however, not the real issue in themselves. The real issue is what kind of God one believes in. The question is not if things like the virgin birth or the resurrection from death are even possible. From a strictly human viewpoint, they are not. The real question is, "Can God do such things?" If He cannot, He is not much of a God. But if God is God, and all that this title infers, includes, and indicates, He can do anything He wants to do. The only possible limits to God are the limits He places on Himself.

If God is all powerful, things like the virgin birth and the resurrection are easy for Him to accomplish. It is an amazing inconsistency to allow that God has created the heavens and the earth and then to doubt His ability to bring about a virgin birth. If He can create the wonder and vastness of the universe and all the complexity of the single cell, the virgin birth and the resurrection are very simple matters. For a Jew who believes in God, there is no reason to doubt the miracle of the virgin birth. The real question is, "Did it happen with the birth of Yeshua?" The

Old Testament said that it *would* happen with the Messiah. The New Testament said that it *did* happen with Yeshua.

Yeshua Didn't Bring Peace, Did He?

The most common objection one hears to the Messiahship of Yeshua is this: He could not be the Messiah since He did not bring peace. Well, since He was not accepted, He could not very well bring peace, could He? Furthermore, the purpose of the Messiah's first coming, or as the early rabbis would have it, the purpose of the coming of the first Messiah, Messiah the Son of Joseph, was not to bring peace but to suffer and die. Peace would come through the coming of the second Messiah, Messiah the Son of David, or as the New Testament would have it, by the second coming of the Messiah.

The Messiahship of Yeshua must first be judged on whether He did suffer and die for sin, and then on whether those who believed in Him received their justification and forgiveness of sins. That He suffered and died for the sins of Israel is the testimony of the eyewitness accounts we have in the New Testament. That Jews have been receiving and experiencing the forgiveness of their sins through faith in the substitutionary death of Yeshua has been testified by many. Both Talmudic Judaism and the New Testament agree that there would be one coming of a Messiah to suffer and die, which would precede the coming of the Messiah to bring peace. The point of difference is the former's claim of two different Messiahs, and the latter's claim of one and the same person, Yeshua.

While it is true that Yeshua did not bring world peace, it was not the purpose of the Messiah's first coming. Therefore, the lack of peace in this world is not a valid argument against His Messiahship. For Yeshua will yet come again and will yet bring peace.

Christians Hate the Jews!

Another objection to the Messiahship of Yeshua is not so much an objection against Yeshua Himself as it is against the way His name has been used throughout Jewish history. For have not Christians persecuted and killed Jews in His name for centuries? Has not the cross been a symbol of death to Jews? Has not the church issued discriminatory laws against the Jews? Has not the name of Yeshua been used to torch Jewish homes and bodies? Has not baptism been used in forced conversions to Christianity and as an excuse to separate Jewish children from their families? All of this is true and so is a lot more. It may be questioned whether those who perpetrated these atrocities were really Christians, but they certainly called themselves that.

But is all that a valid argument against the Messiahship of Yeshua Himself? Can Yeshua be held responsible for the way in which His name has been used or misused by those who profess to follow Him?

In the post-Maccabean period, a man by the name of John Hyrcanus became the ruler of Israel. Israel at that time was fighting for independence from those who would take it from her, such as the Hellenistic Syrians. Among John Hyrcanus' many acts of war was forcing people to convert to Judaism—if they did not, they were killed. When he captured the Greek cities, the residents were given the choice of converting to Judaism or dying by the sword. The entire Edomite nation, then known as the Idumeans, were forcefully converted to Judaism; many who refused died by the sword. Many acts of atrocity were thus committed in the name of Judaism.

Now suppose that many of those who lost their families and loved ones by these tactics began going on an all-out campaign against Moses, whom they would consider the founder of Judaism. Suppose because of all these acts of forced conversion and death, the Greeks and Edomites rejected all that Moses had to say. Suppose that Judaism would be rejected because of the horrible things perpetrated in its name. This would all be unfair, for just because John Hyrcanus used the name of Moses and killed in the name of Judaism did not mean that Moses or Judaism itself taught that such things ought to be done. Indeed, it would be very unfair to reject Judaism strictly on the grounds of the way some used the name of Judaism to accomplish their own desire.

In more recent history, an Orthodox Jew assassinated Yitzchak Rabin, the Prime Minister of Israel, in the name of Judaism. Is Moses to be rejected because of what a fanatic did in the name of Judaism? Obviously not!

By the same token, it would be very wrong to reject the Messiahship of Yeshua strictly on the grounds of the way some have used His name, for Yeshua and the New Testament do not sanction any such acts against the Jews. The New Testament, which taught the Gentiles that "salvation is of the Jews" (John 4:22), forbade the persecution of the Jews. So if some who erroneously called themselves Christians used the name of Yeshua for their own selfish war against the Jews, it still did not make it a Christ-like action. For if the Yeshua of the New Testament is the true Messiah, such actions are as foreign to His character as could be possible. Hence, the Messiahship of Yeshua must be based on who He claimed to be. Does He fit the mold of the Messiah of the Old Testament? He must be accepted or rejected on this ground alone, not by teachings that were clouded or perverted by those who sought a pretense to persecute the Jews.

Theological Objections

Theological objections to Yeshua by rabbinic authorities have so repeatedly attacked the same areas as to become stereotyped. These will usually center on the question of the virgin birth, the claim of Yeshua to be the Son of God, and the fact that Jews cannot believe that a man can become God. Objections to the virgin birth have already been dealt with, in the study of Isaiah 7:14. The kind of God one believes in is still an issue.

As to the claim of Yeshua to be the Son of God, one objection is this: "The New Testament knows Jesus as the son of God and as Messiah. Judaism, however, does not acknowledge a son of

God who was set apart and elevated above other human beings. The Jewish conviction is that all men are equal before God and no mortal can claim divinity." This is an example of how the Messiahship of Yeshua is judged purely on the basis of modern Judaism. The thought is that Yeshua could not be the Messiah since Judaism does not acknowledge a Son of God to begin with. The author of this objection would have been more honest had he said that Judaism, as he knows it—which is only modern Judaism—does not acknowledge a Son of God. In the case of Reform Judaism, there would be no Messiah to begin with. The writer effectively ignores centuries of Jewish theological treatments that certainly do view the Messiah as being a Son of God. Had the writer taken the time to look at the early rabbinic interpretations of Psalm 2, it would have taught him not to make such a rash statement. The Old Testament, which is the basis of Judaism, did teach that God would have a Son. That Son is the Messiah Himself. The issue is not whether Judaism acknowledges it. The issue is whether the Bible teaches it, and the Old Testament certainly teaches it loud and clear.

The third objection is the fact that Jews cannot believe that a man can become God. And indeed, it is very true that a man cannot become God. No man can claim divinity. This is where modern Judaism has misconstrued the teachings of the New Testament. The New Testament never claimed that Yeshua was a man who became God. This is heresy! It goes contrary to Judaism, of any form: biblical, rabbinic, or otherwise. It also goes contrary to the Christian faith. Neither the New Testament nor Yeshua ever taught that there was a man who became God. The New Testament claims the reverse: It was God who became a man in the person of Yeshua of Nazareth. If God became a man, this man would certainly be superior to other men. He would now be the God-Man. Certainly, Judaism does not dare claim that God cannot become a man if He wanted to. The God of Biblical Judaism is all powerful: God can do anything He wants to. If there is anything God cannot do, He is less than God. So, the real question is: "Did God choose to become a man?" Not, "Can He?" The claim is that God became a man. It is amazing how so many rabbinic writings about Yeshua refuse to discuss this very point and insist on discussing how a man could become God.

Other common objections also miss the real point. One such objection is the fact that Yeshua forgave sins, which is something only God can do. Again, this is true—only God can forgive sins. But if Yeshua is the God-Man, the forgiving of sins would be part of His authority.

Another objection of this nature centers around the fact that Yeshua performed His miracles in His own name. This objection, as voiced by one Jewish writer, runs as follows: "The Hebrew prophets, too, performed miracles; but they stressed that they did so as God's instruments. When Elijah revived the son of the widow, he did not say that he had wrought that miracle as Jesus did on a similar occasion." In answering this objection, we should carefully note what Yeshua said in the Gospels: He claimed many times that He was doing His miracles by the power and authority of the Spirit of God. It is true that the prophets did miracles and gave God the credit, but again, Messiah was not going to be just another man or just another prophet. Rabbinic theories taught that the Messiah, because He had the name of God Himself, will be able to do things in His own name. That is why the Messiah kept playing such a prominent role in rabbinic theology. That is why the Jewish people throughout the centuries, before modern liberalism crept into Judaism, continually looked forward to the coming of the Jewish Messiah. The Messiah would have such authority and such power that He would be able to accomplish great things in His own name. Yeshua claimed to be that Messiah and so should, in fact, have been able to do those things in His own name. As the author above admits, Yeshua did accomplish those things in His own name. By doing so in His own name, He substantiates His Messiahship rather than disproving it.

Poor Research

Other Jewish objections to Yeshua show some very poor research with regard to what the New Testament actually says. One example reads like this: "Judaism . . . is committed to a good life and discourages asceticism. Jesus, however, claimed that His kingdom was not of this world: He pointed to poverty as the mark of piety." The fact is that Yeshua discouraged asceticism. He did encourage moderation in all things. The very purpose of the coming of Yeshua was to provide enjoyment of life. Yeshua said, "I have come that you might have life and that you might have it more abundantly" (John 10:10). He never at any time made poverty the mark of piety. He often talked against the false use of riches, but He never made wealth itself a sin or poverty a virtue. The message of Messiah was not: "Be good now so you can go to heaven later." His message was: "Get right with God so you can enjoy the kind of life God wants you to enjoy now, as well as later in heaven."

Another example involving poor research of the New Testament is one that reads as follows: "Judaism exalts the family, integrated into a larger community. Jesus applauded celibacy and disparaged family ties as a barrier to religious dedication." Actually, Yeshua did not encourage celibacy. This type of life, Yeshua said, was just for the very few; it was not a mark of higher spirituality. His main point was correct priorities. His teaching was this: Every person must put God first and his family second. This is hardly going contrary to Judaism.

Not only do some objections show poor research of the New Testament, they also show poor research of the Old Testament, as is clear in the following case: "The Hebrew Bible emphasized unity of mankind and the prophets spoke as God's messengers to all nations and not primarily to his own people. Jesus, however, emphasized that he was sent only to the lost sheep of the house of Israel. He refused to heal the daughter of a Canaanite woman. Judaism does not discriminate against non-Jews." One wonders if this writer ever read the Old Testament or even knows about his own Judaism. Judaism forbids intermarriage, and that is a form of discrimination against non-Jews. Furthermore, the prophets emphasized no such things as the writer claims. By far, the great majority of the Hebrew prophets did not give their messages to Gentiles but exclusively to the Jewish people. Over and over again, the prophets stressed the point that the Jews are God's people in a peculiar way and distinct from the Gentiles. There were messages that were for the Gentile nations, but these were invariably messages of judgment because of Gentile mistreatment of the Jewish people. One need only read the Prophets one time to see this.

The writer is also wrong about Yeshua's dealings with the Canaanite woman. Yeshua did not refuse to heal the daughter; in fact, He goes right ahead and does heal her! (Matthew 15:21-28.) The point that Yeshua wanted to make to the Canaanite woman was that the Messiah's task was primarily to make Himself known to the Jews, not the Gentiles. Gentiles would also be blessed, but Messiah's first priority was to the Jewish people. The same is true for the Jewish prophets.

It would be futile to go on and on, for many of the objections to the Messiahship of Yeshua are based on preconceived notions as to what the New Testament claims rather than on what it actually states. The theological questions can best be answered after determining the kind of God one believes in. Is God limited as to what He can do or can He do anything in accordance with His power? Then it can be asked: Did God become a man in Yeshua or did He not? The Old Testament, not modern Judaism, must be the standard by which it is decided whether Yeshua is the Messiah or not. This is a question that no individual can honestly answer unless he makes his own personal investigation. Rejection on the basis of preconceived notions, because of the way one has been led to believe, is to be dishonest with oneself.

The Majority and the Minority

A different kind of objection is raised repeatedly: If Yeshua was the Messiah, why don't the rabbis believe in Him? Or it may be stated like this: If Yeshua is the Messiah, how come very few Jews believe this? The implication here is that something cannot be true for the Jew unless most rabbis or most Jewish people accept it to be true. In other words, the implication is that truth is determined by majority vote.

However, truth is not determined by majority vote. If something is true, it is going to be true if everybody believes it or if nobody believes it. Even if everybody believes that the earth is flat and it is possible to fall off the edge of the earth, it will still not make it true. Truth just cannot be determined that way. Truth is something that is absolute; it never changes. It is irrelevant how many people believe the truth. It is still true because of what it is in itself.

But some will say that if the Jewish religious leaders have rejected something, it certainly cannot be true religiously speaking, at least not for the Jews. If Yeshua really was the Messiah, maybe not all Jews would have believed, but certainly a great many should have, especially Jewish leaders. As a matter of fact, a great many of the Jews did believe that Yeshua was the Messiah, including Jewish leaders. No, it was not the majority. The majority rejected His Messiahship. But a great many did accept His Messiahship. Again, just because the majority did not accept Yeshua as the Messiah, does not disqualify Him from being the One.

As we look at our sacred history, we will discover over and over again that it was always the minority of Jews who obeyed the revelation of God. The prophets called the small group of believers the remnant of Israel. It was always the remnant of Israel that accepted what God had to say through His prophets. The majority has always rejected it, including the religious leaders of that day.

Let's look at an example that comes from the time of Elijah the Prophet. As we look into the life of Elijah, we find the prophet very depressed because the people would not return to the God of Israel and worship Him. Elijah's depression caused him to run away to Mount Sinai, wishing he could die.

⁹ Then he came there to a cave, and lodged there; and behold, the word of the LORD came to him, and He said to him, "What are you doing here, Elijah?" ¹⁰ And he said, "I have been very zealous for the LORD, the God of hosts; for the sons of Israel have forsaken Your covenant, torn down Your altars and killed Your prophets with the sword. And I alone am left; and they seek my life, to take it away." ¹¹ So He said, "Go forth, and stand on the mountain before the LORD." And behold, the LORD was passing by! And a great and strong wind was rending the mountains and breaking in pieces the rocks before the LORD; but the LORD was not in the wind. And after the wind an earthquake, but the LORD was not in the earthquake. ¹² And after the earthquake a fire, but the LORD was not in the fire; and after the fire a sound of a gentle blowing. ¹³ And it came about when Elijah heard it, that he wrapped his face in his mantle, and went out and stood in the entrance of the cave. And behold, a voice came to him and said, "What are you doing here, Elijah?" ¹⁴ Then he said, "I have been very zealous for the LORD, the God of hosts; for the sons of Israel have forsaken Your covenant, torn down Your altars and killed Your prophets with the sword. And I alone am left; and they seek my life, to take it away." ¹⁵ And the LORD said to him, "Go, return on your way to the wilderness of Damascus, and when you have arrived, you shall anoint Hazael king over Aram; ¹⁶ and Jehu the son of Nimshi you shall anoint king over Israel; and Elisha the son of Shaphat of Abel-meholah you shall anoint as prophet in your place. ¹⁷ "And it shall come about, the one who escapes from the sword of Hazael, Jehu shall put to death, and the one who escapes from the sword of Jehu, Elisha shall put to death. ¹⁸ "Yet I will leave 7,000 in Israel, all the knees that have not bowed to Baal and every mouth that has not kissed him."

1 Kings 19:9-18 (ASV)

So completely was the nation of Israel given over to idolatry in Elijah's day, that the prophet feels that he is all alone (verses 10 and 14). But God answers him and says, "I will leave 7,000 in Israel, all the knees that have not bowed to Baal and every mouth that has not kissed him" (verse 18). The answer of God to Elijah is that there are seven thousand others who have stayed true to the God of Israel. Now notice: of the hundreds of thousands of Jews living in the nation of Israel in Elijah's day, only seven thousand believed the Prophet Elijah. Certainly, here most the Jewish leaders were wrong, and, again, it was the remnant who believed.

When we come to the Major Prophets, we find the same thing to be true. Even Isaiah, the prince of all the prophets, said in his very first chapter:

[9] Unless the LORD of hosts Had left us a few survivors, We would be like Sodom, We would be like Gomorrah.

Isaiah 1:9 (NASB)

Isaiah, too, recognized that there is only a remnant, a small minority of Jewish people, which obeys the prophets. The majority are in disobedience. Isaiah also testifies that if it was not for this remnant, God would have been so disgusted with Israel that He would have destroyed us completely as He destroyed Sodom and Gomorrah. Jeremiah and Ezekiel and all the other prophets had to constantly go against the greater majority, trying to maintain the truth of God.

Rabbi Saul, who was a Jewish believer from the first century, recognized that the very same thing was happening in his day. It was the minority of Jews who were accepting the Messiah Yeshua. In one of his letters to a congregation in Rome, Saul recounts the story of Elijah and applies it to his day. He says:

[2] God has not rejected His people whom He foreknew. Or do you not know what the Scripture says in the passage about Elijah, how he pleads with God against Israel? [3] "LORD, THEY HAVE KILLED YOUR PROPHETS, THEY HAVE TORN DOWN YOUR ALTARS, AND I ALONE AM LEFT, AND THEY ARE SEEKING MY LIFE." [4] But what is the divine response to him? "I HAVE KEPT for Myself SEVEN THOUSAND MEN WHO HAVE NOT BOWED THE KNEE TO BAAL." [5] In the same way then, there has also come to be at the present time a remnant according to God's gracious choice.

Romans 11:2-5 (NASB)

Rabbi Saul explains that what was happening in his day, and is happening today, is what has always happened in Jewish history. The majority has always been disobedient to the revelation of the God of Israel. The minority, the remnant, has always believed. Rabbi Saul goes on to say that the Messianic Jews are the believing remnant of Israel today.

This type of truth, the truth of God, cannot be determined by the majority. So the answer is: So what if the majority of rabbis and Jewish people do not accept Yeshua as their Messiah? It does not change the fact that He is the Messiah.

The Logic of It All

The last objection we want to look at goes like this: It is not logical, it is not Jewish to believe in Yeshua. Well, that depends on the issue of who Yeshua really is. For the sake of argument, let the premise be allowed that Yeshua is the Messiah. Surely, then, the most natural, Jewish thing to do is to believe in Him—that is logical enough. If Yeshua is the Messiah, it is Jewish to believe in Him. And believing in Him, if He is the Messiah, makes a Jewish person not less Jewish, but more Jewish. That actually makes him a completed Jew, because he has the relationship that the first Jew had, a relationship with God by faith.

Many objections raised are often fronts for a real objection that is seldom voiced: the fear that if a Jew accepts Yeshua, he will cease to be a Jew and become a Gentile instead. Yet, those Jews who do believe in Yeshua firmly maintain that Yeshua did not destroy their Jewishness.

Appendix 11

Table of Messianic Prophecies

The table below summarizes the Messianic prophecies that have been studied in this book.

Prophecy	Scripture	Page
His Person		
He would be human.	Genesis 3:15	4
He would be a descendant of Abraham.	Genesis 22:18	9
He would be from the tribe of Judah.	Genesis 49:10	11
He would be a son of David.	Isaiah 11:1-2	36
	Jeremiah 23:5-6	60
	I Chronicles 17:10b-14	80
He would be both God and man (Messiah is Jehovah).	(Genesis 3:15)	6
	Isaiah 7:14	24
	Isaiah 9:6-7	33
	Jeremiah 23:5-6	60
	Micah 5:2	62
	Zechariah 12:10	73
	Zechariah 13:7	75
	Psalm 80:17	92
	Psalm 110:1-7	93
He will live eternally.	I Chronicles 17:10b-14	80

Prophecy	Scripture	Page

His Nature

He would be full of the Holy Spirit.	Isaiah 11:1-2	36
	Isaiah 42:1-4	40
	Isaiah 61:1-2a	58
He would be humble.	Zechariah 9:9-10	63
He would be gentle.	Isaiah 42:1-4	40
He would have a unique relationship with God.	Psalm 16:1-11	85
He would be the Son of God.	Psalm 2:7-12	83
	Proverbs 30:4	96
Messiah would be the Good Shepherd.	Zechariah 11:1-17	66

His Appearing

His would be a virgin birth.	(Genesis 3:15)	6
	Isaiah 7:14	24
He would be born in normal circumstances.	Isaiah 52:13-53:12	50
He would be born in poverty.	Isaiah 11:1-2	36
He would be preceded by a herald.	Isaiah 40:3-5	40
	Malachi 3:1	76
He would be born in Bethlehem, city of David.	Micah 5:2	62
He would be seen riding on a donkey.	Zechariah 9:9-10	63
He would be present 483 years after the decree to rebuild Jerusalem (after the Babylonian Captivity).	Daniel 9:24-27	97

Prophecy	Scripture	Page
He would appear before A.D. 70.	Genesis 49:10	13
	Isaiah 7:14	24
	Isaiah 8:9-10	32
	Isaiah 9:6-7	33
	Zechariah 11:1-17	66
	I Chronicles 17:10b-14	80
	Daniel 9:24-27	97

His Offices

Prophecy	Scripture	Page
He would be a king.	Genesis 49:10	13
	Numbers 24:17a	14
	Isaiah 7:14	24
	Isaiah 9:6-7	33
	Jeremiah 23:5-6	60
	I Chronicles 17:10b-14	80
	Psalm 2:7-12	83
	Psalm 110:1-7	93
He would be a priest.	Psalm 110:1-7	93
He would be a prophet.	Deuteronomy 18:15-19	19
	Isaiah 61:1-2a	58

His Mission and Ministry

Prophecy	Scripture	Page
He would be specially trained.	Isaiah 50:4-9	47
He would remove the curse due to Adam's fall.	Genesis 5:21-29	8
He would bring salvation to the Gentile nations.	Isaiah 42:1-4	40
	Isaiah 49:1-13	43

Prophecy	Scripture	Page
He would be rejected at first.	Isaiah 49:1-13	43
	Isaiah 52:13-53:12	50
	Zechariah 11:1-17	66
	Zechariah 12:10	73
	Psalm 22	87
	Psalm 110:1-7	93
He would only be accepted by a small believing remnant of the people.	Zechariah 11:1-17	66
He would appear to fail but in fact be successful.	Isaiah 42:1-4	40
He would be sold for 30 pieces of silver.	Zechariah 11:1-17	66
His rejection would result in an attack upon Israel and the scattering of the people.	Zechariah 11:1-17	66
	Zechariah 13:7	75
His rejection would be followed by the acceptance of a false Messiah.	Zechariah 11:1-17	66
He would eventually be accepted.	Isaiah 49:1-13	43
	Psalm 110:1-7	93
He would be seated at the right hand of God.	Psalm 80:17	92
	Psalm 110:1-7	93

His Suffering and Death

He would suffer.	Isaiah 50:4-9	47
	Isaiah 52:13-53:12	50
	Psalm 22	87
He would be legally tried and condemned to death.	Isaiah 52:13-53:12	50

Prophecy	Scripture	Page
He would die.	Psalm 16:1-11	85
	Psalm 22	87
He would be executed.	Isaiah 52:13-53:12	52
	Daniel 9:24-27	97
He would die a violent death by means of piercing.	Zechariah 12:10	73
	Zechariah 13:7	75
	Psalm 22	87
His death would be substitutionary.	Isaiah 52:13-53:12	52
His death would result in the destruction of Jerusalem and the Temple.	Daniel 9:24-27	97
He would be buried in a rich man's tomb.	Isaiah 52:13-53:12	52
He would be resurrected.	Isaiah 52:13-53:12	52
	Psalm 16:1-11	85
	Psalm 22	87
He would bring justification to those who believe in Him.	Isaiah 52:13-53:12	52

His Future

Prophecy	Scripture	Page
He will be ruler of the Gentile nations.	Psalm 2:7-12	83
He will rule over Israel in the Messianic kingdom.	Psalm 110:1-7	93

CPSIA information can be obtained
at www.ICGtesting.com
Printed in the USA
LVHW100414120821
694572LV00003B/6